SOUTHERN
STORIES

SOUTHERN STORIES

Slaveholders in Peace and War

Drew Gilpin Faust

UNIVERSITY OF MISSOURI PRESS / *Columbia and London*

Library of Congress Cataloging-in-Publication Data

Faust, Drew Gilpin.
    Southern Stories : slaveholders in peace and war / Drew Gilpin
    Faust.
        p.   cm.
    Includes index.
    ISBN 0-8262-0865-7
    ISBN 0-8262-0975-0 (pbk.)
    1. Slaveholders—Southern States. 2. Southern States—
History—1775–1865. 3. Confederate States of America—History.
4. Slavery—Southern States. I. Title.
F213.F25   1992
975.03—dc20   92–20632
                                                        CIP

♾™ This paper meets the requirements of the
American National Standard for Permanence of Paper
for Printed Library Materials, Z39.48, 1984.

Designer: Kristie Lee

Typesetter: Connell-Zeko Type & Graphics

Printer and Binder: Thomson-Shore, Inc.

Typefaces: Goudy Old Style and Goudy Handtooled

For Christabel Follett Smith

Contents

Men

Women

Author's Note

The texts of the essays reprinted here have not been revised for this volume. In one case, I have restored the footnotes to an article published in a journal that did not permit extensive annotation, and in another I have cut some material handled in greater depth in a subsequent essay. Otherwise, the pieces remain as originally written. I regard at least part of the interest of such a collection to lie in its tracing of the evolution of a scholar's work, warts and all. I also consider scholarly articles to be a bit like historic artifacts, irremediably products of the time in which they were first conceived and written. I believe that once published, articles take on a kind of life and identity apart from their authors. If a writer changes perspective on a subject, I would prefer a new essay to the revision of an old one.

The decision not to alter these articles has meant that there is some repetition from essay to essay, particularly in the section on women where certain background information about the impact of the war on the southern home front is presented in more than one chapter. For those reading straight through the volume, I regret this redundancy, but for those sampling the essays one or two at a time, the repetition may prove useful.

To acknowledge everyone who has helped with the works in this book would be to list the hundreds of individuals who have aided me since I started graduate school. I feel I have been unusually blessed by the generosity of friends and colleagues, a great many of whom are thanked in the notes for individual articles. For particular help and encouragement with this volume, I am grateful to Beverly Jarrett, who is an extraordinary editor and friend, and to Steven Hahn, at once a supportive and exacting critic. Charles Rosenberg's help was invaluable in the original preparation of each essay and in their collection here.

Acknowledgments

I wish to thank these publications and their editors for permission to reprint these works: "Evangelicalism and the Proslavery Argument: The Reverend Thornton Stringfellow of Virginia" originally appeared in the *Virginia Magazine of History and Biography* 85 (January 1977): 3–17; "The Rhetoric and Ritual of Agriculture in Antebellum South Carolina" was published in the *Journal of Southern History* 45 (November 1979): 63–79; "Culture, Conflict, and Community: The Meaning of Power on an Antebellum Plantation" is from the *Journal of Social History* 14 (September 1980): 83–97; "The Proslavery Argument in History" first appeared as the introduction to *The Ideology of Slavery: The Proslavery Argument in the Old South, 1830–1860*, edited with an introduction and bibliography by Drew Gilpin Faust (Baton Rouge: Louisiana State University Press, 1981); "Christian Soldiers: The Meaning of Revivalism in the Confederate Army" is from the *Journal of Southern History* 53 (February 1987): 63–90; "Altars of Sacrifice: Confederate Women and the Narratives of War" appeared in the *Journal of American History* 76 (March 1990): 1200–28; "In Search of the Real Mary Chesnut" was published in *Reviews in American History* 10 (March 1982): 54–59; "Race, Gender, and Confederate Nationalism: William D. Washington's *Burial of Latané*" appeared in the *Southern Review* 25 (Spring 1989): 297–307; "A War Story for Confederate Women: Augusta Jane Evans's *Macaria*" was originally the introduction to a reprint of Augusta Jane Evans, *Macaria*, edited by Drew Gilpin Faust (Baton Rouge: Louisiana State University Press, 1992); "Trying to Do a Man's Business: Gender, Violence, and Slave Management in Civil War Texas," appeared in *Gender and History* 4, no. 2 (Summer 1992): 197–214.

Introduction

The ten essays collected here span almost two decades of work in southern history, ranging from a piece composed when I was a graduate student to an article completed in the past few months. As I reread these essays, I was surprised—at once pleased and dismayed—by the continuities that bind them together. Certain assumptions and issues have engaged me from the start—even when I was consciously unaware of their persistence. Although over time I have shifted the focus of my inquiries from men to women and moved from an emphasis on the antebellum years to an increasing preoccupation with the Civil War itself, many of my motivating questions have remained the same. Most fundamentally, I have been concerned with how members of a slave-holding society made sense out of a world that seems to us in the twentieth century to make very little sense at all.

STORIES

My interest in finding out who white southerners thought they were led me to recognize early on that southerners had been eager to discover this too. In the decades preceding the Civil War and even more emphatically during the war itself, educated white southerners wrote to explain—themselves to themselves, to each other, and to the wider world. Working through southern archives, I found a rich variety of stories, a panoply of voices in which they sought to provide a meaning for their own lives and for the social order in which they lived. Sometimes these stories were collective, as in the case of the antebellum proslavery argument or Confederate discourses about women; sometimes they appear to have been more personal, as in the diaries and letters of figures like Lizzie Neblett, Mary Chesnut, Thornton String-fellow, or James Henry Hammond, who regularly employed their pens to create a degree of coherence and order amidst the complex circumstances of their particular lives. Yet even these individual narratives

1

were profoundly shaped by broader social prescriptions and expectations, and the struggle between the individual diarist and these constraints has been a central focus of my interest. The sense we make out of our own lives must inevitably—and sometimes tragically—be situated within the understandings of self that our society offers to us.

My work has thus consistently exhibited a strongly biographical impulse. Even though biography has been anything but a fashionable historical genre during the past two decades, I have found the point of intersection between the individual and his or her social world an extraordinarily rich—all but irresistible—locus in which to explore the opportunities and limitations that shape social action. Individual lives are the ultimate sites in which the larger forces of historical process and change operate in their fullest and, in my judgment, and to my taste, most intriguing and revealing complexity.

The notion of "stories" with which I have titled this collection thus has for me an importantly double significance: it encompasses not just the ideologies and rationalizations and explanations that comprised southern social thought; it is meant to include as well the way particular southerners acted out—sometimes embracing, often revising—those metaplots as they constructed and construed their own lives. We all live within the stories we tell, for these tales fashion a coherent direction and identity out of the discontinuities of our past, present, and future. The anticipated outcomes of our narratives offer motivations for our actions within them. Yet the sources of our stories transcend each of us as individuals; our imaginations and thus our possibilities are limited by the availability to us of a repertoire of plots that we can act out or seek to revise. As Carolyn Heilbrun has so effectively explained, "What matters is that lives do not serve as models; only stories do that. And it is a hard thing to make up stories to live by. We can only retell and live by the stories we have read or heard. We live our lives through texts. They may be read, or chanted, or experienced electronically, or come to us, like the murmurings of our mothers, telling us what conventions demand. Whatever their force or medium, these stories have formed us all; they are what we must use to make new fictions, new narratives."[1]

For Lizzie Neblett, managing slaves in Civil War Texas, the conventional story of the southern woman seemed so incompatible with the story of the southern slave master that she found herself unable to forge a unified and coherent narrative to guide and explain her new wartime existence. But at the same historical moment, writer Augusta Jane Evans confronted the challenges the Civil War posed to existing renditions of women's lives by self-consciously creating a new story for southern women. Her novel *Macaria* was designed to replace the prevailing narrative of marital fulfillment with one of single blessedness, a story more suited to a region losing a large part of a generation of young men. Evans intended her tale to offer southern women new possibilities for self-definition as well as a basis for reconciliation to a changed and previously scorned set of life choices.

IDEAS AND HISTORY

When as a graduate student I first began to express interest in studying southern thought, I generally encountered skepticism that at times verged upon incredulity. More than once, established scholars whimsically responded that the notion of "southern ideas" was in and of itself oxymoronic—implying that I must myself be moronic to be contemplating such a barren field of inquiry. Yet in the decades since the early seventies, not only has southern intellectual history emerged as a lively field, but the study of belief and ideology has flourished more generally.[2]

A major factor in the transformation of the place of ideas in southern history has been the influence of Eugene Genovese. Over the past thirty years, Genovese has published a succession of books that have provided a powerful and controversial Marxist reframing of southern history. Characterizing the Old South as a distinctive precapitalist society on a collision course with the emerging bourgeois order of the North, Genovese set the terms of debate within the field. Because his particular Marxism rested upon a Gramscian understanding of social power, his work placed ideology—Gramscian concepts of hegemony—at the center of the class relationships underlying the southern social order. In investigations of "the world the slaveholders made" and "the world the slaves made," Genovese explored the legitimating ideology of planter paternalism and the liberating power of slave Christianity as essential elements defining white and black southerners and their interaction. Through processes of both assertion and negotiation, the bound and the free struggled for psychological dominance at the same time they contended for the more material foundations of power. Ideas are for Genovese outgrowths of material conditions—and class relations in particular—but are also transformative of these realities. With Genovese's definition of planter hegemony comprising a critical concern for southern historiography, I found that my interest in slaveowners' ability to think the seemingly unthinkable fit neatly into a lively area of discussion and debate.[3]

But it is not only southern historians who have in the past two decades found ideas a subject for intensive examination; the study of belief and ideology has flourished more generally. Early on, the enormous influence of anthropologist Clifford Geertz gave an interdisciplinary legitimation and reinforcement to historians who had resisted the siren song of cliometrics, the lure of positivistic quantifiable truth that exerted such a powerful sway over the historiography of the late 1960s and early 1970s. Geertz's appeal lay partly in offering an alternative, qualitative social science model that, particularly in its elegant attention to language, seemed more congenial to many historians than the methodological rigidities of quantification. But Geertz also provided a rationale for rehabilitating the role of ideas in historical explanation, ideas that since the day of the Progressive historians had been largely devalued as mere epiphenomena, as rationalizations of material interests, or else relegated to a disembodied realm of "intellectual history" that seemed to have no clear relation to the rest of historical experience. The 1970s are often characterized as the decade that yielded new scholarly insight into groups previously believed to have been inarticulate and thus historically invisible—groups such as slaves, workers, women. But the decade established the foundations for a new history of the articulate as well.[4]

For me, probably the most influential of Geertz's many contributions was his representation of belief as "model of and model for" the world in which it appears. In this formulation I found the means of escape from the kind of reductionist thinking about ideas that had shaped much historical writing current during my years of graduate training. Yet, at the same time, Geertz's approach resisted an Idealism that would render thought so powerful and transcendent as, almost paradoxically, to remove it from social processes and social relevance, and, especially, from issues of power. In his commitment to reading all the world as a text, Geertz gave historians a means of moving beyond the formal written legacies of an elite few; he made thought an integral part of all social action; he helped transform the study of ideas in history from the rather narrow analysis of intellectuals to a much broader investigation of people thinking. Ideas reflected and affected the world; they possessed their own internal dynamic at the same time they were shaped by social and historical experience.[5]

Thinking about actions as texts soon prompted me to consider the possibilities inherent in regarding texts as actions—socially shaped into generic forms, socially produced and socially received. In agricultural orations, for example, I recognized a genre that could be regarded as a form of verbal ritual, a genuine speech act, and I discovered that the social setting in which they were performed became analytically inseparable from their substance. Words, as one nineteenth-century orator reminded me, took on "the power of things."[6]

At times, indeed, my work has been criticized for taking the power of words—of language, of ideas—too seriously, of giving too much credence and attention to what was, after all, just talk. But I hope the essays collected here will help dispel such criticism in the accumulated case they make for the force ideas have exerted in southern history. White southerners acted on a set of assumptions—we might today consider them illusions—about the nature of their society and their world, assumptions that ultimately proved to be more powerful than life itself. In the antebellum years, these ideas worked to legitimate masters' authority, naturalize black inferiority, and undergird white solidarity. In war, ideas rationalized the South's defense, as Christian soldiers willingly gave up the life they knew for a promise of a life to come; women sacrificed their subsistence and their loved ones in order to realize their image of appropriate female virtue. For these ideas, for these understandings of themselves, white southerners ultimately lost their civilization and, in hundreds of thousands of cases, their lives. Ideas proved themselves more powerful, more important than personal or cultural survival.

Yet these essays demonstrate as well the limits upon the power of ideas. To return to the terms of the Geertzian framework that initially exerted such an influence upon me, ideas are not just a "model for" the world, imposing their force upon it, but also serve as a "model of," reflecting its impositions upon them. Perhaps it has been these lingering Geertzian influences that have helped prevent me from fully embracing the postmodern dissolution of "the real." I have found the emphasis of postmodern and poststructuralist theory upon the "constructed" nature of the world largely convincing, for it has fit well with the ways I have seen southerners from Thornton Stringfellow to Lizzie Neblett define their lives. But unlike postmodern discourse theorists, I do not believe that this creation of meaning takes place entirely apart from the material circumstances that surround it. The Civil War has proved a reality difficult to dismiss. Although the traditional understandings, the constructions white southerners placed upon their lives persisted well past the point of reason or usefulness, the impact of death, starvation, and terror finally brought change in attitudes and identities, in the fundamental ways in which southerners represented and understood their world. War compelled new narratives.[7]

Not infrequently, the Civil War has been described as a "moment of truth," and indeed, its function as a test, a forum of evaluation of priorities and commitments has been the source of much of my attraction to it as a field of study. But perhaps within the context of my use of the war as an empirical counterweight to the claims of postmodern theory, I should instead call the conflict the "moment of reality." I have been told that when a professor at a neighboring university recently learned that a new course was being offered on "War as Text," she was moved to ask the poststructuralist instructor if he had tried out his approach on any members of the Veterans of Foreign Texts. Reality is hard to dismiss when it has happened to you.[8]

Yet at the same time that the Civil War suggests limits to the tenacity of our discursive constructions, it serves as extraordinarily forceful testimony to the power of ideas to survive in spite of their seemingly dysfunctional or irrational character—their growing incongruity with surrounding circumstance. As slavery disintegrated around them, Thornton Stringfellow and James Henry Hammond both strove to maintain their illusions about the contentment of their slaves and the paternalistic essence of the peculiar institution. Even though technological advances in the range and firepower of weaponry made it absurd, southerners kept on charging. But the carnage of Pickett's suicidal assault at Gettysburg proved an undeniable reality, at last compelling new constructions of strategic and tactical choices. The worlds we create in our heads and in our shared discourses are not impervious to the intrusions of material reality, and these intrusions indeed become a major source of change in our collective understandings. History—either as experience or discipline—without reference to such reality and such change is difficult to imagine.

IDEAS IN THE OLD SOUTH

What sort of picture of the Old South emerges from the kinds of questions and approaches I have embraced? A region, a culture, a slaveholding class so involved in defining itself and its legitimacy was a class in struggle—in struggle with itself, in struggle with those over whom it sought to exercise power. The South's master class was by the early nineteenth century at pains to explain its rule, to negotiate a control that was far from absolute. Masters invoked paternalism to convince slaves to accept their inferiority, to enforce sacrifice upon white women, to persuade nonslaveholding agriculturists that class divisions did not even exist. Through deft rhetorical and thus ideological moves, they redefined oppression as mutual obligation, suffering as sacrifice, and masters and yeomen as politically indistinguishable. "Who is the non slaveholder?," David F. Jamison asked an audience of South Carolina agriculturists in 1856, "Or, more properly, Who is interested in the institution of slavery? Everyone, I answer, who is interested in the welfare, good government and prosperity of the South."[9]

Southern slaveholders were involved in a war of words and ideas long before they resorted to military conflict. And this war was as much within the South as between the South and the rest of the nation. The very nature of this rhetorical and ideological contest suggests how much southern slaveholders had conceded before they even began their defense. Implicit in their position was an acceptance of their own accountability. As a system of social assumptions, paternalism admitted that an obligation to serve accompanied the legitimation to rule. In his agricultural address, for example, planter Jamison conceded the right of lower-class whites to have their interests represented, even as he redefined those interests to coincide with his own. Slaves, women, yeomen farmers were paradoxically empowered by slaveholders' efforts to enhance their own domination and control. Planter ideology worked against as steadily as it worked for planter power.

Such negotiations about the foundations of social order in the Old

South suggest a society in transition, a society whose leaders struggled to maintain the old hierarchy with the appearances of emerging democracy, to perpetuate their preeminence by reshaping it. The dual character of southern society, its "Janus face," is certainly evident throughout my work. The Old South was a civilization that looked backwards and forwards simultaneously. In this bifurcated vision lay both the South's weakness and its strength. Southern ideology generally, just like the particular representations of it I describe in the essays on the proslavery argument and on agricultural orations that follow, casts itself as all-encompassing—invoking the traditionalism of religion and history and the modernity of science in its own defense. Yet this attempt at universality, this constant effort to provide what I have called a "bridge across the chasm of change," served as a mode of denial and ultimately as a source of cultural and social disintegration. Southerners struggled so hard to transform change into continuity that they were rendered impotent to deal with the abrupt and brutally real upheavals around them.[10] .

SOUTHERN WOMEN AND MEN

For many individual white southerners, these failures of ideology translated on a personal level into acute dilemmas of identity. James Henry Hammond lived his life—as a master, as a politician, as a father—uncertain whether he wanted to be feared or loved. Mary Chesnut professed to despise slavery, yet benefited from it daily and supported the immolation of her world in its defense. And Chesnut shared with Augusta Evans an emergent female ambition that each woman readily "strangled" out of continuing deference to male prerogative. Lizzie Neblett was all but consumed by the wartime contradictions between the survival of southern womanhood and the salvation of southern slavery. The inconsistencies inherent in the South's definition of itself and in the master class' rationale for its power imposed contradictions and almost irreconcilable expectations upon its members.[11]

The story of the Old South, the "southern stories" I invoke in my title, thus seem to me all part of a larger cultural narrative shared widely by articulate white southerners of the mid-nineteenth century. The narratives these men and women told about their lives, the way they construed and shaped their personal choices made sense only within this larger framework of culturally defined options. And for southern slaveholders, these possibilities were distinctively gendered. In the prewar years, few white southerners, male or female, maintained any doubts about the appropriate and deep-seated contrasts between men's and women's life choices. But war would reveal the tenuousness of these assumptions, their status as social constructions rather than natural and inevitable realities. In some ways the fulfillment of the masculine ethos of honor, military life proved to be not all glory; soldiers were neither all nor always heroes. War experience simultaneously extolled traditional southern male gender categories and undermined them. Pickett's charge marked both the apotheosis and the absurdity of a conception of male honor that had been central to the Old South but could never after July 1863 be understood in quite the same way again.

The exigencies of war required new men as well as new weapons. Many soldiers found themselves subjected to the discipline of what amounted to their initial experience with wage labor and compelled in the ranks to accept direct subordination for the first time. For yeoman smallholders, who had defined themselves in terms of their autonomy and independence, such a transformation was often profoundly disturbing and contributed to the notorious ill discipline of southern troops. Men of the master class, in turn, saw their understandings of themselves and their social identities altered when they had of necessity to abandon their paternalistic responsibility for the welfare of the women they left behind as they departed for war. And the erosion of the slave system challenged the paternalistic foundations of upper-class male identity as well. As Union victory drew ever closer, sullen and unmanageable slaves made clear to James Henry Hammond that their now abandoned "cheerful greetings" had been not a sign of acceptance of his legitimate domination and fatherly concern, but a charade.

The disappearance of many of the material foundations for paternalism among men of the master class and for independence among the middling orders threatened the very bases of male identity in the Confederate South. At the same time that paternalism had been central to southern ideology, it had rested firmly upon individual notions of male identity—of fatherhood and its privileges and obligations. Paternalism thus represented the intersection of cultural imperative and personal identity, of the metaplot and the individual story. The destruction of paternalism's base in the war's obliteration of slavery thus posed a crisis of personal, and specifically male identity, as well as cultural survival. An upheaval in gender definition was thus a critical part of the destruction of the Old South.

But transformations in female identity were equally profound. The Confederacy needed white women to lead new sorts of lives if it was to survive as a nation. Women had to be persuaded to follow new plots, accept different narratives about their purposes and responsibilities. Women were now inexorably part of the public sphere. Traditionally male obligations had to be recoded as female so that women could be induced to provide the home front labor required to support the mass military mobilization of total war. Confederate propagandists redefined teaching and nursing as female—stressing nurturance, sacrifice, and self-abnegation as essential attributes of these newly feminized undertakings. But southern women acting out these new plots still frequently felt themselves ill-suited to their roles. Old gender assumptions coexisted with new gender necessities to challenge the very foundations of any sort of fixed gender distinction. Tales of women disguised as soldiers titillated southern ears, representing the at once alarming and thrilling possibilities inherent in the warborn challenge to the most essential components of the self. When Augusta Jane Evans's pseudonymous critic FIDELIA complained that the author had created a third gender in her heroine Irene, she echoed a sense of gender displacement that reached well beyond reactions to Evans's pathbreaking novel *Macaria*.

While dozens of Confederate women confessed their longing to be men, Lizzie Neblett displayed a similar perception of genders blurred yet tenacious in her frustrations at "trying to do a man's business." For many southerners like Lizzie, gender identities did not shift as rapidly as circumstances and required behaviors. Desperate to be relieved of her duties as slave manager, Lizzie would no doubt have shared Amanda Walker's firm belief that a woman was not a "fit and proper person" to govern slaves. Mary Chesnut similarly hated nursing and abandoned her hospital visits, regarding those who relished the work as equivalent to men. War tore away the moorings of gender in which personal identity had been based, revealing the centrality both of gender to social relations and of culture to individual self-definition in the Old South.

WAR AND CULTURE

War offers an extraordinary window through which to see not just the significance of gender relations, but the essential foundations of southern social and cultural assumptions. Forced under the pressures of four years of conflict to set priorities, to make difficult choices, to define themselves as a nation and a people, Confederates left posterity unequaled means of insight into the Old South. And my gradual recognition of this opportunity has shaped the evolution of my scholarly concerns, shifting my focus on the antebellum years into a fascination with the war era itself as a time in which the implicit conflicts and unarticulated values of the prewar South would necessarily become explicit and thus accessible to the eager historian. Even in my early essays—before I thought I was interested in the war—I found myself explaining Stringfellow and Hammond as slave owners by reference to their reaction to slavery's wartime disintegration. The war began in a sense to take control of me, as it indeed had of the white southerners I was studying.

War became, to use an oft-quoted aphorism, my "educator," as it had been in a much more direct sense for so many through the ages. The life of the common soldier taught me about class relations and social change in southern society; the "gendering" character of war drew my attention for the first time to the study of southern women and then helped make me aware of the significance of gender to social relations in the prebellum as well as the wartime South. Studying the Civil War has taught me, and I would argue that it should teach anyone professionally interested in southern history, that we cannot end our considerations of the Old South, in either our research or our courses, in 1861. We must accept an extended chronology in which the Old South is realized in the Confederacy, in which the war years are seen as a refraction of the essential elements of what has gone before, as well as the source of the new South that is to come. The military questions that have been the major concern of most Civil War scholars must be sited in broader social and cultural interpretations. Military histories are unquestionably important, for the best of them reveal a great deal about the kinds of choices that define a society. But in leaving the Civil War almost exclusively to military historians for so long, we have ignored an unparalleled opportunity to see the South in the crucible and to explore a moment in which cultural and personal survival became so closely identified as to cast into dramatic relief the fundamental interactions between human beings and the worlds they construct around them. The Civil War was the fulfillment of the Old South and the origins of the New; it was created by men and women who were in turn transformed by what it became. The Civil War educated southerners white and black by introducing them all to a new way of life. We in the twentieth century must permit the Civil War to educate us in new understandings of southern history and of the timeless human dilemmas that war stories tell so well.[12]

MEN

Evangelicalism and the Proslavery Argument

The Reverend Thornton Stringfellow of Virginia

istorians have long recognized evangelicalism as an integral component of the world view of many nineteenth-century Americans and a major motivating force behind the myriad of reform movements which characterized the period. For the most part, scholars have studied these phenomena in the North, even though, as Donald Mathews has recently reemphasized, "The South and evangelical Protestantism have had a peculiarly intimate relationship for perhaps two hundred years."[1]

While the existence of a basically religious orientation among individuals throughout antebellum America is in one sense witness to the cultural similarity of North and South, the social applications of evangelicalism below the Mason-Dixon line reflect significant differences between the two regions. Evangelical thought provided an ideological and emotional context in terms of which individuals approached many of their society's most pressing problems and within which they legitimated their consequent social actions. Thus an examination of the differences and similarities in the expressions of evangelicalism North and South should serve as a useful index to the contrasting preoccupations of the sections.

One form this religiously oriented world view assumed in the South is exemplified by a prominent Baptist of the period, whose activities and social attitudes demonstrate the dynamic of the evangelical impulse within the context of a single life. While sharing many of the beliefs of northern reformers, the Reverend Thornton Stringfellow of Virginia was at the same time a southern nationalist and a staunch defender of the peculiar institution. As contributor to the anthology *Cotton is King*[2] and as author of numerous proslavery pamphlets, Stringfellow was a leading figure in the South's defense of its civilization. Almost unknown to twentieth-century historians, he was recognized in his own time as a writer of considerable importance, and so eminent a southerner as James Henry Hammond acknowledged that Stringfellow had advanced the "best scriptural argument"[3] for human bondage.

Stringfellow invites study not just because of his long neglect by historians,[4] but because his life suggests the existence of a southern reform impulse analogous to that which historians have frequently described in the North. In his evangelical and social concerns, Stringfellow appears to have been a southern counterpart of certain northern reformers of the middle decades of the nineteenth century. Assuming for themselves the right to be their "brothers' keepers,"[5] to act as the conscience of others, and to require adherence to what they determined to be appropriate standards of behavior, these men demonstrated their humanitarian commitment through such activities as temperance work, the Sunday school movement, and tract and mission societies. Although a Virginian with no ties to the centers of this reform agitation in Boston and New York, Thornton Stringfellow found many of these same issues of crucial importance. A number of contemporary historians have described a sense of stewardship, a belief in the appointment of some men to be the guardians of others, as a generating force behind northern reform.[6] In the case of Stringfellow, at least, these same motivations can be seen to have existed in the South.

Yet in spite of the similarities of their evangelical orientation, the northern and southern reformers were to find certain major differences in the interpretation of their Christian duty. While accepting many of the same religious premises as did his northern brethren, Stringfellow was bewildered by their apparent inability to recognize what he perceived as the most significant aspect of the conception of moral stewardship—the justification of slavery as a positive good.

Thornton Stringfellow was born in Fauquier County, Virginia, in 1788 and, except for a brief period of residence in South Carolina, lived in Fauquier and nearby Culpeper counties until his death in 1869. Son of a slaveholder who possessed nearly 1,000 acres of land at the time of his death in 1813,[7] Thornton belonged to a family of considerable means. With part of his wealth inherited from his father and part from the first of his four wives, Amelia, Stringfellow was always prosperous and was described by the Virginia Baptists' *Religious Herald* as "a man of high social position."[8] A large slaveholder, Stringfellow lost between sixty and seventy bondsmen as a result of the Civil War. His will reveals him to have been the owner of two houses and more than 2,000 acres of land at the time of his death.[9]

Despite his social prominence, no information survives concerning any formal education he may have received. According to an obituary composed by the Shiloh Baptist Association, his mother wished him to pursue a higher education, and Stringfellow fully intended to enter a university in South Carolina when "a general derangement of his nervous system . . . affecting especially his eye-sight, scattered all his mother's visions with respect to his collegiate training."[10] Unable to earn an advanced degree, Stringfellow nevertheless demonstrated the high regard in which he held academic endeavor by consistently using the honorary A.M. and D.D. degrees awarded him by Columbian and Richmond Colleges.

Although prevented from pursuing an education in South Carolina, young Stringfellow remained away from home for several years in hope of succeeding in commerce. In 1811 on a visit to his parents, both of whom were Baptist "New Lights," Stringfellow experienced an emotional conversion which led him to remain in Virginia and enter the ministry. In 1814 he was ordained and soon thereafter assumed responsibility for several congregations in Fauquier County.

The Baptist Church in Virginia at this time was entering a period of internal dissension.[11] Although the Separate and Regular Baptists had in 1787 sufficiently suppressed their doctrinal disagreements concerning the issues of free will and predestination to unite into one body, major differences in outlook persisted. The discord was specifically expressed in the early years of the nineteenth century over questions of education of ministers and promotion of missions, both of which were seen by some Baptists as the presumptuous activities of Arminians who doubted God's ability to choose those who would lead His flocks and those He would save. The issue of education was especially explosive, for uneducated pastors—who made up the majority of the Baptist clergy—perceived the movement to train preachers as a direct challenge to their status.

As the son of Baptist "New Lights," Stringfellow believed strongly in evangelicalism and vigorously supported the mission movement throughout his career. Unlike the conservative predestinarians of the denomination, Stringfellow consistently advocated activism in service of God. His belief in the importance of man's role in saving himself and others was the assumption that produced not only his evangelicalism, but his humanitarian concerns, among which he would have included his proslavery ideas. The congregations under his charge in the early years of his ministry were members of the Ketocton Association, and Stringfellow was active as early as 1817 in promoting support for missions within the organization. Although Ketocton was later to emerge as one of the staunchest defenders of predestinarian anti-mission sentiment, at this time Stringfellow was sufficiently persuasive in his case for Christianizing the heathen to secure support from Ketocton for the Baptist Triennial Convention, the central pro-mission body of the church, and an appointment as the association's delegate to its meeting.

Viewing himself as God's steward on earth, Stringfellow felt it his duty to inform others of his perception of God's will through missionary work and through education in the ways of piety. Thus his mission sentiment was complemented by an advocacy of increased education both for his congregation and for individuals who aspired to join him as spiritual leaders.[12] During the years he lived in Fauquier County, Stringfellow conducted a grammar school and first indicated his interest in the Sunday school movement, an area in which he would later assume a leadership role. As a supporter of both clerical education and evangelism, Stringfellow should not have been surprised to find that "some of the ministers" in the Ketocton Association "were contentious and the annual sessions were disturbed by vain janglings."[13] Because of the discord caused by his missionary views, Stringfellow led in 1819 in the formation of a new body, the Columbia Association, in which his opinions might prevail.

In 1833 Stringfellow purchased a sizeable tract of land, approximately 1,000 acres, on the Rapidan River in Culpeper County and moved into his mansion "Bell Air." Surrendering some of his pastoral duties in Fauquier County, he organized a new congregation at Stevensburg, a small settlement not far from his new farm. Bell Air was to be his permanent home, and Stringfellow's period of greatest prominence was to begin shortly after his assumption of the Culpeper County pastorate. Soon a leader in the Shiloh Association, to which the Stevensburg Church belonged, Stringfellow continued his active support for education and mission movements. A member of the Virginia Baptist Education Society, Stringfellow later became one of its Board of Managers and in 1846 was chosen a vice-president of the Southern Baptist Convention's Domestic Mission Board.[14] He also persisted in his advocacy of Sunday schools, withdrawing from his Stevensburg pastorate in 1846 because he felt his congregation to be neglecting the parish Sunday school.[15]

During the period of his ministry at Stevensburg, Stringfellow's interest in benevolent activities spread well beyond support for missions and education. The manner in which he perceived these new areas of concern, however, was consistently shaped by his original interests and always appeared to him as a simple extension of his earliest work. Thus Stringfellow's philosophy of benevolence was based on his conviction of the close relationship between discovering God's will—educating oneself—and bringing this word to others through domestic or foreign missionary activity. Stringfellow felt God's intentions were clearly expressed in the Bible and always available to men; benevolence became a "simple" matter of explicating the Bible and guiding men in following its dictates. Stringfellow saw his duty as communicating to others his Master's wishes and ensuring that they were followed. As God's earthly representative, his own "moral character . . . in justice and equity . . . [should] ressemble that of his heavenly master." It was through his terrestrial surrogates that God intended to effect "moral reform to the world."[16] The explication of God's will and its promulgation and enforcement through missionary and reform activity became for Stringfellow the core of his Christian duty.

Stringfellow first acted upon this conception of his role as reformer in the temperance movement, explaining in an essay published in the *Religious Herald* in 1842 how opposition to alcohol fit within his scheme of reform. Affirming the intimate involvement of the church in the affairs of the world, Stringfellow stated, "Many professors [of faith] look upon the connexion they have formed with the churches as having dissolved their connexion with the world. This is a mistake. . . . We are all responsible to God in his providence, for social or national duties."[17] But Stringfellow denied that the individual conscience or moral sense should attempt to define and arrest vice. Man must heed God's word as expressed in the Bible about what constitutes evil, and must act in conjunction with fellowmen in attempting to eradicate it. Perhaps, like

many northern clergymen involved in "active benevolence," Stringfellow perceived the unchecked individual conscience, the force behind a substantial portion of the nonclerical northern reform movement, as a potentially disruptive social force.[18] Therefore supporting
his reform prescriptions with specific biblical references, Stringfellow
concluded that the temperance movement was God's work. The saints
of the modern church, the stewards of God's earthly kingdom, must
unite in removing the "leprous spot" of alcohol from society. Having
studied the Bible to determine the will of God, Stringfellow advocated
the formation of temperance societies to spread the word and enforce it
through reform activity.[19]

Although Stringfellow specialized in treating man's spiritual afflictions, he saw care of man's physical needs as comprising an equally
important part of the work of benevolence. Thus interest in disease and
its cures became part of his mission. God's goodness, he declared, encompasses His provision for our physical maladies, and we must be
trained in how to use the remedies He has supplied. One of these,
Stringfellow contended, was the mineral waters in Fauquier County,
which would, in his estimation, cure everything from snake bite to dys-
pepsia.[20] Yet for the benevolence of these springs to be fully realized,
men must come to understand God's purpose in creating the waters.
Just as he, as interpreter of the Bible, devoted himself to explaining the
spiritual remedies God had designed the Scriptures to reveal, so scientists must interpret for man the physical remedies offered "immediately
by the hand of God"[21] in nature. Just as ministers were stewards of
spiritual affairs, so scientists were responsible for the more material
expressions of God's design. In the *Religious Herald*, Stringfellow published case after case of miraculous cures by the waters in order to
"invite the superintending care of science in the administration, and
more speedily apprize the world of the immense value of these waters."[22] Benevolence once again appeared as the interpretation and
promulgation of God's goodness, and scientists, like ministers, were
appointed by the Lord to superintend His creation and communicate
His will to men.[23] Even as local booster, Stringfellow defined and rationalized his activities in terms of his conception of stewardship.

Stringfellow's perception of himself as a missionary and reformer was
central to his involvement with slavery, as its intellectual advocate, as
pastor of a large "colored" membership, and as a slaveholder himself.

Many students of abolitionism and other social reform movements in the North during this period have suggested that reform was in essence a movement of social control, the assertion by a self-righteous privileged group of the power to prescribe the behavior of others.[24] Certainly Stringfellow's view of himself as God's steward partakes of a similar sense of superiority, which in his case was encouraged by his high social and economic status. As master of seventy slaves, he no doubt possessed a certain habit of command. His fear of the unleashed individual conscience indicates as well the basic conservatism of his commitment to reform; individuals were to be limited in their advocacy of social change by traditional biblical prescriptions as interpreted by men like Stringfellow himself.[25]

If, then, a basic component of the reform impulse was a commitment to the maintenance of social order, the reformer would consequently take a particular interest in the elements of society which seemed to threaten its stability. Therefore in the South, a region obsessed with the fear of slave insurgency, the reform movement sought to control blacks as individuals and as a race. Endeavoring to inculcate personal habits of orderliness, obedience, and morality in the slave by means of Christian missionary activity, the southern reformer defended as well the institutionalization of social control over blacks through the slavery system. Moreover, if benevolence was to be seen as moral stewardship, what better exemplified this humanitarian guardianship over others than the paternalism of slavery?

In accordance with his dedication to interpretation and education as the first phase of mission work, Stringfellow began to publish articles on slavery in the *Religious Herald* which were reprinted and issued as pamphlets. The first of these, appearing in 1841, was, predictably, an extensive examination of scriptural prescriptions on the subject. Considering his role to be that of Biblical interpreter, Stringfellow began his involvement in the slavery issue by determining where God stood on the question. To Stringfellow, the answer seemed clear. The Almighty had sanctioned slavery in the patriarchal age, had particularly blessed the slaveholding nation of Moses, had shown his approval of the fugitive slave laws by ordering the runaway Hagar to return to her master, and had allowed Christ to recognize its legality. Prompted into writing by the debate on the subject between Francis Wayland, president of Brown University, and Richard Fuller, leading Baptist of the South,

Stringfellow decried the misconceptions about the nature of benevolence which were held by the abolitionists. "With men from the North,
I have observed for many years a palpable ignorance of the divine will,
in reference to the institution of slavery."[26] Rather than depending on
the Bible for definitions of right and wrong, these reformers from the
North proclaimed the power of their individual consciences to determine God's will.

> I would respectfully and affectionately ask all who love our Lord Jesus
> Christ in the southern section of our beloved country, If we are not
> verily guilty in reference to the abolition crusade?
>   We have seen since the adoption of the federal constitution, a
> religious, fanatic, abolition zeal, which we have known was not ac-
> cording to scripture knowledge, organizing itself and accumulating
> strength. . . . We have known that the success to such a spirit in this
> country was impossible if the sword of the Spirit was brought to
> bear—yet we have allowed that weapon to remain in the scabbard,
> until a generation has risen up, whose minds and consciences in this
> subject are defiled with ignorance. . . . In view of these facts, I ask
> why is it that good men and true . . . are seen taxing their energies to
> accomplish every Lilliputian scheme within the range of benev-
> olence, while they neglect to do the only thing that can save our
> beloved country from ruin? . . . Will no steps be taken to place the
> Sword of the Spirit in the hands of the people?[27]

To Thornton Stringfellow, the most important work of benevolence
was to spread the word of God's approval of slavery. The South as a
whole must unite to reform the North, by learning God's ways and
showing the path of righteousness to the misguided abolitionists and
their compatriots.

But Stringfellow saw his missionary responsibility in regard to slavery
not just as convincing whites of its justness. Proselytizing the heathen
should begin at home, and Stringfellow was greatly concerned with saving and reforming the slaves who belonged to his church. The black
membership at Stevensburg was nearly as large as the white, and a
major occupation of the church elders seems to have been the disciplining of wayward colored members for drinking, profanity, and sexual
license. From a twentieth-century point of view, it is easy to label this
concern with "any disorder that may exist among our colored mem-

bers"[28] as a simple mechanism of social control, a way in which south-erners used social institutions to reinforce the slave system. Although this was certainly one function of church discipline, it was not seen by Stringfellow and his congregation as their overt purpose or their pri-mary motivation. Orderly behavior and social stability were by-prod-ucts of Godliness, but were secondary results of a religious process de-signed principally to ensure salvation. Racial subordination appeared to the Stevensburg congregation as a part of the missionary work to which the church and its pastor were so devoted. "It is a lamentable fact," declared the church minutes, "that we know too little of the conduct of our coloured members. We pay too little attention to the subject of personally conversing with them, Encouraging and exhort-ing them to works of Righteousness, reproving their errors, becoming acquainted with their conduct and enforcing discipline."[29] String-fellow's transcending interest was evangelical, and the question of ra-cial control was but a subordinate issue within his religiously oriented world view. "Enforcing discipline" among blacks was seen as important because it was part of "Encouraging and assisting them to works of Righteousness."[30]

Just as the church as an institution had a missionary duty toward the black man, so the institution of slavery itself was designed to educate the bondsman for salvation. The South must come to recognize that in caring for slaves, in leading them out of barbarism, it fulfilled God's will and served as an instrument of His mercy. Ownership of slaves was itself a kind of moral stewardship. "There is truly moral power put forth for good, in the obedience enjoined upon the slave and especially in the duty to the slave enjoined upon the master."[31] Here again the North had failed in its Christian duty, for "after pocketing the price of these savages, [it] refused to bear any part of the burden of training and ele-vating them."[32] The Scriptures showed clearly that God had made men socially, morally, and politically unequal, and thus slavery was invented so that by uniting the interest and sympathy of the superior white mas-ter with his property right in the slave, it might protect and elevate the black man. Regulation of blacks was a necessary part of their education and improvement. "The guardianship and control of the black race, by the white, . . . is an indispensable Christian duty, to which we must as yet look, if we would secure the well-being of both races."[33] In attack-ing the southern system, the North not only threatened the future of an institution created by God, but undermined the effectiveness of its present benevolent operation. "Was it not for the seditious spirit of the North, we would educate our slaves generally, and so fit them earlier for a more improved condition, and higher moral elevation."[34] In spite of this, however, the southern states had so helped the slaves that "their condition, *as a class*, is now better than that of any other equal number of laborers on earth."[35]

Stringfellow's justification for slavery, his belief in natural inequality, in the importance of the master's sympathy being encouraged by his property right in the slave, his comparison of the condition of the slave laborer with the free, seem very similar to the ideas of George Fitzhugh, who lived about fifty miles away at Port Royal, near Fredericksburg. Stringfellow's church at Stevensburg was on the Culpeper-Fredericksburg road, so the two men could conceivably have visited. Unfortunately, Stringfellow's library and personal papers were destroyed in a fire early in this century,[36] so we may never know whether or not the two men directly influenced one another. The similarity of their approaches to slavery as a patriarchal institution, however, suggests that the two men were familiar with each other's views.[37]

Stringfellow and Fitzhugh also shared a strong conviction of the necessity of making the South believe in its own righteousness and justify its position before the onslaughts from the North. Stringfellow increasingly saw the South as good and the North as evil, commenting on how his region contained less population but twice as many churches as did the free states. It was the "southern section as a whole" that Stringfellow called upon to serve as missionary for his cause.[38]

Stringfellow's conception of the South as a discrete section possessing its own religious goals and mission was manifested in 1845 in his active support for the separation of southern Baptists from their infidel northern counterparts through the formation of a Southern Baptist Convention.[39] In April of 1845 Stringfellow published a letter urging other churches to unite in support for a Southern Convention to deal with northern refusal to admit slaveholders as missionaries.[40] Because Stringfellow thought of holding slaves as itself a kind of mission work, he perceived the northern position only as another manifestation of the sorely misguided and infidel "benevolence" of abolitionism. The Stevensburg church took the lead with its local association in promoting the united southern meeting, and Stringfellow was chosen from his area to attend the convention in Augusta, Georgia. Imbued with a sense of historic purpose, Stringfellow began a diary to record the details of each day's session.[41] Although he does not seem to have played a role of any great significance at Augusta, his missionary fervor was soon recognized by the newly formed Southern Baptist Convention, which selected him as vice-president of its Domestic Mission Board.

Continuing to publish new and revised editions of his thoughts on slavery up until the Civil War, Stringfellow persisted in his perception of the South as bearing the "Sword of the Spirit" against northern heretics. The true test of his beliefs, however, was to come in 1863 when at the age of seventy-five, crippled by rheumatism, he and his invalid wife and granddaughter were surrounded at Bell Air by Yankees and held prisoner for several months while the northerners supplied their troops from the produce of his farm. Undaunted by age and illness, and always eager to convert the unbeliever, Stringfellow greeted his first Yankee with copies of his slavery pamphlets. He never abandoned faith in the possibility of converting the North to the southern cause, proclaiming hopefully in early July 1863, "In the morning saw extracts from northern papers—all favorable to the South."[42]

Although a few Yankee souls appeared salvageable to the old minister, most of the northerners seemed to be "of the baser sort," affirming Stringfellow's long-held conviction of the moral superiority of the South. Commenting on a group of soldiers garrisoned on his land, Stringfellow stated, "I have never met with such atheistical profanity—they play cards Sunday & all other days all over my yard—they curse God—They breathe out cruelty."[43] Yet, Stringfellow assured himself, "We are surely strengthened by a divine hand or we could not bear up under the present pressure."[44] But Stringfellow's trials were to increase, for only a week later he awoke one morning to find all his slaves had departed. Unable to confront the thought that his servants had fled from his benevolent care, Stringfellow insisted that they had been all but kidnapped by the Yankees. "We feel great relief in the Exodus of our servants as the Yankees crowded their houses day and night using persuasion & threats if they refused to go—they kept before their eyes, houses ready to receive them—everything provided to meet their wants—schools for their children—social equality in the best families—the highest price for their labour."[45] The next morning, Stringfellow remarked on the novelty of his changed domestic situation: "My wife & myself made our fire—made up our own bed."[46]

But Stringfellow was certain that the Lord remained on his side. "I have never felt a stronger conviction than now that all things work together for good to them that love him. I feel that it is he only that could have sustained us all in the measure of quit [quiet?] resignation with which we have been thus far blessed."[47] Convinced of the righteousness of the South, Stringfellow remained firm in his belief in northern baseness. "Vain confidence and inhumanity are the elements which make up the northern army. Truth has taken its flight—sentiments of honour are not known. . . . We are at the mercy of as base beings as God has ever permitted to live on this planet."[48]

Toward his own situation, Stringfellow developed an attitude of Job-like patience and drew an explicit analogy between the Civil War as a test of his faith and the Biblical trial of Shadrach, Meshach, and Abednego. "Many mercy drops have been vouchsafed to me & mine since the Lord put us into the furnace—but my heart is still what God in his word tells me it is—'deceitful and desperately wicked who can know it.' But he has emptied it some of the world so as to furnish more room for him whom my soul loveth—Oh that these afflictions may work for us all a far more exceeding & eternal weight of glory."[49]

A week later, on the last day of 1863, this volume of Stringfellow's diary ended with a final jibe at the northern "rogues."[50] Since he had made entries nearly every day for almost a year, it seems likely that he began another volume, but this book, as far as is now known, has not survived. Nevertheless, in late 1863, despite months of captivity and signs of impending defeat for the South, Stringfellow's faith in his section and the structure of his system of belief had not changed. Although his slaves ran away, he could not admit to himself that it was the result of any defect in the institution as one of benevolence and of benefit to both black and white. His contact with Yankees merely strengthened him in his conviction of southern moral superiority. Confederate defeat was not a sign of God's displeasure but merely a trial of the strength of southern faith and righteousness.

Little information exists concerning Stringfellow's activities in the four years of life that remained to him after southern surrender. This may in part have been because of deteriorating health, for even in 1863 he found himself confined to bed a great deal of the time and prevented by rheumatism even from kneeling in prayer. Acquaintances reported, however, that the minister's support for slavery and his belief in the South were undiminished at the time of his death.[51] Stringfellow's continuing faith in his own proslavery position is manifested in his will where he specifically designated all his own writings on slavery as well as those of others in his library to be given to his grandson along with such other treasures as his watch and family Bible.[52]

Stringfellow's proslavery sentiments were not shaken by the events of the Civil War because they were part of a much more extensive structure of belief. God had intended him as a clergyman and the church as an institution to act as His earthly surrogates, to expound and enforce His will among other men. Participation in benevolent activities, such as advocacy of temperance or of Sunday schools, appeared to Stringfellow as the logical consequences of his special position of responsibility. Because he had been chosen, it was his duty to point out to others the way of righteousness. Just as his social role as pastor reinforced his image of himself as divinely appointed to provide moral guidance, so his position as slaveholder strengthened his sense of himself as a trustee over other human lives. For Stringfellow, the two roles, minister and slaveholder, were analogous, for both required the exercise of a patriarchal moral concern about the behavior and welfare of others. Thus the advocacy of slavery seemed to him as integral a part of God's work as the encouragement of Sunday schools or Bible societies or any other institution of Christian education.

Because his evangelical world view was shared by a large proportion of nineteenth-century Americans, Stringfellow was continually reinforced in his commitment to moral stewardship and the missionary purpose by others involved in the church and in the myriad of reform activities. Only in the implications of his beliefs and values regarding slavery did he differ substantially from many northern advocates of benevolence.

Because the significance of Stringfellow's thought about slavery becomes clear only when it is seen within the context of his entire belief system and of his conception of his role, it may prove worthwhile to examine the thought of other proslavery theorists in relation to their institutional affiliations and their views of their purpose in the world. Perhaps then we might better understand how the defense of the peculiar institution formed an integral part of southern civilization. In the case of Stringfellow, the justification of slavery was inextricably related to the position he assumed as God's steward and the evangelicalism which served as the foundation of his world view. In his religious orientation to life around him and in his perception of political and social issues as essentially spiritual questions, Stringfellow epitomized the evangelical outlook that historians have come to see as one of the salient features of his era. Although the existence of this belief system and the steward's role that institutionalized it have been described primarily in regard to the North, Stringfellow's life suggests that it may instead have characterized the nation as a whole in the middle years of the nineteenth century.

The Rhetoric and Ritual of Agriculture in Antebellum South Carolina

W ords," literary critic I. A. Richards once remarked, "are not a medium in which to copy life. Their true work is to restore life itself to order." Language, Kenneth Burke has concurred, may be less a way of describing reality than of creating it. Speech, the two scholars suggest, is not so much a vehicle for conveying information as a mode of social action which in conceptualizing the world imposes a particular structure and meaning upon it. If language does indeed have such social functions, historians might reasonably expect to find in periods of cultural upheaval linguistic forms that seek to ease the crisis. Designed to cope with social chaos, these verbal rituals would codify a society's most fully articulated conceptions of order and disorder—and thus its most highly developed definition of itself.[1]

The changes that characterized early nineteenth-century America could not but appear threatening to a nation that had traditionally regarded the farmer as the favorite of God and agriculture as the basis of an ideal social order. The farmer's declining status amidst the rising importance of the professions, the eroding preeminence of agriculture in an economy of expanding commerce and manufacturing, and the movement of population away from older areas of settlement along the eastern seaboard seemed not just to signal the overthrow of existing patterns of economic relationships but to represent the emergence of an entirely new system of values and cultural commitments. To many Americans, the situation of agriculture seemed inseparable from—and even representative of—the condition of society at large. As one New Hampshire pastor observed to a gathering of farmers, "The fields we cultivate are an emblem of the moral field of the world. The labor we bestow upon them is a striking representation of that moral and religious culture which should be given to individuals and society."[2]

Because agriculture appeared to be a foundation of both social and moral order, perception of decline in its objective social and economic importance created considerable uneasiness among Americans already apprehensive about the widespread changes affecting their early nineteenth-century world. Drastic alterations in religious outlook, family life, political relationships, and economic structures seemed a protean threat to accustomed patterns of existence. The apparent shift in the position and role of agriculture within the social order thus came to represent for many anxious Americans a far wider spectrum of uncertainties. As a result, discussion of this change was often cast in an agricultural idiom. The imagery of agriculture provided a metaphorical mode of cultural self-examination and definition; it offered symbols with which Americans apprehended their world in social and moral as well as economic terms.[3]

This use of agricultural terminology as a vehicle through which to formulate deep-rooted cultural anxieties appears most prominently in what was known to nineteenth-century Americans as the agricultural address. Delivered at ceremonial gatherings of agricultural societies in all sections of the nation, these addresses constituted a specific oratorical genre that followed a prescribed pattern both of form and subject matter. Reflecting in their style and content many of the era's most deeply felt concerns, the speeches became, moreover, the focal point of a social ritual designed to confront and resolve many of the same issues of status and value articulated in the addresses themselves. Taken together, the agricultural orations and their social setting within agricultural gatherings constitute what sociolinguist Dell Hathaway Hymes has called a "speech event." The agricultural address was an act of verbal communication that served as a particular focus of social interaction, while at the same time the substance of the oration formulated the wider patterns of cultural values within which this immediate social reality was located. The rhetoric and the ceremony that bracketed it therefore manifested the interaction of language and culture through the designation of agriculture as both verbal and ritual symbol.[4]

While the relationship of language to culture and society is evident in agricultural addresses delivered throughout antebellum America, the specific details, the texture and meaning of the confrontation with change differed from region to region. While the nation as a whole had shared a common agricultural heritage, the social and economic implications of this traditional commitment differed markedly in North and South. And while Americans throughout the nation confronted disquieting change in the antebellum period, the particular shape of progress was to vary considerably between the growing commercial and industrial civilization of the North and the slave society of the South. While a challenge to the status of agriculture was certainly unsettling to old farm communities of New England and the Middle States, it appeared to the South as a crisis of even greater proportion, and inevitably became caught up with the region's growing consciousness of itself as a minority section in the years leading up to the Civil War. Any threat to the preeminence of agriculture was thus construed as a direct attack upon the southern way of life generally. By the early nineteenth century the South had thoroughly committed itself to an economic, social, and racial order based on profitable staple-crop agriculture carried out by a labor force of black slaves. Any alteration of these arrangements seemed to threaten what had become a comprehensive system of racial subordination and control. Thus, the fear of change that existed throughout antebellum America took on a particularly intense form in the South, for change itself seemed especially menacing to a region in which violence lay as the recognized yet unspoken foundation of the social order.

The agricultural address similarly reflected these dimensions of universality and specificity. A form employed widely in both North and South, the agricultural oration was nevertheless culture and section specific; it expressed the particular response of the society in which it was articulated to a set of problems that in their most general sense confronted all Americans. But in the South this fear of change was experienced most directly as a series of immediate threats to regional confidence and even survival. Within the state of South Carolina, which remained a focus of sectional conflict from the nullification controversy in 1832 to the attack on Fort Sumter in 1861, this sense of crisis was particularly acute. Everywhere a response to change, the agricultural address in South Carolina reflected the peculiarly intense dilemmas confronted by the planter leadership of this most radical southern state. For the master class the agricultural address became a jeremiad, a lamentation of regional failure as well as a call for South Carolinians to reclaim their rightful place as the chosen people of God. Through verbal symbols, planters imbued the soil that supported them with spiritual meaning and transformed nature into both a model of and a model for their social and moral lives.[5]

The purpose of this essay will be to explore the role and meaning of these orations within increasingly sectionalist South Carolina where the vicissitudes of agriculture correlated directly with alternating moods of cultural chauvinism and despair. A description of the formal structure of the agricultural address and its relationship to the ritual of the agricultural society meetings where it was delivered will suggest a way in which language may become part of a continuum of social action. A case study of South Carolina, moreover, may serve to elucidate how a single American subculture defined itself in response to processes of change and to suggest how its peculiar employment of a nationally utilized genre simultaneously reflected both the area's uniqueness and its typicality. The agricultural oration in this sense embodied the dialectical relationship between nationalism and sectionalism so central to the culture of the Old South.[6]

The severe agricultural depression of the late 1830s and early 1840s came as a climax to twenty years of uncertainty in the cotton market. After the nationwide financial panic of 1819, cotton prices never regained the heights of the first decades of the century. Despite signs of a reviving market in the mid–1830s, prices had by the end of that decade begun a precipitous decline that was further accelerated by the national economic crisis beginning in 1837. With only brief interruptions the cotton market remained depressed until the 1850s. Before about 1826 increasing productivity had somewhat compensated for the drop in price, but after that year South Carolina's output of cotton declined as well, and it continued to decline for the next fifteen years.[7]

In the early 1830s the tendency of South Carolinians to fix blame for their difficulties on oppressive tariffs imposed by the North led to the upheavals of the nullification movement. But when a compromise tariff did not bring economic revival, South Carolina's planters began to search for other explanations of their predicament. Compared with fresh lands in the southwestern states of Alabama and Mississippi, overworked Carolina soil seemed exhausted, clearly incapable of competing in productivity per hand or per acre. "The sterile aspect of the country . . . ," one planter observed, "indicates too truly our wretched system of agriculture, and the necessity of an immediate change if we wish to preserve the little remnant of fertility still left in our lands."[8]

With the effects of western competition magnified by falling prices, Carolinians sought to account for the depressed state of the cotton market. "It is a well-known fact," one orator reminded his audience, "than [sic] the quantity of cotton already grown is fully equal to the consumption, and by many, it is believed, to exceed it." The golden age of cotton, it seemed, had passed. The planters of South Carolina, James Henry Hammond warned, "will be speedily compelled almost, if not altogether, to abandon its longer cultivation."[9]

Yet the state's agriculturists acknowledged that they were peculiarly unequipped to deal with cotton's demise. Their reliance upon the staple was so exclusive that they found themselves "tributaries" to other regions of diversified economies both for many foodstuffs and for nearly all manufactures. "It is the true policy of the cotton planters," resolved an agricultural convention in 1843, "to curtail the cotton crop and increase the provision crop—so as to supply all the breadstuffs and raise all the different kinds of stock . . . which may be necessary for family and plantation use."[10]

These structural deficiencies in South Carolina's agricultural economy seemed to perceptive analysts the cause of another alarming development. The productivity of western land was not only capturing the cotton market, it was attracting many of South Carolina's most industrious and enterprising citizens. The problem of emigration from Carolina was so severe that by 1850 the census revealed that of all living Americans born in South Carolina, 41 percent had moved elsewhere. The slow growth of population took on ominous meaning when South Carolina lost two representatives in congressional reapportionment.[11]

Prevailing agricultural practices contributed significantly to these harsh economic and demographic realities. Most Carolinians had little understanding of soil chemistry and clung to what State Agricultural Surveyor Edmund Ruffin described as the "barbarous usage" of growing cotton on the same land every year. Even those who did practice rotation of crops tended to follow one exhausting product with another, little understanding the principles behind variation in planting. Carolinians retained as well an almost "universal prejudice" against the plow, so that even when fertilizer was applied to the soil, it was not

Edmund Ruffin, agricultural reformer and proslavery advocate
in the uniform of Palmetto Guard (1861). Courtesy
Library of Congress, Washington, D.C.

effectively worked in. Shallow cultivation also contributed to extensive erosion, as rains washed loose topsoil into rivers and streams. Because of this "ignominious course of culture" an agricultural journal estimated in 1850 that eight hundred thousand "square acres" of Carolina land had been entirely worn out—or at least seemed effectively exhausted because of an inability to compete in productivity with virgin lands in the West.[12]

Severe as they appeared, the realities of soil depletion and declining profits seemed to agricultural orators as only a part of the crisis afflicting the state. Behind these obvious difficulties lay another, less apparent dimension of Carolina's dilemma. Those who discussed her plight rarely restricted their analyses to social and economic concerns. Orators defined the agricultural situation in moral terms; speakers sought to describe Carolina's condition in language that would contain implicit within it a strategy of action for dealing with the crisis at hand. The constantly reiterated threat of both moral and economic "despair and ruin" was intended to compel Carolinians to the reform that was presented as their only salvation.[13]

Agricultural decline, these orators found, challenged an entire system of values; it called into question not just men's means of relating to the soil but their relationships with one another and with God. Like Puritan jeremiads, lamentations of degeneration in agricultural addresses equated material with spiritual blessings, identifying economic decline as both symbol and consequence of social disharmony and moral decay. It was an error, one speaker warned, that "instead of looking to ourselves for a want of success, [we] attribute the failure to our lands—we proclaim them sterile."[14]

Agriculture and its failures could not be separated from man's moral condition; the land necessarily influenced and reflected man's spiritual nature. These rhetorical formulae defined agriculture as the cornerstone of society itself, not simply through its provision of the material bases of life but through "its great and primary value, in affecting the condition of the human family, and conserving the social harmonies, and promoting and sustaining the moral basis" of southern civilization. The agricultural address had traditionally offered the assurance of ultimate immutability within nature's cycles of repeated decay and rebirth. To a society beset by change, the orations thus provided a familiar and comforting image of the land as a stable reality, transcending individual human lives or fortunes. The "God of Nature," a correspondent of the *Southern Agriculturist* contended, had made it possible for the southerner to remain aloof from the social disorders that increasingly plagued the cities of the North. Independent of other men and reliant only upon the land, the planter could be "more above the reach of contingencies than the monarch upon his throne."[15]

But by the mid-1830s such a vision of stability had come to serve more as the affirmation of a consoling possibility than as a realistic description of the situation at hand. Indeed, the very appearance of change, of challenges to this ideal of eternal immutability, required agricultural rhetoric to encompass these new threats within its explanatory mode. Orators of the 1830s began to recognize that the earth had not proved unchangeable but had decayed; society had similarly been drastically altered as Carolinians abandoned their tired lands to move to the virgin soils of the West. But this had occurred, the speakers explained, because the relationship between culture and agriculture was not simply one-directional; agriculture was a *reflection* of society and values as well as an influence upon them. Nature's riches were not the free gift of God but demanded careful management and cultivation. "The Earth is ours as a sacred trust." Even Carolina's slave institution, orators warned ominously, seemed to be weakening, eroding like the soil because of the planter's failure to exercise his responsibility to supervise the human bounty God had entrusted to his care. The state's deficiencies, the exhaustion of her soil, the decay of her way of life, the orators argued, arose from the neglect of what were in essence religious duties.[16]

The rhetoric transformed failures of mind into failures of morality and thus rendered them appropriate subjects for the evangelical intervention of the agricultural orator. "We have not," one Carolinian lamented, "done justice to that noble inheritance which has descended to our hands. We have, in the mournful language of scriptural self-chiding, left undone those things which we ought to have done; and we have done those things which we ought not to have done." But, he continued, departing from the Anglican prayer for absolution that he had invoked, "We will not add, that 'there is no help in us,' for we trust there is both help and hope . . . in any people, who acknowledge their errors, and are . . . prepared to amend them."[17]

Like jeremiads, these agricultural lamentations transformed the experience of crisis into a divine warning. Depression was not a vindictive punishment or a sign of damnation, but a corrective affliction imposed, like the tribulations of Job, on God's chosen. The present situation, Basil Manly explained, "is a state of *trial*." South Carolinians had erred, but a final verdict had not yet been rendered; the lamentation of apostasy contained implicit within it the possibility of redemption and reform. This characterization of the situation implied a sense of human obligation, a requirement for action. "God does nothing in vain," William H. Wigg reminded the Agricultural Society of St. Luke's Parish. In Carolina's affliction "*He* has revealed his will. *He* has made our duty plain."[18]

These orations were designed, like rhetoric more generally, to move humans to certain attitudes and actions. Words were intended, as Edmund Rhett explained to the Beaufort Agricultural Society, to assume "the power of things." The addresses therefore display many of the time-honored devices of traditional rhetoric learned by educated Carolinians from Classical texts. But the Carolinians' specific use of these ancient modes of persuasion demonstrate as well the speakers' understanding of the particular values most deeply cherished by their fellow citizens.[19]

The literary device upon which the agricultural address was founded was one that rhetoricians since the age of Aristotle have labeled "identification," an assertion of likenesses among both ideas and individuals that imparts the sense of intellectual coherence and of emotional and social unity prerequisite to common action. To advance his case a speaker redefines or reclassifies a problematical concept in terms of recognized positive affect; he moves the idea into a realm acknowledged as appealing and desirable. He "identifies" the object of his concern with the positive response actually evoked by the context in which he has placed it, and thus he demonstrates its consistency with accepted beliefs and values. At the same time, he enhances his persuasive powers by using identification in another manner as well, stressing the similarities between himself and his audience, not just in terms of belief but of more objective external factors. Thus out of both conceptual and social divisions he seeks to establish unity, imposing upon the diversity of experience a single order and meaning that will clearly prescribe future attitudes and patterns of conduct.[20]

South Carolina's agricultural orators sought in their use of identification to establish an ideological as well as a social consensus that would override the cultural and social conflict they found so alarming. As historian James M. Banner, Jr., has emphasized, the emergence of black majorities in two-thirds of South Carolina's parishes by 1860 had only intensified a long-standing fear of the existence of any discord among whites. Expressed in what Banner describes as a Carolina tradition of an "antiparty ideology" and a "no-party system," these anxieties were manifested as well in the dedication of the agricultural address to the promotion of unity. Both the ideas presented within the orations and the form of the addresses themselves were designed to advance this traditional rhetorical—and social—goal.[21]

The structure of the genre itself reveals the most basic relationships of sameness the orators sought to present. These addresses were highly stylized, and speakers recognized that they were expected to follow certain well-established forms. When Joel Roberts Poinsett intended to deviate slightly from the explicit rules, he felt compelled to excuse himself and to explain he would not be making "what is usually called an Agricultural address."[22]

Almost without exception, agricultural orations from this period in South Carolina opened with what one speaker described as an "apologetic preface." Each orator felt obligated to proclaim his "sense of . . . deficiency" at the task before him and thus to identify himself with his audience and engage their sympathies by denying his uniqueness or individuality and by portraying himself as in a sense the creation of their will. Although in New England agricultural orations were often delivered by clergymen, South Carolina's orators were almost inevitably planters—the most successful and wealthy citizens, to be sure, but, they insisted, as tillers of the soil, simply *primi inter pares*. Here was the persistent paradox of the South's aristocratic egalitarianism again reaffirmed; the orator sought simultaneously to be first and to be equal. The existence of class divisions in the region could be all but denied through an insistence upon the essential similarity that overrode differences not just between the highly successful agriculturist on the podium and the planters who composed most of his audience but between the richest and the poorest Carolinians. Be they wealthy planters or dirt farmers, southerners were, the myth contended, agrarians all. In these familiar terms, the orator endeavored to portray himself to—and identify himself with—both his listeners and his section.[23]

Having emphasized this solidarity, the orator set forth upon his address, usually beginning with a paean to agriculture. "Nothing is more common on occasions like the present, than for the speaker to labour at the very outset, to impress his audience with the importance of his subject," one South Carolinian explained. Agriculture had to be transported from the realm of the mundane to a position of appropriately inspirational dignity. Orators sought regularly to accomplish this task by considering it in terms of the legitimating frameworks of history, science, and religion.[24]

Usually, "an historical sketch of the progress of agriculture in different ages and nations, or with abstract speculations on its antiquity, dignity and importance" immediately followed the apologetic preface. Cain, Noah, the Patriarchs, the Egyptians, the Greeks, the Romans, and America's Founding Fathers were invoked to demonstrate that in its very persistence through the ages agriculture had gained at least a degree of transcendence. As chronologically the first endeavor of mankind, orators argued, agriculture deserved to be considered the foremost.[25]

But agriculture was not simply legitimated by tradition; it was identified with the way of the future as well. After reiterating the history of husbandry, the oration almost inevitably included a section discussing agriculture in light of modern experimental discoveries, seeking, as Basil Manly explained, "accomplishment of an immediate and settled union between the profoundest science and the labors of the field." In associating agriculture with rational investigation the orator sought to enhance the position of husbandry by portraying it as a profession requiring knowledge and training and bestowing upon its practitioners the "dignity" accorded by the modern age to such accomplishment.[26]

Yet while agriculture was theoretically consistent with modern science, it was, the orators complained, rarely practiced by South Carolinians in conformity with scientific dictates. The discussion of agriculture in the light of history and science was thus usually structurally juxtaposed with a third section of the address lamenting existing inadequacies. Here the orator stressed the contrast between the achievements of husbandry in past ages, its future potential as a branch of science, and its manifold present deficiencies. Inspired by the account of agriculture's glorious past and its future greatness, the listener was to be moved to change the disappointing present, to make rational husbandry a reality. Science, the orator reminded his audience, promised to be more than a means to truth; it would serve as an avenue to success as well, for it was on the principles of science that the rise of the professions was founded. "You hear him [the farmer] talk," Andrew P. Calhoun declared to a gathering of planters, "of law and medicine as the two learned professions. He habitually defers to them as something superior to his own. . . . Now, cannot this be changed? Cannot the farmer and planter train his intellect[?]" Agricultural orators did not doubt that "the application of science . . . will soon correct the errors of public sentiment, and organize the social relations of society on a new basis," enhancing the image of the farmer by identifying him with the march of progress that characterized the modern age. Science was desirable not only because it was true, but because it would be socially and economically profitable.[27]

The paean to rational knowledge that appeared in every agricultural address, however, was ordinarily cast in what the twentieth century would regard as curiously unscientific terms. The orator hoped not only to associate agriculture with both past tradition and future progress but also to unite religion with science into a single legitimating framework. "The scientific planter . . . ," J. Jenkins Mikell explained, could not but be aware of "the Divine mind . . . displayed before him." As a result, the portions of the address devoted to history and science were often followed by a specific discussion of the ties between agriculture and religion. More frequently, however, the consideration of these relationships was not restricted to a single section of the address; religious language and symbolism pervaded the entire oration, providing the terminology for much of the rest of the discussion. Science was presented as simply the modern form of divine revelation, for the farmer, as one orator affirmed, routinely "looks through nature up to nature's God." The listener had learned that improved agriculture could elevate his material condition; now he was promised that the pursuit of wealth would produce spiritual amelioration as well. In agriculture, the speakers suggested, lay the means of reconciling not just science and religion but traditional morality with the alluring materialism of the modern world.[28]

In a reformed agriculture and consequently replenished soil lay the resolution of all these tensions—a way of satisfying the desire for wealth within the framework of man's most time-honored occupation. The westward emigration so destructive to social order within the state would no longer be necessary, for profitable farming would be possible at home. Through agriculture, Carolina's planters assured themselves, they could be rich without succumbing to corrupt materialism. Under such circumstances, riches would serve as testimony to their spiritual excellence and favor with God. Planting, Whitemarsh Benjamin Seabrook affirmed before the United Agricultural Society, was one "business, which of all others, best conduces to the legitimate purposes of man's creation."[29]

Through the symbolic identification of nature, society, and God, moral commitment was defined as being as important as the very nourishment man derived from the earth. The agricultural jeremiad served, in the words of anthropologist Victor Turner, as a "mechanism that . . . converts the obligatory into the desirable." Like the ritual and symbolic forms Turner has described among African peoples, the structure of the agricultural address juxtaposed and thus associated ethical norms with the emotional allurements of financial profit. Duty was defined as a pleasure and pleasure as a duty. James Henry Hammond of South Carolina neatly exemplified the way such symbols work when in 1841 he explained the effects of casting what modern Americans would regard as economic problems in social and religious terms. Agricultural decline, he proclaimed, "cannot be contemplated but with feelings of profound emotion. Not only on account of its immediate pecuniary consequences, but its great moral effects." Through such evocation of feeling agricultural oratory sought to achieve the purposes of all rhetoric: to influence men to think and feel what is right and thereby move them to do what is right. Nature, like God, the addresses advised, must be actively worshiped. Herein lay the imperative for agricultural reform. "We ought to bear in mind," James Hamilton counseled, "that the great source of production is the earth; that in order to keep her in a kind temper for yielding, we must pay her tribute without stint." To manure the land, South Carolina's orators explicitly proclaimed, was to make an offering to God, as well as to Mammon.[30]

The agricultural orator thus sought to establish cognitive consistency in the minds of his listeners by identifying agriculture with all those configurations of belief and sources of meaning his compatriots seemed to regard as important. Indeed, the structure of the address was a movement from one to another of these frameworks of meaning, a juxtaposition of several sources of authority. Through its compatibility with both older and newer systems of belief, agriculture was offered as a bridge over the chasm of change. Here, the orator proclaimed, was a means of resolving conflicting ideological allegiances. By combining— both substantively and structurally—discussion of past achievement with that of future progress, by uniting religion and science, the agricultural oration associated reassuring tradition with dynamic innovation, deriving from each realm its own particular affective imperative, designed to infuse agriculture with new meaning. The agriculturist, the orator proclaimed, could be simultaneously wealthy and holy, religious and rational, traditional and modern.[31]

Carolinians, however, shared fears more immediate and perhaps more alarming than their anxieties about shifting foundations for belief in an era of change. The world seemed not just to be escaping easy comprehension; it threatened to slip entirely out of their control. "Dangers," Hugh Swinton Legaré remarked to a friend, "are around and above and below and within our poor little State." The agricultural address in South Carolina reflected these peculiarly local fears and was therefore designed to resolve tension and conflict in the social as well as the cultural realm. At the same time, therefore, that its introductory synthesis of religion, science, and history offered a convincing framework of explanation for mundane events, the oration sought a more immediate social impact, and this effort structured the more pragmatic second half of the address.[32]

Spurred by their growing fears of disorder, Carolinians endeavored to reaffirm existing social arrangements by emphasizing the state's unity of material interest. To this end, agricultural orators attempted to identify the people of South Carolina with the land and to demonstrate that a particular social and economic system grew inescapably out of this special relationship. As Henry William Ravenel stated explicitly, "An agricultural people are always more strongly attached to the soil on which they have been reared. They become identified with it." Indeed, man's body itself, another speaker explained, was literally "composed of the materials of agriculture." The social order, the orators implied, was founded in nature and therefore must be at once legitimate and inevitable.[33]

But nature exerted her influence in another manner as well, decreeing not just the unity but the particularity of southern agriculturists.

The soil of the South, its flora and fauna, were—like the social institutions that had grown out of them—specific to the region and dictated by its unique characteristics. "Peculiar climate, peculiar productions, and still more peculiar institutions," William Elliott argued, rendered agriculture the fundamental determinant of the entire southern way of life, the source of the unity and distinctiveness of the southern people. "We, stand as agriculturists," Frederick A. Porcher proclaimed to the Black Oak Agricultural Society, "isolated from the mass of mankind." Growing political and ideological nonconformity was founded, Carolinians asserted, in the unchanging realities of the physical environment.[34]

Yet, to portray southern society as united and self-conscious was a rhetorical gesture, more prescriptive than descriptive. Emphasis on "homogeneity of interest," Ravenel explained, was specifically calculated to persuade southerners to a "unanimity of action" in a state where even the leadership class was riven with conflict. By affirming the existence of a shared southern identity that had grown out of a common association with the soil, orators sought to compensate for existing divisions and to obviate the threat of emerging ones.[35]

A committee of the State Agricultural Society readily acknowledged the strong tendencies toward fragmentation within the Carolina elite when it observed in 1845 that "the habits of planters are those of separate action: they combine less than any other class of men. Each regards his plantation as his empire." These long-standing pressures toward disunity, moreover, had been greatly intensified by the fierce political conflicts of the early 1830s. Unionists and Nullifiers had struggled bitterly within the state, and wounds incurred during the hostilities still smarted, serving as a significant divisive factor throughout South Carolina and within her leadership. Recurring national crises, such as the controversy later in the same decade over the effort to "gag" congressional discussion of abolition, continued to erode the solidarity of Carolina's master class.[36]

To a state that had long regarded unity as all important and had systematically eschewed the development of a party system because of the necessary division it implied, such developments seemed most alarming. Orators sought specifically to use agriculture as a diversion from these frictions. "Could we talk less about politics and more about crops?" one speaker implored. In contrast to the "agitating" subject of political issues, orators found the topic of agriculture altogether "more calm, and peaceful"—and therefore, more desirable. Political controversy, another orator warned, undermined that "unity of feeling, thought and action" so essential to defend the state and her peculiar institutions against what one planter called "the intonations of a gathering tempest."[37]

Orators regularly avoided the difficulties posed by political questions by insisting upon subsuming them into a discussion of agriculture. It was on this topic, "if any where," R. A. Maxwell proclaimed to an up-country gathering, that "all parties may unite on a common platform." In recognizing the unity of interest that underlay any political question or potential division, Carolinians could escape the "low and vulgar banners of party." Andrew P. Calhoun painted an appealing portrait of the way that an understanding of the central importance of agriculture would enhance the future of South Carolina. "We will have society great and grand beyond description," he proclaimed, "—one homogenious [sic] interests [sic] extending through the whole. Every question started by demagogism in our midst, hushed—unity, concert, and strength will mark our councils." A focus on the importance of agriculture would, he implied, not just unify the planters. Class differences among all whites were defined as meaningless before this overwhelming commonality of interest. A demagogue's factional appeal to the masses could not succeed, Calhoun explained, in a society where the people understood their common identity. The hegemony of agriculture would thus ensure the hegemony of the planter, of his particular husbandry and its peculiar institutions.[38]

In its consideration of specifically Carolinian problems of social unity, the second half of the agricultural address often turned to the subject of slavery. As one orator explained, it seemed "naturally required of me" to discuss the system of human bondage. The advancement of a common agricultural interest as a means of suppressing political dissension thus addressed another agenda as well. Agriculture was not simply the means of support of the great majority of the population; it was the *raison d'être* for the slave institution upon which the social order was built. "The system of Southern Agriculture," as William Elliott acknowledged, "is dependent on and moulded by the institution of domestic slavery." Orators identified the people with the southern soil, the soil, in turn, with a particular sort of agriculture, and the agriculture, finally, with the peculiar institutions of the southern states. To improve husbandry was thus to defend slavery. As Whitemarsh B. Seabrook explained, "South-Carolina is emphatically an agricultural State. The prosperity and permanency of her domestic institutions are identified with its success. . . . To encourage it, is a political duty."[39]

The language of agriculture became a kind of code for the discussion of slavery, a means of talking about the most sensitive political concern of the day in a manner ostensibly apolitical, a manner designed to obviate any sources of division on this all-important subject. The orators' overwhelming concern with unity arose ultimately from anxieties about this very issue, about the future of the slave institution. Implicit within every agricultural address, these tensions frequently became explicit as well. As early as 1825 Seabrook warned that "the tenure by which we hold our slaves, is daily becoming less secure." Two decades later he found "our domestic institutions . . . in imminent peril." Agricultural uplift was a crucial part of meeting this crisis, Seabrook explained, for "if, from unprofitable harvests, the servant should become a burden to his master, the shouts of the fanatic may yet be heard in our own domicil." Agricultural reform could be equated with the survival of both slavery and the South. The *"existence and continuance"* of the peculiar institution, one up-country orator warned explicitly, *"depend upon our agriculture."*[40]

Although only a few organizations actually titled themselves "Agricultural and Police Societies," a common dedication to upholding slavery was clear in the addresses delivered before every association. Mastery of slaves was on the one hand "a profound and difficult science" requiring the same level of learning and skill as any kind of animal husbandry. Yet slaves were human as well, undeniably a part of the social and moral realm. "A heavy weight of moral and religious responsibilities devolve" upon the southern planter, Robert William Roper reminded the Agricultural Society of South Carolina, "especially where a number of his fellow creatures are subject to his control." Proper administration of slaves, like a reformed agriculture more generally, was thus, as one orator concluded, not just a scientific but "a sacred duty."[41]

And by its association with the universal importance of agriculture, slavery too became a focus of unity. Because everyone was in one way or another dependent upon South Carolina's agricultural productivity, the orators argued, everyone—whether or not he owned slaves—was dependent upon the peculiar institution. David F. Jamison explained this point of view to the state society. "The brunt of this conflict" with the North, he declared, "must be borne by the slaveholders. They constitute the more numerous class and are most directly interested in the issue. But who is the slaveholder? Or more properly, Who is interested in the institution of slavery? Every one I answer, who is interested in the welfare, good government and prosperity of the South." Jamison, like most agricultural orators, sought to identify nonslaveholders as well as planters with the peculiar institution and here did so by the rhetorical trick of redefining the terms of the discussion. By insisting that slavery was indispensable to all southerners, he argued that through their identification with a slaveholding region even nonslaveholders became slaveholders themselves.[42]

From the transcendent realm of history, religion, and science, the agricultural address thus narrowed its focus to specific issues, such as slavery, that troubled the state. Like traditional Protestant sermons, the orations moved from the general exegesis of doctrine to its particular mundane applications. The systems of meaning explored in the beginning of each address provided the language and the framework within which the details of Carolina's impending crisis were discussed; orators hoped to infuse the particular actions advocated in the second half of the agricultural addresses with the compelling force of the imperatives contained in the overarching systems of belief already outlined. Thus, they called their fellow citizens to united action in undertaking the moral, social, and economic uplift of the state.

In its mission of inspiration and even conversion, the agricultural address was thus transformed from rhetoric into part of a quasi-religious ritual. Verbal action was intended to provoke behavioral response; both were part of the same continuum of social action. Like the Protestant sermon not just in general structure but in external context, the agricultural oration served as a central component in a gathering of the faithful; it was the focusing element in the meetings of the agricultural societies that began to proliferate in the 1830s. Between 1826 and 1847 the number of these nearly tripled, from eleven to thirty-two, and a State Agricultural Society was created in 1839 to coordinate the expanding activities of the local groups.[43]

The agricultural association provided a social setting and context for the agricultural address and even an embodiment of the values these orations expressed. The society meeting was to translate the action of words into the action of behavior. Agricultural organizations were intended to promote the unity of all South Carolinians, a unity that the orations had defined as both necessary and desirable. Because leaders saw agricultural improvement as indispensable to South Carolina's survival in the escalating sectional struggle they made an effort to enlist every citizen in the cause. Thus, they held agricultural festivals, advertised by widely distributed handbills; thus, they self-consciously named the two most prominent journals of the movement *Southern Agriculturist* and *Farmer and Planter,* emphasizing in the very titles the unity of all tillers of the soil. But from the first it was evident that the evangelism of agriculture was not easily to succeed—as many of its prophets had dared hope—in converting Carolinians of all classes to the gospel of improvement. Agricultural reformers therefore explicitly dedicated themselves, at least as an immediate goal, to the consolidation of the planter class within the state, an endeavor that dangerous political divisions originating in nullification had made especially urgent. "The constant interchange . . . of sentiments and opinions between planters, from different sections of the country, which will be elicited," one advocate of organization explained, "will be a great mean of forming a closer union than has heretofore prevailed." Just as agricultural oratory sought to replace partisan polemics, so gatherings of agricultural societies were designed to supplant political assemblies with their inevitable tendencies toward faction and discord.[44]

The societies themselves became almost exclusively the preserve of the planter class. When Virginian Edmund Ruffin spoke before the Monticello Society, he remarked that he "did not see one who appeared to be of the lower class," even though he expected such individuals to be "attracted by the plentiful barbacue [sic]." In the Pendleton Association—one of the few agricultural organizations to assume the humble appellation of Farmers' Society—the average landholding was 809 acres, while the average for the area was 426. While only 28 percent of club members owned 250 acres or less, 43 percent of landholders in the vicinity possessed farms smaller than that size. Thus even in Pendleton, in the more egalitarian up-country region of the state, agricultural society members were the most substantial property holders.[45]

In most agricultural organizations, the form of the meetings was much the same, directly reflecting the outlook and values of this master class. An inspirational address by a leading citizen often opened the proceedings by lamenting Carolina's decline and asserting the need for both agricultural and moral reform. Individual members of the organization then spoke, affirming the principles of a reformed husbandry or offering witness of their personal conversion to scientific farming by describing their own experiments and innovations. Through this procedure, John S. Brisbane explained to the St. Andrews Association, "we not only may communicate any improvement made individually, but we excite a disposition to have something worth communicating, and arouse into action those dormant powers of investigation which otherwise would remain in torpidity. Who has not felt himself stimulated to exertion by the desire of gaining the applause of his neighbors[?]" To encourage such "emulation" more generally, agricultural clubs sponsored exhibitions and fairs and offered premiums for outstanding examples of produce or stock.[46]

The societies sought to create an atmosphere of mutual improvement by encouraging competition and communal pressure. One of the vehicles for realizing this goal was the committees of inspection that reported at society gatherings. These groups were appointed to investigate members' methods of husbandry. "The fear of shame," Brisbane explained, "of being held up to view as negligent planters, will stimulate to exertions, which otherwise would not have been made." Despite the untidy appearance of his crop because of the outbreak of measles in his family, Mr. Crawford was forgiven by the Visiting Committee of the Fishing Creek Agricultural Society because his purchase "of a fine Berkshire pig" seemed "a sufficient index that, with him, the spirit of improvement is abroad." Like the classes within evangelical sects, the visiting committees of South Carolina's agricultural societies were designed to ensure that spiritual conversion to reform would not fail to be expressed in changed behavior.[47]

Following the reports of these inspections, agricultural meetings frequently dissolved for a "pic-nic," a feast of such magnitude as itself to serve as testimony to the potential bounty of the earth—and the wealth of the planters who provided it. As with the premiums and committee visits, the planters here too vied with one another to display their agricultural success and social status, in this instance by providing the most sumptuous foods. At St. Helena Society meetings members rotated the responsibility for dinner, which eventually became so lavish that the organization decided to impose a fifty-cent fine on those who sent more than six courses of meat to the clubhouse. At the St. Andrew's Society each member contributed a single dish, but all had to be consigned to "the hands of the stewards, and by them arranged on the table" in order to prevent any individual from placing his contribution in a position of undue prominence on the buffet. While the societies sought to unify Carolina's planters and the agricultural interest in the state as a whole, they simultaneously provided an arena for the display and affirmation of the hierarchical structure of Carolina society and of its elite. The aggressiveness that the Carolina aristocrat exhibited in political contests thus appeared in the more "calm and peaceful" realm of agriculture as well. But here the planter could express his competitiveness in a less socially destructive manner, in a potlatch centered on food or in rivalry over success in husbandry. Just as the orations at these meetings articulated the system of values of the culture, so the activities that followed—the interaction among the planters, the reports of the inspection committees, and the "pic-nic"—served as the social expression of these values and as a ritual ratification of the Carolina social order.[48]

Both the addresses and the societies demonstrate the peculiar combination of aristocratic and democratic allegiances that troubled mid-nineteenth-century Carolinians. The emphasis of the orations on the central importance of agriculture to the state denied the legitimacy of class conflict while simultaneously ensuring the preeminence of the planter. Yet fear of an emergence of class resentment is evident throughout the addresses. Speakers felt obligated to outline the allegedly nearly equal advantages offered to all classes by the southern way of life, thus implicitly acknowledging that democratic principles held some legitimacy. As they demonstrated their commitment to perpetuating their own preeminence, they felt curiously compelled to maintain that it did not exist.

Agricultural reform was an undertaking designed to meet the needs of Carolina's master class during an era of extended crisis; it served as an assertion of control by a class unsettled by economic difficulties at home, eroding political power within the nation, and doubts about the foundations of its own legitimacy. Through the rhetoric and ritual of agriculture South Carolina planters sought to shore up their confidence and security, transforming their power into authority, identifying it with images of social prosperity and of morality rather than relying on the more objective realities of unquestioned economic or political superiority to support their dominance. Unexamined hierarchicalism could no longer win consent; Carolina's master class felt compelled to demonstrate that its preeminence was—paradoxically—democratic, as well as moral and rational in foundation.

In a similarly paradoxical manner, the agricultural reform movement was both a failure and a success. Agricultural historians looking back on objective conditions have found that actual improvement of land or methods of tillage was minimal and was for the most part restricted to those privileged planters who believed they could afford the luxury of experiment. Most Carolinians, ignoring entreaties on behalf of deep plowing and crop rotation, continued their destructive practices. Nevertheless, attitudes toward agricultural conditions changed out of all proportion to an actual amelioration of the situation. While some implacably realistic orators continued to assail Carolina agriculture, even these felt compelled to combat a growing sense of optimism about successes of the reform movement. "Much has been said about improvement in agriculture," J. P. Barrott admitted to the Greenwood Society in 1852. But, he challenged, "we ask for the proof. . . . We talk much of improvement in agriculture," he concluded, "but it is all fudge."[49]

Most orators did not share his cynicism. "We now have," William Elliott proclaimed to the St. Paul's Society in 1850, "a marked and visible improvement in every department of business." There was justification for his belief that in important ways the situation had changed. With the rise of cotton prices in the early 1850s Carolinians could afford to be optimistic. "Farmers are generally out of debt," J. E. Byrd wrote in *Farmer and Planter*. A declining interest in agricultural improvement accompanied this new mood and was reflected in the demise of the State Agricultural Society, which stopped meeting after the fall of 1849 because of the inactivity among many of the local organizations that composed it.[50]

These changed attitudes about agriculture were in part a reflection of Carolina's revitalized faith in the social order that agriculture had come to symbolize. Improved prices affected Carolinians' perceptions of agricultural conditions, but these perceptions simultaneously reflected a larger social and political atmosphere. The acute nature of regional crisis in the years just before the Civil War seemed to require a level of confidence incompatible with intense criticism of agricultural and economic realities and prospects. To risk real reform, Andrew P. Calhoun explained in an 1856 oration, South Carolina had to feel secure, for only under such circumstances could she safely admit weakness and acknowledge the need for change. Another citizen explained in *Farmer and Planter* that it was dangerous amid the upheaval following the Compromise of 1850 to contend "that neglect and dilapidation mark our internal condition. At this moment, when our gallant little state seems destined to fight, single handed, the battle of the South, we have need of all our courage, all our spirits, all our *faith in Carolina.*"[51]

Agricultural reform, they implied, was an undertaking suited to an era in which crisis was less acute, an era of merely chronic difficulties, like those of the late 1830s and 1840s, for example. It was a movement that could anticipate only long-term effects in building social unity and uplifting a distressed economy. When the northern threat seemed immediate—at the time of nullification, during the crisis of 1850–1852, and in the period of secession—the focus of concern of the planter class shifted to the more narrowly political issues it could use as its sectional defense within the arena of national government. The agricultural jeremiad, with its language of desolation and decline, conceded too much to the enemy and was thus supplanted by a political rhetoric emphasizing not the state's shortcomings but its successes, the emblems of its special favor with God. "Who will gainsay," demanded an orator, "that the Southern people of the American Union are the chosen race of modern times?" The special status that had so long been implied by the image of agricultural depression as corrective affliction was here at last realized as a full-blown southern nationalism. James Henry Hammond employed the now familiar synecdochic identification of the South with her agricultural staples in his proclamation of this burgeoning sectional confidence. Although in 1841 he had advised his fellow Carolinians to abandon the unprofitable cultivation of cotton, in 1858 he felt the necessary assurance to proclaim to the United States Senate and the world at large, "You dare not make war on cotton. . . . Cotton *is* king."[52]

In the comparatively quiet years of the mid–1850s the agricultural reform movement had reemerged briefly with the reestablishment of the State Society in 1855, but this effort, like its predecessors, was to fail and to disappear beneath the overwhelmingly political concerns of its era. Despite its failure to improve agricultural practice, the reform movement contributed to an important shift in outlook within the state. With the final crisis of Lincoln's election Carolina's master class was sufficiently convinced of the legitimacy of its authority and the viability of its way of life to defy national law and opinion and, ultimately, federal troops. South Carolina's planters were able to agree to withdraw from the Union without creating the internecine division that had appeared during nullification, and they succeeded as well in securing the acquiescence—if not the enthusiastic support—of the rest of the citizens of the state. Although the lands and practices of the state's husbandmen were for the most part unchanged, attitudes were not. The planter class found in 1861 a unity and effectiveness of action that had eluded it thirty years before. The rhetoric and rituals of agriculture had played an important role in establishing this symbolic consensus and social solidarity.[53]

Attribution of such crucial significance to tediously repetitive, long-winded, stereotyped orations may seem bewildering, if not perverse. Yet it is their very formulaic quality that renders these addresses so suggestive to the historian, for it implies that there existed a set of socially understood and shared rules about the meaning and purpose of the orations. They are not simply random pronouncements but are rather a group product, a verbal genre, and therefore a social form. In this rural society the kinds of communication and interaction that form the essence of any culture were severely limited by geographic distances and by a level of illiteracy that inhibited the development of a periodical press or a large reading public. Thus, the verbal genres of oratory were of special importance in the Old South. As one historian has remarked, "It is doubtful if there has ever been a society in which the orator counted for more than he did in the Cotton Kingdom."[54]

Yet an emphasis on verbal forms seems unfashionable, given the reaction by historians of recent years against their discipline's conventional reliance on texts in its interpretations of the past. Such approaches, scholars have justly argued, neglect the "inarticulate" masses, the less privileged orders of society who did not leave extensive written records. But this enthusiasm for the "history of the inarticulate" has produced an unwarranted aversion to use of documents and a self-defeating blindness about new ways to interpret them. Not every verbal artifact is an abstract and intellectualistic treatise irrelevant to the society in which it appears. Speech is a form of social action, goal-directed and socially organized in the same way as voting or any other sort of behavior. The "new social history," with its emphasis on interdisciplinary methods of retrieving the experience of the inarticulate, has important implications for a new history of the articulate as well. Clifford Geertz, perhaps the most prominent anthropological influence on recent historians, has advised scholars to treat behavior like a text. But perhaps for our purposes, we should invert this prescription. Possibilities for a new history of the articulate rest in treating texts like behavior. When these texts appear—as do agricultural orations—in recurrent and identical forms, they become a new sort of aggregate data, governed by social rules and suffused with cultural meaning. As the central performance in the ritual of the agricultural societies, these orations are symbolic social forms, part of a larger pattern of action and context of meaning that stretches out through society meetings into South Carolina civilization more generally. In part, the rhetoric of agriculture was designed to impel men to reformist action in the world outside them. But, at the same time, these symbols sought to reaffirm and refine the conceptual categories inside men's heads, a process that had profound effect upon the outlook of the antebellum Carolinian, the nature of the world he saw, and, thus, the way he subsequently acted within it. In these two senses—by manipulating both the world and the words that defined it— the language of agriculture became a form of cultural action. Words indeed took on, as Edmund Rhett had suggested, "the power of things."[55]

Culture, Conflict, and Community

The Meaning of Power on an
Antebellum Plantation

A dozen miles south of Augusta, Georgia, the Savannah River curves gently, creating two bends that were known to antebellum steamboat captains as Stingy Venus and Hog Crawl Round. Nearby, on the South Carolina shore, a cliff abruptly rises almost thirty feet above the water. Mineral deposits in the soil give the promontory a metallic tinge, and the bank and the plantation of which it was part came as early as colonial times to be called Silver Bluff.[1]

In 1831, an opportune marriage placed this property in the hands of twenty-four-year-old James Henry Hammond. An upwardly mobile lawyer, erstwhile schoolmaster and newspaper editor, the young Carolinian had achieved through matrimony the status the Old South accorded to planters alone. When he arrived to take possession of his estate, he found and carefully listed in his diary 10,800 acres of land, a dwelling, assorted household effects, and 147 bondsmen. But along with these valued acquisitions, he was to receive a challenge he had not anticipated. As he sought to exert his mastery over the labor force on which the prosperity of his undertaking depended, he was to discover that his task entailed more than simply directing 147 individual lives. Hammond had to dominate a complex social order already in existence on the plantation and to struggle for the next three decades to control what he called a "system of roguery" amongst his slaves.[2]

Hammond astutely recognized that black life on his plantation was structured and organized as a "system," the very existence of which seemed necessarily a challenge to his absolute control—and therefore, as he perceived it, a kind of "roguery." Because Hammond's mastery over his bondsmen depended upon his success at undermining slave society and culture, he established a carefully designed plan of physical and psychological domination in hopes of destroying the foundations of black solidarity. Until he relinquished management of the estate to his sons in the late 1850s, Hammond kept extraordinarily detailed records. Including daily entries concerning the treatment, work patterns, and vital statistics of his slaves, they reveal a striking portrait of slave culture and resistance and of the highly structured efforts Hammond took to overpower it. The existence of such data about one master and one community of slaves over a considerable period of time makes possible a tracing of the dialectic of their interaction as one not so much among individuals, but between two loci of power and two opposing systems of belief. While Hammond sought to assert both dominance and legitimacy, the slaves at Silver Bluff strove to maintain networks of communication and community as the bases of their personal and cultural autonomy. This struggle, which constantly tested the ingenuity and strength of both the owner and his slaves, touched everything from religion to work routines to health, and even determined the complex pattern of unauthorized absences from the plantation.

A master-slave relationship is never static, but of necessity evolutionary. Each participant confronts the other with demands and expectations, seeking continually to enhance his own power within the framework of their interaction. In the emotional and ideological context of paternalism, this dialectic of oppression, challenge, and concession produce the interdependence of lord and bondsman that Eugene Genovese has so arrestingly described. But because of the comprehensive nature of *Roll, Jordan, Roll*, Genovese has dealt with this relationship in necessarily general terms. A detailed examination of the development of patterns of mutual response between a single master and his slaves thus promises an opportunity to supplement and refine some of Genovese's insights about the sources of that "reciprocity" he has urged as a defining feature of the South's slave system.[3]

When Hammond took possession of Silver Bluff, he assumed a role and entered a world largely unfamiliar to him. His father had owned a few slaves and even deeded two to young James Henry. But Hammond

Portrait of James Henry Hammond by William Scarborough. Courtesy South Caroliniana Library, Columbia, South Carolina.

was entirely inexperienced in the management of large numbers of agricultural and domestic workers. The blacks at Silver Bluff, for their part, confronted a new situation as well, for they had become accustomed to living without a master in permanent residence. Hammond's wife's father, Christopher Fitzsimons, had been a prominent Charleston merchant who visited his upcountry property only intermittently. Upon his death in 1825, the plantation was left to his daughter Catherine and came under the desultory management of Fitzsimons's sons, who had far less interest than would their future brother-in-law in making it a profitable enterprise. In 1831, therefore, both Hammond and his slaves faced new circumstances. But it was Hammond who was the outsider, moving into a world of established patterns of behavior and interaction in the community at Silver Bluff. Although by law all power rested with Hammond, in reality the situation was rather different.

As a novice at masterhood, Hammond received advice and encouragement from his friends. "Be kind to them make them feel an obligation," one acquaintance counseled, ". . . and by all means keep all other negroes away from the place, and make yours stay at home—and Raise their church to the ground—keep them from fanaticism for God's sake as well as for your own." Hammond took this exhortation to heart, seeking within a week of his arrival at the Bluff to enhance his power by extending control over the very souls of his slaves. "Intend to break up negro preaching & negro churches," he proclaimed in his diary. "Refused to allow Ben Shubrick to join the Negro Church . . . but promised to have him taken in the church . . . I attended. . . . Ordered night meetings on the plantation to be discontinued."[4]

The desire to control black religious life led Hammond to endeavor to replace independent black worship with devotions entirely under white direction. At first he tried to compel slaves into white churches simply by making black ones unavailable, and even sought to prevent his neighbors from permitting black churches on their own lands. But soon he took positive steps to provide the kind of religious environment he deemed appropriate for his slaves. For a number of years he hired itinerant ministers for Sunday afternoon slave services. By 1845, however, Hammond had constructed a Methodist church for his plantation and named it St. Catherine's after his wife.[5]

The piety of the Hammond slaves became a source of admiration even to visitors. A house guest on the plantation in the 1860s found the services at St. Catherine's "solemn and impressive," a tribute, she felt, to Hammond's beneficent control over his slaves. "There was a little company of white people," she recalled, "the flower of centuries of civilization, among hundreds of blacks but yesterday . . . in savagery, now peaceful, contented, respectful and comprehending the worship of God. . . . By reason of Senator Hammond's wise discipline," the visitor assured her readers, there was no evidence of "religious excesses," the usual "mixture of hysteria and conversion" that she believed characterized most black religion. These slaves, it appeared to an outsider, had abandoned religious ecstasy for the reverential passivity prescribed for them by white cultural norms.[6]

Hammond had taken great pains to establish just such white standards amongst his slaves, and the visitor's description of the behavior he had succeeded in eliciting from his bondsmen would undoubtedly have pleased him. But even Hammond recognized that the decorous behavior of his slaves within the walls of St. Catherine's was but an outward compliance with his directives. He seemed unable to eradicate black religious expression, evidences of which appeared to him like tips of an iceberg indicating an underlying pattern of independent belief and worship that persisted among his slaves. Twenty years after his original decision to eliminate the slave church, Hammond recorded in his plantation diary, "Have ordered all church meetings to be broken up except at the Church with a white preacher." Hammond's slaves had over the preceding decades tested their master's initial resolve, quietly asserting their right to their own religious life in face of his attempt to deny it to them.[7]

In the course of these years, they had reestablished their church, forcing Hammond to accept a level of black religious autonomy and to permit the slaves to hold as many as four different prayer meetings in the quarters each week. Hammond returned to his original commitment to "break up negro preaching" only when the intensity of black religious fervor seemed to threaten that compromise level of moderation he and his slaves had come tacitly to accept. "Religious troubles among the negroes"—as in 1851 he described his sense of the growing disorder—revived his determination to control the very emotional and ideational sources of unruliness among his slaves. "They are running the thing into the ground," he remarked, "by being allowed too much organization—too much power to the head men & too much praying and Church meeting on the plantation." Black religious life reemerged as an insupportable threat when it assumed the characteristics of a formal system, with, as Hammond explicitly recognized, organization and leadership to challenge his own power. The recurrent need for Hammond to act against the expanding strength of the black church indicates his failure either to eliminate this organization or to control his slaves' belief and worship.[8]

The struggle for power manifested in the conflict over religious autonomy was paralleled in other areas of slave life on the Hammond domain. Just as Hammond sought from the time of his arrival in 1831 to control religious behavior, so too he desired to supervise work patterns more closely. "When I first began to plant," he later reminisced, "I found my people in very bad subjection from the long want of a master and it required of me a year of severity which cost me infinite pain." The slaves, accustomed to a far less rigorous system of management, resented his attempts and tried to undermine his drive for efficiency. "The negroes are trying me," Hammond remarked in his diary on more than one occasion during the early months of his tenure. In response, he was firm, recording frequent floggings of slaves who refused to comply with his will. When several bondsmen sought to extend the Christmas holiday by declining to return to work as scheduled, Hammond was unyielding, forcing them back to the fields and whipping them as well.[9]

As the weeks passed, the instances of beatings and overt insubordination noted in plantation records diminished; a more subtle form of conflict emerged. Over the next decade, this struggle over work patterns at Silver Bluff fixed on the issue of task versus gang labor. The slaves clearly preferred the independent management of their time offered by the task system, while Hammond feared the autonomy it provided the bondsmen. "They do much more" in a gang, Hammond noted, and "are not so apt to strain themselves." Task work, he found, encouraged the blacks to complete required chores too rapidly, with "no rest until 3 or 4 o'clock," and then gave them the opportunity for hours of unsupervised recreation. But despite what owners generally tended to see as its wholesomeness and security, gang work had the significant disadvantage of displeasing the laborers, who at Silver Bluff performed badly in a calculated effort to restore the task system. "Negroes dissatisfied to work in a gang & doing badly," Hammond observed in 1838. Almost exactly a year later he made a similar remark, noting that hoers were leaving "all the weeds and bunches of grass" growing around the cotton plants. "Evidently want to work task work which I will not do again."[10]

Although at this time Hammond succeeded in establishing the gang as the predominant form of labor at Silver Bluff, the victory was apparently neither final nor total. Indeed, it may simply have served to regularize the pattern of poorly performed work Hammond had viewed as a form of resistance to the gang system. He continued to record hoeing that ignored weeds, picking that passed over bulging cotton bolls, and cultivating that destroyed both mule and plough. But eventually the slaves here too won a compromise. By 1850, Hammond was referring once again in his correspondence and in his plantation diary to task work, although he complained bitterly about continuing poor performance and the frequent departure of many bondsmen from the fields as early as midafternoon.

Hammond seemed not so much to master as to manipulate his slaves, offering a system not just of punishments, but of positive inducements, ranging from picking contests to single out the most diligent hands, to occasional rituals of rewards for all, such as Christmas holidays; rations of sugar, tobacco, and coffee; midsummer barbecues; or even the pipes sent to all adult slaves from Europe when Hammond departed on the Grand Tour. The slaves were more than just passive recipients of these sporadic benefits; they in turn manipulated their master for those payments and privileges they had come to see as their due. Hammond complained that his bondsmen's demands led him against his will to countenance a slave force "too well fed & otherwise well treated," but he nevertheless could not entirely resist their claims. When after a particularly poor record of work by slaves in the fall of 1847 Hammond sought to shorten the usual Christmas holiday, he ruefully recorded on December 26 that he had been "persuaded out of my decision by the Negroes."[11]

Hammond and his slaves arrived at a sort of accommodation on the issue of work. But in this process, Hammond had to adjust his desires and expectations as significantly as did his bondsmen. His abstract notions of order and absolute control were never to be fully realized. He and his slaves reached a truce that permitted a level of production acceptable to Hammond and a level of endeavor tolerable to his slaves.

Like his use of rewards and punishments, Hammond's more general instructions for plantation management reveal his understanding of the process of mastery as consisting in large measure of symbolic and psychological control. The necessity of resorting to physical punishment, he maintained, indicated a failure in ideal management. Hammond constantly tried to encourage the bondsmen to internalize their master's definition of their inferiority and thus willingly come to acknowledge his legitimacy. Yet Hammond recognized that to succeed in this aim, he had necessarily to mask his own dependence upon them. Hammond was well aware the black driver Tom Kollock was a far more experienced agriculturist than his master or than the plantation overseers. "I wish you to consult him [Tom]," Hammond instructed a new overseer, "on all occasions & in all matters of doubt take his opinion wh. you will find supported by good reasons." But, he warned, Kollock must be kept "in ignorance of his influence . . . I would not have Tom injured by the supposition that he was the head manager any more than I would have you mortified by such a state of things." Yet Kollock knew more than he showed, for Hammond found two decades later that the driver had long exploited the power of which the master had presumed him ignorant. While pretending to effective management of both crops and personnel, Kollock had instead worked to undermine productivity by demanding the minimum of his workers. Kollock had fooled Hammond, who in a fury of discovery proclaimed him a "humbug." "I now see," Hammond declared in 1854, "that in him rests the fault of my last . . . crops. He has trained his hands to do very little & that badly."[12]

Unaware how transparent and easily manipulable he must have appeared to slaves, Hammond sought continually to refine and perfect his system of management. A devoted disciple of scientific agriculture and administration, he developed in the 1840s a formal set of rules for treatment and supervision of slaves, allocating carefully defined areas of responsibility to master, overseer, and driver.

Nearly every detail of these regulations indicates a conscious desire to impress the bondsmen with their total dependence upon their master, and, simultaneously, with the merciful beneficence of his absolute rule. Lest the overseer's power seem to diminish the master's own authority, Hammond defined the role of the black driver to serve as check upon him. Because he could only be whipped by the master, the driver was removed from the overseer's control and his status enhanced amongst his fellow slaves. In addition, the driver had the explicit right to by-pass the overseer and to appeal directly to the master with suggestions or complaints about plantation management—or the overseer's behavior. Hammond invested the driver with enough power to encourage the slaves to accept as their official voice the leader Hammond had chosen and, he hoped, co-opted. It was Hammond's specific intention, moreover, to use administrative arrangements to set the overseer and driver at odds and thus to limit the power of each in relation to his own. One of his greatest fears was that the two would cooperate to conspire against him.[13]

Such divisions of authority were clearly designed to emphasize the master's power, but at the same time were meant to cast him as a somewhat distant arbiter of justice, one who did not involve himself in the sordidness of daily floggings. Instead, Hammond sought to portray himself as the dispenser of that mercy designed to win the grateful allegiance of the slave and to justify the plantation's social order. He constantly tried to make himself appear not so much the creator of rules— which of course in reality he was—but the grantor of exceptions and reprieves.[14]

At Silver Bluff, the distribution of provisions was an occasion for Hammond to display this paternalistic conception. The event assumed the form and significance of a cultural ritual, a ceremony in which Hammond endeavored to present himself to his slaves as the source from whom all blessings flowed. Once a week, the bondsmen were required to put on clean clothes and appear before the master to receive their food allowance. "They should," he recorded in his plantation regulations, "be brought into that contact with the master at least once a week of receiving the means of subsistence from him." Although the overseer could perfectly well have executed such a task, the ceremonial importance of this moment demanded the master's direct participation. The special requirement for fresh apparel set the occasion off from the less sacred events of daily life and underlined the symbolic character of this interaction between lord and bondsmen. The event illustrated Hammond's most idealized conception of the master-slave relationship and represented his effort to communicate this understanding to the slaves themselves, convincing them of his merciful generosity and of their own humble dependence and need. The interaction was a statement designed to help transform his power into legitimized authority.[15]

But Hammond's slaves were not taken in by this ritual; they remained less dependent on his dispensations of food and far more active in procuring the necessary means of subsistence than their master cared to admit. Slaves tended their own garden plots and fished for the rich bounty of the Savannah River. And to Hammond's intense displeasure, they also stole delicacies out of his own larder. Pilfering of food and alcohol at Silver Bluff did not consist simply of a series of random acts by slaves seeking to alleviate hunger or compensate for deprivation. Instead, theft assumed the characteristics of a contest between master and slave. Indeed, the prospect of winning the competition may have provided the organized slaves with nearly as much satisfaction as did the actual material fruits of victory; it was clearly a battle over power as well as for the specific goods in question. Although Hammond began immediately in 1831 to try to reduce the level of depredations against his hogs, flogging suspected thieves made little impact. He could not prevent the disappearance of a sizeable portion of his pork or break what he saw as the "habit" of theft among his slaves. Over the years, his supply of livestock consequently diminished, and he found himself compelled to buy provisions to feed his slaves. Hammond recorded with grim satisfaction that the resulting reduction of the meat allowance would be just retribution for the slaves' conspiracy against his herds. Theirs would be, he consoled himself, a hollow victory. "The negroes," he noted in 1845, "have for years killed about half my shoats and must now suffer for it." But the impact of black theft was perhaps even greater on other plantation products. Hammond was resigned to never harvesting his potato crop at all, for the slaves stole the entire yield before it was even removed from the ground.[16]

Alcohol, however, was the commodity that inspired the most carefully designed system of slave intrigue. When Hammond began to ferment wines from his own vineyards, slaves constantly tapped his bottles, then blamed the disappearance of the liquid on leaks due to miscorking. But the slave community's most elaborate assault on Hammond's supplies of alcohol went well beyond such crude tactics to call upon a unique conjunction of engineering skill with the power of voodoo. In 1835, Hammond found that several of his slaves had dug tunnels beneath his wine cellar. Other house servants had provided aid, including necessary keys and information and some spiritual assistance as well. A female domestic, Urana, Hammond recorded, used "root work" and thus "screened" the excavators by her "conjuration." Hammond determinedly "punished all who have had anything to do with the matter far or near." But his response could not replace the lost wine, nor compensate for the way the incident challenged the literal and figurative foundations of his plantation order. The force of voodoo lay entirely outside his system of domination and his efforts to establish cultural hegemony. The slaves were undermining his power as well as his house.[17]

Folk beliefs flourished in other realms of slave life as well. Hammond's bondsmen succeeded in perpetuating African medical ideas and customs, even though their master's commitment to scientific plantation management necessarily included an effort to exercise close medical supervision over slave lives in times of sickness and of health. The blacks of Silver Bluff may well have been encouraged in their resistance to Hammond's therapeutics by his record of dismal failure: he had great difficulty in achieving a slave population that reproduced itself. For the first twenty years of his management, slave deaths consistently exceeded slave births at the Bluff, despite Hammond's sincere and vigorous efforts to reverse these disheartening statistics. Hammond continually purchased new bondsmen, however, in order to offset a diminution in his labor supply probably caused as much by the low, damp, and unhealthy location of much of his property as by any physical mistreatment or deprivation of his slaves.

In part, these difficulties arose from the shortcomings of medical knowledge in antebellum white America more generally. Initially, Hammond and the physicians he consulted employed a series of those heroic treatments that characterized accepted nineteenth-century medical practice—compelling the slaves to submit to disagreeable purges, bleedings, and emetics. When these failed to cure, and seemed often to harm, Hammond gave up in disgust on conventional medicine and turned first to "Botanic Practice," then in 1854 to homeopathy, a medical fad that in its misguidedness at least had the virtue of advocating tiny dosages and thus minimizing the damage a practitioner might inflict.

Although Hammond never faltered in his certainty that Western science would eventually provide the solution to his dilemmas, his slaves retained an active skepticism, resisting his treatments by hiding illness and continuing to practice their own folk cures and remedies. In 1851, Hammond recognized that an entire alternative system of medical services thrived on his plantation. "Traced out the negro Doctors . . . who have been giving out medicine for years here & have killed I think most of those that have died. Punished them and also their patients very severely." Hammond was even able to use the existence of black medicine as a justification for the failures of his own methods. Although he did not refer to these doctors again, it seems likely that he achieved no greater success in controlling them than in eliminating black preaching or voodoo.[18]

For most of Hammond's slaves, insubordination served to establish cultural and personal autonomy within the framework of plantation demands. Resistance was a tool of negotiation, a means of extracting concessions from the master to reduce the extent of his claims over black bodies and souls. At Silver Bluff, such efforts often were directed more at securing necessary support for black community life than at totally overwhelming the master's power. Hammond learned that he could to a certain degree repress but never eliminate black cultural patterns; his slaves in turn concealed much of their lives so as not to appear directly to challenge their master's hegemony.

For some Silver Bluff residents, however, there could be no such compromise. Instead of seeking indirectly to avoid the domination inherent to slavery, these individuals confronted it, turning to arson and escape as overt expressions of the rebelliousness. Throughout the period of his management, Hammond referred to mysterious fires that would break out in the gin house on one occasion, the mill house or the plantation hospital the next. While these depredations could not be linked to specific individuals and only minimally affected the operation of the plantation, running away offered the angry slave a potentially more effective means of immediate resistance to the master's control. Between 1831 and 1855, Hammond recorded fifty-three attempts at escape by his bondsmen. Because he was sometimes absent from the plantation for months at a time during these decades, serving in political office or traveling in Europe, it seems unlikely that this list is complete. Nevertheless, Hammond's slave records provide sufficient information about the personal attributes of the runaways, the circumstances of their departure, the length of their absence and the nature of their family ties to demonstrate the meaning and significance of the action within the wider context of plantation life.[19]

The most striking—and depressing—fact about Silver Bluff's runaways is that Hammond records no instance of a successful escape. A total of thirty-seven different slaves were listed as endeavoring to leave the plantation. Thirty-five percent of these were repeaters, although no slave was recorded as making more than three attempts. Newly purchased slaves who made several efforts to escape were often sold; those with long-term ties to the Silver Bluff community eventually abandoned the endeavor.[20]

Runaways were 84 percent male, averaged thirty-three years of age, and had been under Hammond's dominance for a median period of two years. Hammond's initial assumption of power precipitated a flurry of escapes, as did subsequent changes in management. When the owner departed for long summer holidays or for business elsewhere, notations of increased numbers of slave escapes appeared in plantation records. This pattern suggests that slavery was rendered minimally tolerable to its victims by the gradual negotiation between master and slave of the kinds of implicit compromises earlier discussed. A shift in responsibility from one master to another or from master to overseer threatened those understandings and therefore produced eruptions of overt rebelliousness.

While the decision to run away might appear to be a rejection of the ties of black community as well as the chains of bondage, the way in which escape functioned at Silver Bluff shows it usually to have operated somewhat differently. Because there were no runaways who achieved permanent freedom and because most escapees did not get far, they remained in a very real sense a part of the slave community they had seemingly fled. Forty-three percent of the runaways at the Bluff left with others. The small proportion—16 percent of the total—of females were almost without exception running with husbands or joining spouses who had already departed. Once slaves escaped, they succeeded in remaining at large an average of forty-nine days. Sixty-five percent were captured and the rest returned voluntarily. The distribution of compulsory and elective returns over the calendar year reveals that harsh weather was a significant factor in persuading slaves to give themselves up. Seventy-seven percent of those returning in the winter months did so voluntarily, while in the spring and summer 80 percent were brought back against their will. Weather and workload made summer the runaway season, and 58 percent of all escape attempts occurred in June, July, and August.

While certain individuals—notably young males, particularly those without family ties—were most likely to become runaways, the slave community as a whole provided these individuals with assistance and support. Hammond himself recognized that runaways often went no farther than the nearby Savannah River swamps where they survived on food provided by those remaining at home. The ties between the escapees and the community were sufficiently strong that Hammond endeavored to force runaways to return by disciplining the rest of the slave force. On at least one occasion Hammond determined to stop the meat allowance of the entire plantation until the runaways came in. In another instance, he severely flogged four slaves harboring two run-aways, hoping thereby to break the personal and communal bonds that made prolonged absences possible.[21]

In the isolation of Silver Bluff, real escape seemed all but hopeless. Some newly arrived slaves, perhaps with family from whom they had been separated, turned to flight as a rejection of these new surround-ings and an effort permanently to escape them. Individuals of this sort were captured as far as a hundred miles away. The majority of runaways, however, were part of the established black community on Hammond's plantation. Recognizing the near certainty of failure to escape the chains of bondage forever, they ran either in pursuit of a brief respite from labor or in response to uncontrollable anger. One function of the black community was to support this outlet for frustration and rage by feeding and sheltering runaways either until they were captured or until they were once again able to operate within the system of compromise that provided the foundation for the survival of black culture and iden-tity at Silver Bluff.

Two examples demonstrate the way runaways eventually became integrated into the plantation order. Cudjo was returned to the Bluff as a plough hand in 1833 after a year of being hired out in Augusta. Thirty-two years old, he perhaps missed urban life or had established personal relationships he could not bear to break. In any case, he began to run away soon after his return. He first succeeded in departing for two weeks but was seized in Augusta and imprisoned. Hammond retrieved him and put him in irons, but within days he was off again with his fetters on. Captured soon on a nearby plantation, Cudjo tried again a few days later and remained at large for ten months. In March of 1834, Hammond recorded in his diary, "Cudjo came home. Just tired of running away." Although Cudjo was still on the plantation two decades later, there appeared no further mention of his attempting to escape.[22]

Alonzo had been with Hammond only eight months when he first fled in 1843. Thirty-four years old, he had not yet developed settled family ties on the plantation, and he ran away alone. Captured in this first attempt, he escaped twice more within the year, disappearing, Hammond recorded, "without provocation." His second absence ended when he was caught in Savannah after thirty-two days and placed in irons. After less than two months at home, he was off again, but this time he returned voluntarily within two weeks. Reironed, Alonzo did not flee again. After 1851, Hammond recorded an ever-growing family born to Alonzo and another Silver Bluff slave named Abby. But while he stopped trying to run away and became increasingly tied to Silver Bluff, Alonzo was by no means broken of his independence. In 1864, he provoked Hammond with a final act of resistance, refusing to supply his master with any information about the pains that were to kill him within a month. "A hale hearty man," Hammond remarked with annoyance, "killed by the negro perversity."[23]

In the initial part of his tenure at the Bluff, Hammond recorded efforts to round up runaway slaves by means of extensive searches through the swamps on horseback or with packs of dogs. After the first decade, however, he made little mention of such vigorous measures and seems for the most part simply to have waited for his escapees to be captured by neighbors, turn up in nearby jails, or return home. In order to encourage voluntary surrender, Hammond announced a policy of punishment for runaways that allotted ten lashes for each day absent to those recaptured by force and three lashes per day to those returning of their own will. The establishment of this standardized rule integrated the problem of runaways into the system of rewards and punishments at Silver Bluff and rendered it an aspect of the understanding existing between master and slaves. Since no one escaped permanently, such a rule served to set forth the cost of unauthorized absence and encouraged those who had left in irrational rage to return as soon as their tempers had cooled. When the respected fifty-three-year-old driver

John Shubrick was flogged for drunkenness, he fled in fury and mortification but within a week was back exercising his customary responsibility in plantation affairs.[24]

For some, anger assumed a longer duration and significance. These individuals, like Alonzo or Cudjo, ran repeatedly until greater age or changed circumstances made life at home more bearable. Occasionally Hammond found himself confronted with a slave whose rage seemed so deep-rooted as to be incurable. When Hudson escaped soon after his purchase in 1844, he was not heard of for seven months. At last, Hammond was notified that the slave was in Barnwell on trial for arson. To protect his investment, Hammond hired a lawyer to defend him. But when Hudson was acquitted, Hammond sold him immediately, determining that this individual was an insupportable menace to plantation life.[25]

While runaways disrupted routine and challenged Hammond's system of management, his greatest anxieties about loss of control arose from the fear that slave dissatisfaction would be exploited by external forces to threaten the fine balance of concession and oppression he had established. From the beginning of his tenure at the Bluff, he sought to isolate his bondsmen from outside influences, prohibiting their trading in local stores, selling produce to neighbors, marrying off the plantation, or interacting too closely with hands of the steamboats that refueled at the Bluff landing. Despite such efforts, however, Hammond perceived during the 1840s and 1850s an ever-growing threat to his power arising from challenges leveled at the peculiar institution as a whole. To Hammond's horror, it seemed impossible to keep information about growing abolition sentiment from the slaves. Such knowledge, Hammond feared, might provide the bondsmen with additional bases for ideological autonomy and greater motivation to resist his control. In an 1844 letter to John C. Calhoun, Hammond declared himself

> astonished and shocked to find that some of them are aware of the opinions of the Presidential candidates on the subject of slavery and doubtless most of what the abolitionists are doing & I am sure they know as little of what is done off my place as almost any set of Negroes in the State. I fancy . . . there is a growing spirit of insubordination among the slaves in this section. In the lower part of this district they have fired several houses recently. This is fearful—horrible. A quick and potent remedy must be applied. *Disunion* if *needs* be.[26]

Yet when disunion came, it proved less a remedy than a further exac-erbation of the problem. Both the possibility of emancipation by Union soldiers and the resort to slave impressment by the Confederates inter-vened to disrupt the established pattern of relationship between master and bondsmen. Hammond seemed almost as outraged by southern as by Yankee challenges to his power. He actively endeavored to resist providing workers to the Confederate government and proclaimed the impressment system "wrong every way & odious."[27]

At the beginning of the war, Hammond was uncertain about the sympathies of his slaves. In 1861, he noted that they appeared "anx-ious" but remarked "Cant tell which side." As the fighting grew closer, with the firing of large guns near the coast audible at Silver Bluff, Ham-mond began to sense growing disloyalty among his slaves and to con-front intensifying problems of control. "Negroes demoralized greatly. Stealing right and left," he recorded in 1863. By the middle of that year, it seemed certain that the slaves expected "some great change." Despite his efforts, they seemed at all times "well apprised" of war news, sinking into "heavy gloom" at any Union reverse. Hammond observed the appearance of "a peculiar furtive glance with which they regard me & a hanging off from me that I do not like." They seemed to "shut up their faces & cease their cheerful greetings." Hammond felt the war had rendered his control tenuous, and he believed that even though his slaves sought to appear "passive . . . the roar of a single cannon of the Federal's would make them frantic—savage cutthroats and incendi-aries."[28]

Hammond never witnessed the Union conquest of the South or the emancipation of his slaves, for he died in November of 1864. Despite his dire prophecies, however, the people of Silver Bluff did not rise in revolution against those who had oppressed them for so long. Unlike many slaves elsewhere who fled during the war itself, the Hammond bondsmen did not depart even when freedom was proclaimed. "We have not lost many negroes," Hammond's widow complained in Sep-tember 1865, as she worried about having too many mouths to feed. "I wish we could get clear of many of the useless ones."[29]

Given the turbulent nature of the interaction between Hammond and his slaves in the antebellum years, it would be misguided to regard the blacks' decision to remain on the plantation as evidence either of docility or of indifference about freedom. Instead, it might better be understood as final testimony to the importance of that solidarity we have seen among bondsmen on the Hammond estate. These blacks were more concerned to continue together as a group than to flee Hammond's domination. In the preoccupation with the undeniable importance of the master-slave relationship, historians may have failed fully to recognize how for many bondsmen the positive meaning of the web of slave interrelationships was a more central influence than were the oppressive intrusions of the power of the master. Silver Bluff had been home to many of these slaves before Hammond ever arrived; the community had preceded him, and now it had outlived him. Its maintenance and autonomy were of the highest priority to its members, keeping them at Silver Bluff even when any single freedman's desire for personal liberty might have best been realized in flight. The values central to this cultural group were more closely associated with the forces of tradition and community than with an individualistic revolutionary romanticism.[30]

On South Carolina's Sea Islands, blacks whose masters had fled perpetuated plantation boundaries as geographic definitions of black communal identity that have persisted to the present day. Although the exslaves at Silver Bluff never gained the land titles that would have served as the legal basis for such long-lived solidarity, they, like their Sea Island counterparts, chose in 1865 to remain on the plantation that in a powerful emotional way they had come to regard as their own. These freedmen saw themselves and their aspirations defined less by the oppressions of slavery than by the positive accomplishments of autonomous black community that they had achieved even under the domain of the peculiar institution.[31]

The Proslavery Argument in History

The controversy over slavery in the antebellum United States did not end with abolition of the South's peculiar institution. In the century that has followed Appomattox, historians have debated the sources and meaning of the slavery agitation nearly as vigorously as early nineteenth-century Americans argued about human bondage itself. But a disproportionate amount of this scholarly attention has been devoted to antislavery movements and ideologies. Whereas studies of abolitionism have established it as both a product and an index of fundamental aspects of nineteenth-century culture, historical treatment of proslavery has emphasized its aberrant qualities, identifying it as the evanescent product of the unique civilization that flourished in the South during the last three decades before the Civil War. Many scholars have felt uncomfortable contending with zealous defenses of a social system that the twentieth century judges abhorrent, and, like David Donald, they have found the proslavery movement "astonishing."[1]

In recent years, however, interpretations of proslavery thought have shifted. Perhaps more accustomed to the notion of a timeless and geographically extensive American racism, scholars have begun to place proslavery within a wider context, to regard it as more than simply a distasteful manifestation of a collective paranoia gripping the South in the years before the Civil War. Historians have come to view the proslavery argument less as evidence of moral failure and more as a key to wider patterns of beliefs and values. The defense of human bondage, they recognize, was perhaps more important as an effort to construct a coherent southern social philosophy than as a political weapon of short-lived usefulness during the height of sectional conflict. In defending what they repeatedly referred to as the "cornerstone" of their social order, slavery's apologists were offering posterity an unusual opportunity to examine the world view of articulate southerners, their sources of social legitimation, and their self-conscious definition of themselves.[2] Slavery became a vehicle for the discussion of fundamental social issues—the meaning of natural law, the conflicting desires for freedom and order, the relationship between tradition and progress, the respective roles of liberty and equality, dependence and autonomy. "The question of negro slavery," one apologist recognized in 1856, "is implicated with all the great social problems of the current age."[3] Addressing topics of deepest import to Americans North and South, the proslavery argument embodied the South's particular perspective on those philosophical, moral, and social dilemmas confronting the nation as a whole. "Proslavery thought," as one recent scholar has remarked, "was nothing more or less than thought about society."[4]

A significant aspect of the reorientation of modern scholarship toward a widening interpretation of proslavery's significance has been a growing interest in its persistence over time. Although a few scholars of the 1930s and 1940s noted proslavery's early origins,[5] most historians continued to associate the defense of slavery with a movement of the South away from Jeffersonian liberalism in the late 1820s and 1830s. After abolitionist William Lloyd Garrison began to denounce slavery in *The Liberator* in 1831, these scholars explained, the South rapidly abandoned its Revolutionary American heritage and took up the almost polar opposite position of proslavery reactionism.[6]

Recent work, however, has revised this chronology, exploring in new detail the significance of proslavery doctrines during the colonial period.[7] Acknowledging a brief period of quiescence during the egalitarian ferment of the Revolutionary years, this interpretation chronicles a reemergence as early as 1808 of a proslavery literature that grew steadily in volume and vehemence throughout the remainder of the antebellum period. This writing, moveover, was not restricted to the South. One of the earliest slavery debates took place in colonial Massachusetts;[8] northerners continued publicly to defend slavery in significant numbers through the time of the Civil War. Britons in England and the West Indies also justified slavery throughout the eighteenth and early nineteenth centuries, and these arguments served as useful sources for American advocates of human bondage.[9]

This broadened chronology and geography of proslavery contains important implications for the understanding of the movement and of the Old South itself. Some scholars in the past have tended to regard the defense of slavery as a product of southern guilt, an effort by slave-holders to assuage consciences riddled with shame about violations of America's democratic creed. Recent attention to the colonial origins and wide extension of proslavery views suggests the existence of a strong alternative tradition of social and even moral legitimation upon which antebellum southerners might draw. Less philosophically and morally isolated than Charles Sellers and W. J. Cash would have us think, southerners may have felt far less guilty and ambivalent as well.[10]

But emphasis on the extensiveness of proslavery thought through time and space has not diminished scholarly interest in the role of the argument in the South during the last three decades of the antebellum period. Even historians insisting upon its early origins and wide diffusion recognize its increased significance in these years. During this era, the slavery controversy not only became a matter of survival for the southern way of life; it served for Americans generally as a means of reassessing the profoundest assumptions on which their world was built.

Although proslavery thought demonstrated remarkable consistency from the seventeenth century on, it became in the South of the 1830s, 1840s, and 1850s more systematic and self-conscious; it took on the characteristics of a formal ideology with its resulting social movement. The intensification of proslavery argumentation produced an increase in conceptual organization and coherence within the treatises themselves, which sought methodically to enumerate all possible foundations for human bondage—"a *discussion on Slavery in all its bearings*," as one southern apologist explained, "in the lights of History, Political Economy, Moral Philosophy, Political Science, Theology, Social Life, Ethnology and International Law."[11] At the same time, more structured arrangements developed among the apologists and their publishers for the production and distribution of these tracts. Southerners united to call upon the region's finest minds for defenses of slavery, to discuss with one another the appropriate contents and goals for their writings, and to arrange their wide dissemination in newspapers, pamphlets, and even book-sized collections of previously printed favorites. One publisher explained his intention of producing an anthology of arguments on fine paper "fit to take its place in the Library or Drawing Room, and to serve as a Text Book on the subject, so that every one in our community may have at hand good strong arguments. . . . Coming in a respectable shape and in good style it will attract much more attention than if simply sent in pamphlet form."[12] The need for a vigorous southern publishing industry became particularly obvious as a result of these efforts to diffuse proslavery views, and the defense of the peculiar institution had an important impact upon southern letters. "We shall be indebted," one southern intellectual and proslavery essayist proclaimed, "to the continuance and asperity of this controversy for the creation of a genuine Southern literature. . . . For out of this slavery agitation has sprung not merely essays on slavery, valuable and suggestive as these have been, but also the literary activity, and the literary movement which have lately characterized the intellect of the South."[13]

Whereas earlier proslavery writers had attracted little attention, the South now rewarded her defenders with acclaim. Francis Lieber, a German emigré with little sympathy for the peculiar institution of his adopted South, remarked bitterly that "nothing would give me greater renown than a pamphlet written . . . in favor of slavery."[14] After a long and unrewarding career as an agricultural essayist, Edmund Ruffin found that "I have had more notice taken of my late pamphlet [on slavery] than of anything I ever wrote before."[15]

Current scholarship regards the change in southern writings about slavery in the 1830s as more one of style and tone than of substance. Southerners did not move from an anti- to a proslavery position. Slaveholders were less troubled about *whether* slavery was right than precisely *why* it was right and how its justice could best be demonstrated. Unsympathetic to the Perfectionism embraced by many of their abolitionist counterparts, proslavery advocates always saw evils in slavery, as they were sure they would in any terrestrial system of society and government. All earthly arrangements, they believed, necessarily required men to cope as best they could with sin; it was the relative merits of social systems, their comparative success in dealing with inherent evil, that should be discussed. As William Harper explained in his *Memoir on Slavery*, "The condition of our whole existence is but to struggle with evils—to compare them—to choose between them, and so far as we can, to mitigate them. To say that there is evil in any institution, is only to say that it is human." With the intensification of the slavery controversy, however, apologists began to acknowledge the institution's shortcomings less openly and to consider only the positive aspects of

the system. "I see great evils in slavery," George Fitzhugh confessed to a
friend, "but I think in a controversial work I ought not to admit them."[16]

Antebellum southerners themselves recognized and justified their
heightened involvement in slavery's defense in the years after 1830. In
spite of "speculative doubts by which the slaveowners were troubled," a
Virginian observed in 1856, "the general sentiment among them . . .
had always tenaciously maintained the sanctity and inviolability of
slavery, but they have not arrived at a clear comprehension of the reasons by which slavery is justified and proved to be right and expedient,
without the aid of the . . . treatises which the controversy still raging
has called forth." Southerners, Mississippian Henry Hughes agreed,
could successfully defend slavery only when they learned "to give the
reasons for it." "Few of our own people," a South Carolinian advocate
similarly complained, "understand it in its philosophical and econom-
ical bearing." These explanations suggest, as historian Ralph Morrow
argued in 1961, that proslavery writings were directed primarily at other
southerners. "We think it hardly to be expected," one apologist candidly admitted in 1843, "that anything which can be said at this late
date will at all diminish the wrongheaded fanaticism and perverse in-
tolerance of the Northern abolitionists." Northern antislavery had pro-
gressed "past the cure of argument."[17]

This concern with the sources and impact of proslavery writing within the South has generated new interest in the authors of proslavery
tracts and in the nature of their lives within the southern social order.
The psychological "guiltomania" interpretations of Sellers and Cash
represent one aspect of this trend. David Donald offered a somewhat
different but related perspective, combining sociological with psychological explanation by exploring the particular social locations of a
group of slavery's southern defenders. "All," he found, were "unhappy
men." But their "personal problems" had a social dimension and were
even a direct result of "their place in southern society." Frustrated by
their own failure to rise to positions of prominence in the South, slavery's apologists sought to compensate for their relegation to the "fringes
of society"; they "looked back with longing to an earlier day of the
Republic when men like themselves—their own ancestors—had been
leaders in the South."[18]

Since Donald presented his ideas in a brief 1970 presidential address
to the Southern Historical Association, other scholars have inquired

more closely into the biographical questions he raised. Larry Edward Tise associated proslavery with the clergy in a study of 275 proslavery ministers and explored as well the institutions and experiences that exposed these men to the Federalist influences so evident in their writings. Although Federalism as a political force disappeared well before the 1830s, many of its conservative principles and hierarchical social assumptions, Tise noted, were perpetuated in the proslavery argument. The relationship of proslavery and social role has also been examined by Drew Gilpin Faust, who has suggested that the argument served as a vehicle for expression of alienation by the South's neglected intellectuals. The logic by which these advocates justified the right of whites to hold blacks in bondage, she argued, inevitably implied the social superiority of intellectuals as well. In taking up the public defense of the peculiar institution, the southern thinker thus sought to advance his particular values and to define for himself a respected social role within a culture known for its inhospitality to letters.[19]

These studies assumed a significant relationship between social role and the particular details of the ideology invoked to legitimate it, and consequently undertook to reassess the contents of proslavery thought in light of these new sociological concerns. William Sumner Jenkins's pioneering study of proslavery in 1935 had definitively classified and explored the most familiar species of arguments. As late as 1971, David Donald still found "the substance of the proslavery argument has little interest." Nevertheless, changing conceptions about the relationship of society and ideology arising in part from the impact of Eugene Genovese's Marxism and in part from shifting concerns of intellectual history have prompted a renewed interest in the contents and symbolic structure of the arguments themselves and in the nature of their development in the three decades before the Civil War.[20]

Many scholars have long acknowledged Thomas Roderick Dew's *Review of the Debate in the Virginia Legislature* as a herald of this new post-1830 era in proslavery ideology. Prompted by legislative discussion of emancipation in the winter of 1831–1832, Dew's essay sought to establish the impracticality of the antislavery sentiments that had swept the state after Nat Turner's slave uprising left more than sixty whites dead in Virginia's Southside. Dew himself proclaimed his argument to be a new departure in proslavery writing, and his pragmatic tone was to serve as the inspiration for the inductive mode of almost all proslavery tracts henceforth. Rejecting the deductive principles of the Lockean contractual social theory that had influenced the Founding Fathers, Dew embraced the conservative organic view of social order that had been implicit in proslavery thought from its earliest beginnings. Social institutions and arrangements evolved slowly over time, he believed, and could not be beneficially altered by abrupt human intervention. Like the proslavery advocates that followed him, Dew called upon his audience to study society as it had existed through the ages and to derive social principles and bases for action from these empirical observations. Theoretical notions of equality could not controvert the striking differences in men's capacities evident to any impartial observer. Idealized conceptions of justice—such as those of the abolitionists—could never serve as reliable bases for social organization. It was all very well, Dew counseled his fellow Virginians, to admit the abstract evils of slavery, but the relative dangers of the alternatives— abolition with or without colonization—were far greater.[21]

Dew called upon southerners to recognize the implications of their own social order and to assume responsibility for it. "One generation," as historian Eugene Genovese has remarked about the South in the years after the Revolution, "might be able to oppose slavery and favor everything it made possible, but the next had to choose sides."[22] Dew was important because he demonstrated the implausibility of straddling the issue any longer, of maintaining the stance of relativism that many southerners had found so comfortable during the Revolutionary era and its aftermath. As antislavery sentiment began to strengthen in the years after the Missouri debates of 1818–1820, it was impossible any longer to endeavor to reconcile the North to the existence of the peculiar institution by conceding slavery's shortcomings. Once the issue was joined, Dew proclaimed, the South must acknowledge her commitment to her way of life and come out firmly on the proslavery side; the South must recognize that her superficial flirtation with the Revolutionary ideology of liberty and equality could be no more than just that.

Although Dew inaugurated a new era in proslavery, a flood of defenses did not appear at once. Only when northern abolitionists in 1835 inundated the South with antislavery propaganda sent through the federal mails did southerners respond in force, exhibiting a new vehemence in their defenses of their way of life. The attack from the

North made southern mobilization an immediate necessity, and latent proslavery feeling was quickly translated into action.

In the course of the next decade, slavery's apologists would, in their collective oeuvre, develop a comprehensive defense of the peculiar institution that invoked the most important sources of authority in their intellectual culture and associated slavery with the fundamental values of their civilization. Their specific arguments showed striking continuity with earlier proslavery positions, elaborating rather than contradicting existing writing. The defenses of slavery of this period were, in addition, remarkably consistent with one another. While one advocate might specialize in religious arguments and another in the details of political economy, most acknowledged, accepted, and sometimes repeated the conclusions of their fellow apologists. The high level of conformity within proslavery thought was not accidental. Consistency was seen as the mark of strength and the emblem of truth. "Earlier and later writers," the editor of a collection of proslavery classics remarked proudly in 1860, "stood on substantially the same ground, and take the same general views of the institution."[23]

To ensure this uniformity, slavery's apologists articulated a series of what we might regard as rules guiding the post-1835 proslavery movement. Endeavoring to avoid the "domain of sectional controversy and political warfare," the defenders of slavery sought broader arguments and wider appeal.[24] Basing their essays in "sober and cautious reflection" upon "purely scientific principles" with "no appeal to passion or to sordid interest," the South's proslavery theorists hoped to attract those who "wished for argument instead of abuse." Many of the South's apologists communicated with one another about their essays and ideas, so that the mature proslavery argument might well be seen as a community product.[25]

As a result of this group criticism and evaluation, there emerged what could be considered a proslavery mainstream. The Bible served as the core of this defense. In the face of abolitionist claims that slavery violated the principles of Christianity, southerners demonstrated with ever more elaborate detail that both Old and New Testaments sanctioned human bondage. God's Chosen People had been slaveholders; Christ had made no attack on the institution; his disciple Paul had demonstrated a commitment to maintaining it.[26]

But for an age increasingly enamored of the vocabulary and methods of natural science, biblical guidance was not enough. The accepted foundations for truth were changing in European and American thought, as intellectuals sought to apply the rigor of science to the study of society and morality, as well as the natural world. The proslavery argument accordingly called not only upon divine revelation, the traditional source and arbiter of truth, but sought at the same time to embrace the positivistic standards increasingly accepted for the assessment of all social problems. Man could and must, these authors contended, determine his social and moral duties scientifically through the examination of God's will revealed in nature and in history. A subspecies of general social thought, the defense of slavery assumed the methods and arguments of broader social theories and reflected an intellectual perspective that in these years first began to regard "social science" as a discrete and legitimate domain of human learning. Reverend Thornton Stringfellow would devise a proslavery theory designed to be at once "Scriptural and Statistical"; George Fitzhugh would write a *Sociology for the South*; Henry Hughes's proslavery tract would appear in the guise of *A Treatise on Sociology* in which the author's striving for relevance and legitimacy beyond the confines of the Old South even led him to replace the term *slavery* with that of *warranteeism*.[27]

But most advocates did not go so far. Sociology was not yet the academic discipline it has since become; moral science—from which sociology would later emerge—still remained the central framework for social analysis in colleges and among the educated both North and South. Thus the mainstream of proslavery argument sought to imbed the peculiar institution within the legitimating context of nineteenth-century moral philosophy, with its emphasis on man's duties and responsibilities and its invocation of historical precedent as guide for future action.[28]

Turning to the past as a catalog of social experiments, slavery's defenders discovered that from the time of Greece and Rome, human bondage had produced the world's greatest civilizations. The peculiar institution, they argued, was not so very peculiar but had provided the social foundation for man's greatest achievements. Moreover, the experience of the ages showed the fundamental principles of the American Revolution to be sadly misguided. Social law as revealed in history demonstrated that men had not in reality been created equal and free, as Jefferson had asserted; this was a mistaken view arising from erroneous modes of abstract and deductive thought. Nature produced individuals strikingly unequal in both qualities and circumstances. "Scientific" truths demonstrated through empirical study prescribed a hierarchically structured society reproducing nature's orderly differentiations. The Revolutionary concepts of natural law were thus replaced by the tenets of social organicism; the prestige of modern science served to legitimate tradition and conservatism in a manner that held implications far wider than the boundaries of the slavery controversy.[29]

Such an approach to social order stressed the importance of man's duties rather than his rights. And for rhetorical purposes, it was often the duties of masters, rather than those of slaves, that apologists chose to emphasize. Within the organic community of a slave society, they argued, the master could not ignore the human obligation to care for his bondsman. "Fed, clothed, protected," the slave was far better off, William J. Grayson proclaimed, than the northern factory worker whose employer had no interest in his health or even his survival. "Free but in name," northern laborers had liberty only to starve. As William Harper argued, there existed "some form of slavery in all ages and countries."[30] It was always necessary, Abel Upshur explained, "that one portion of mankind shall live upon the labor of another portion." Every civilization needed what James Henry Hammond dubbed a "mud-sill" class to do the menial labor of society.[31] The southern system of human bondage, they argued, simply organized this interdependence and inequality in accordance with principles of morality and Christianity.

The humanitarian arrangements of slavery, the southerners proclaimed, contrasted favorably with the avaricious materialism of the "miscalled" free society of the North. Whereas the Yankees cared only about the wealth that their operatives might produce, southerners accepted costly responsibility for the human beings whom God had "entrusted" to them. A number of defenders even maintained, like Harper, that "slave labor can never be so cheap as what is called free labor." Nevertheless, Hammond piously advised, slavery's moral purposes dictated that "we must . . . content ourselves with . . . the consoling reflection that what is lost to us is gained to humanity." The proslavery argument asserted its opposition to the growing materialism of the age and offered the model of evangelical stewardship as the best representation of its labor system. The master was God's surrogate on earth; the southern system institutionalized the Christian duties of charity in the master and humility in the slave. "You have been chosen," Nathaniel Beverley Tucker declared to his fellow slaveholders, "as the instrument, in the hand of God, for accomplishing the great purpose of his benevolence."[32] The nineteenth-century concern with philanthropy, defenders of slavery argued, was most successfully realized in the South's system of human bondage. Reflecting the lessons of human experience through the ages, as well as the prescriptions of both divine and natural order, slavery seemed unassailable. The truths of science, religion, and history united to offer proslavery southerners ready support for their position.

But by the 1850s, challenges to the unity of proslavery ideology had begun to appear. In large part, these emerging rifts mirrored wider intellectual currents. Forms of knowledge and legitimation long assumed to be necessarily compatible were everywhere displaying nagging contradictions. Most significant was an increasingly unavoidable conflict between the claims of science and those of the Scriptures. Rather than supporting and amplifying the truths of biblical revelation, science seemed to many midcentury thinkers already a threat to the conclusions of other modes of knowledge; challenges had begun to appear to the nineteenth century's holistic conception of truth.[33]

But in the proslavery argument, as in patterns of American thought more generally, these inconsistencies were to remain largely dormant; comparatively little overt strife between religion and science appeared before the Civil War, for most Americans voiced confidence that the achievement of greater understanding would eventually reveal an underlying compatibility. So, too, southerners defending slavery sought to minimize the impact of philosophical contradictions in order to maintain the strength that derived from proslavery unity. "There is no forked tongue in the language of learned men—whether physician or divine," one proslavery scientist insisted. "Truth is the same whether uttered by one or the other—the phraseology may differ but truth is an unit."[34]

By the end of the antebellum period, however, even those recognizing the necessity for unity and consistency sometimes found it difficult to make their views conform to the moral-philosophical mainstream of proslavery thought. The emergence of ethnology by the late 1840s as a recognized science of racial differences was to pose inevitable difficulties for the Fundamentalist bases on which the proslavery movement

had been built. On the other hand, scientific validation of Negro inferiority offered an alluring and seemingly irrefutable argument to those
favoring the social subordination of blacks in slavery. "The mission of
Ethnology," as one southern proponent declared, "is to vindicate the
great truths on which the institutions of the South are founded."[35] Yet
theories that urged the existence of two permanently separate and unequal races of men directly challenged Genesis and its assertion that all
humans were descended from a single set of common parents. The
dilemma implicit in this conflict of knowledge and values was neatly
illustrated in the personal dilemma of Josiah Nott. A leading southern
spokesman for racial science, he was anxious to deemphasize challenges to religious orthodoxy, yet equally desirous of establishing the
validity of his own field. The pressure for unity in the proslavery movement influenced Nott to suppress overt antagonism toward religion,
and as a result the Alabama physician dotted his writings with protesta-
tions of his devotion to sacred truth. "No one can have more positive
distaste than myself for religious or any other controversy," Nott proclaimed, insisting that he used his "best efforts to avoid unpleasant col-
lisions." Science and revealed religion, he asserted, would necessarily
be consistent if their truths were properly ascertained. "The works of
God form one great chain, of which revealed religion is but a link; and
while the Bible, on one hand, has shed a flood of light on Ethnology,
this in turn has afforded immense aid to Biblical criticism."[36]

Ultimately, however, Nott was unable to fulfill the expectations for
conformity held by the proslavery mainstream. Irascible and somewhat
belligerent, Nott translated a latent hostility toward religion in general
into an open assault upon the clergy as the purveyors of false doctrines.
While he piously proclaimed his devotion to revelation, he mercilessly
attacked its clerical interpreters. Such a position, he thought, would
offer the possibility of establishing scientific principles without directly
undermining religion; conflicts between ethnology and the Bible could
be reconciled without challenging the unity of all truth. Science and
religion were consistent, he maintained, but ministers were clearly fal-
lible and in challenging science misinterpreted the divine word.

For the most part, Nott's audience did not perceive his subtle distinction between anticlericalism and antireligionism. Nott provoked violent controversy, and clerical defenders of slavery moved to affirm the
unity of the human race and of proslavery ideology by disproving his

polygenist theories. To many, Nott seemed to be causing altogether unnecessary difficulties. He and his associate George Gliddon, one critic remarked, had "involved their cause with the discussion of the inspiration, authenticity, authorship & translation of Scripture, to such an extent that their work looks more like a labored attempt to annihilate that volume than to discuss mooted questions in ethnology."[37]

Most defenders of slavery sought to use the scientific prestige of ethnology to enhance their position without becoming ensnared by the difficulties it presented; they were eager to sidestep the problems Nott addressed head-on. George Frederick Holmes, long sympathetic to the notion of race as a major determinant of human civilization, nevertheless advised fellow southerners that the truths of ethnology remained "enveloped . . . in all the mist of obscurity. I should steer a cautious middle course between the extreme views on this subject." Edmund Ruffin found that despite great potential value, ethnology offered "more amusement than reliable information," and George Fitzhugh bluntly declared that if forced to choose between the Bible and ethnology, southerners had best stick to the Holy Writ.[38] Although most proslavery advocates did not admit the inherent conflict so openly, in practice they followed Fitzhugh's advice. Racial arguments had been a part of proslavery thought since its earliest manifestations in the colonial period. The impact of ethnology was chiefly to enlarge and systematize this facet of the argument and to offer a variety of skull measurements, geological and anthropological "facts" as incontrovertible evidence for the mainstream position. Nature was invoked to provide additional support for the moral justifications that remained the core of the proslavery argument.[39]

The intricacies of racial and ethnological arguments were not the only difficulties confronting the mainstream of proslavery thinkers. Conformity and unanimity within the movement were occasionally threatened by departures from the prescribed style, as well as the substance of proslavery tracts. In their effort to present the defense of slavery as a part of the transcendent truths of religion and science, many apologists believed that a tone of dispassionate inquiry was an absolute necessity. Polemics would injure rather than advance the ultimate goals of the proslavery cause. "Christian candor and fairness of argument," one apologist insisted, were the emblems of "the search after truth." When Josiah Nott replied angrily to attacks upon his ethnological assertions, the *Southern Quarterly Review* was quick to chastise him, proclaiming the tone of his work "unfortunate." But the most vigorous criticism from the proslavery mainstream was directed against George Fitzhugh, whose "extravagant heresies" sparked an outburst of protests from other apologists.[40]

A Virginian who began publishing well after the main lines of pro-slavery theory had been defined, Fitzhugh proclaimed himself the first true defender of slavery, the first to have "vindicated slavery in the abstract." He was the only southerner vigorously to advocate slavery as the most desirable arrangement for white as well as black labor, and the only apologist to transform the discussion of slavery into an unremit-ting attack on free labor and capital. But while presented in extreme form, his arguments were basically derived from those of the theorists who had preceded him and had been developing a general defense of slavery for decades. Fitzhugh's assault upon northern and British wage slavery and his discussion of the sorry plight of free workers, for exam-ple, had been a popular argument since Robert Walsh's comparison of southern slavery and European free labor in 1819. But it was Fitzhugh's outspoken tone and aggressive style that drew even more attention than the substance of his essays. His contemporaries regarded him as something of a crackpot.[41]

Fitzhugh candidly acknowledged that his involvement in proslavery was far from dispassionate or disinterested. "Confessing myself the greatest egoist in the world," Fitzhugh hoped to attract attention and promote book sales by self-consciously making his work "odd, eccen-tric, extravagant, and disorderly."[42] Southerners reviewing his books deplored their "utter recklessness of both statement and expression." George Frederick Holmes, whom Fitzhugh admired as the proslavery advocate with views closest to his own, found his discussions "incendi-ary and dangerous," and Edmund Ruffin pronounced Fitzhugh's views "absurd."[43]

Never included in the anthologies of proslavery classics of his own era, Fitzhugh's work has been often reprinted in ours, and he has at-tracted lavish attention from present-day historians. This modern in-terest in Fitzhugh may in part be a result of his very unrepresentative-ness. In their perception of the proslavery argument as aberrant and "astonishing,"[44] historians have turned to its most extreme, provoc-ative, and even outrageous presentation. Many politically motivated northerners of the mid-nineteenth century chose a similar course, pointing to Fitzhugh's arguments as proof of the impassable gulf separating North and South. There is even evidence that Abraham Lincoln himself turned to Fitzhugh's writing for the portrait of intersectional opposition that led him to conclude that the nation was a "house divided."[45] It was much easier for nineteenth-century northerners, as it is for modern Americans as well, to discount an argument that is "odd, extravagant and disorderly" than to confront the ways in which the mainstream proslavery position drew upon basic values of Western civilization shared by the North and the South to justify human bondage.

Yet Eugene Genovese has argued persuasively for Fitzhugh's importance as a "ruthless and critical theorist who spelled out the logical outcome of slaveholders' philosophy and laid bare its essence."[46] Fitzhugh's attacks upon capitalism and free labor, he has asserted, were necessary corollaries to the defense of slavery. Because Fitzhugh was extreme, he was able to articulate the unspoken—and even unrecognized—assumptions on which proslavery rested.

Genovese was careful not to argue for Fitzhugh's representativeness. Indeed, other southerners and other proslavery advocates endeavored to refute what Genovese has called the "logical outcome" of their own philosophy. As they sought to avoid the implicit conflicts of religion and ethnology, so too they eschewed Fitzhugh's all-out attack upon civilization as it was developing in the nineteenth-century capitalist West. Fitzhugh's "opposition to interest or capital" one defender summarily dismissed as "foolish."[47] In hoping to save southern civilization as they knew it, southerners sought to perpetuate rather than resolve the inconsistencies between their prebourgeois labor system and the bourgeois world market in which it flourished. The mainstream of the South's defenders had to dissociate themselves from Fitzhugh, for he showed them to be caught in a paradox at a time when they could ill afford the luxury of the self-examination and questioning necessary for its resolution. Yet this was a paradox that did not envelop the South alone. The paternalism of much of the North's industry, the ideas of evangelical stewardship underlying its widespread reform movements, indeed the strength of northern proslavery sentiment itself bespoke the existence of a similar conflict above the Mason-Dixon line between antimaterialist, prebourgeois values and the "cash-nexus" at the center of the modern civilization fast emerging.[48] The paradoxes that the proslavery argument encountered and unwittingly exposed—conflicts of tradition and modernity, of human and material values, of science with religion—were but further evidence of the argument's centrality within nineteenth-century American culture. These were problems in social philosophy and values confronting all Americans of this era, and unassailable solutions were as scarce in the North as in the South.

While we can continue to abhor the system of human bondage that flourished in the Old South, there is much we can learn from a more dispassionate examination of the arguments used to defend it. We have sought to distance the slaveholders and their creed, to define them as very unlike ourselves. Yet their processes of rationalization and self-justification were not so very different from our own, or from those of any civilization of human actors. The persistence of modern racism is but one forceful reminder of the ways that human beings always view the world in terms of inherited systems of belief and explanation that only partially reflect the reality they are meant to describe. By understanding how others have fashioned and maintained their systems of meaning, we shall be better equipped to evaluate, criticize, and perhaps even change our own.

Christian Soldiers

The Meaning of Revivalism in the
Confederate Army

From the fall of 1862 until the last days of the Civil War, religious revivalism swept through Confederate forces with an intensity that led one southerner to declare the armies had been "nearly converted into churches."[1] A remarkable phenomenon in the eyes of contemporary observers, these mass conversions have been largely ignored by modern scholars.[2] The attention recent historians have devoted to other manifestations of nineteenth-century evangelicalism makes this neglect of Civil War religion seem all the more curious, for scholarly findings about the relationship between revivalism and the process of social and cultural transformation suggest that an exploration of army evangelicalism should yield important insights into the meaning of the South's experience in an era of profound dislocation and change.[3]

The centrality of religion within antebellum southern culture gave sacred language and perception a prominent place in the region's response to war. The South had not only embraced evangelical Protestantism with a uniformity and enthusiasm unmatched in the rest of the nation but had also used religion as a crucial weapon in the sectional propaganda battle. Defining itself as more godly than the North, the South turned to the Scriptures to justify its peculiar institution and its social order more generally. With its declaration of nationhood and the subsequent outbreak of war, the Confederacy identified its independence and success as God's will. Their cause, southerners insisted until the very last days of the conflict, was God's cause; the South's war of defense against invasion was unquestionably a just war.

The prominence of such sentiments in public discourse—in the Confederate Constitution itself, in Jefferson Davis's proclamations of fast days, in generals' announcements of military victory, not to mention in church sermons and denominational publications—established religion as the fundamental idiom of national and personal identity. Southerners' responses to the unanticipated horrors of the first modern, total war were almost necessarily articulated within a religious framework and in religious language. But if religion was central to the Confederacy as a whole, it was perhaps of greatest importance to the common southern soldier, whose life was most dramatically altered—if not actually ended—by war's demands. The widespread army revivals directly reflected the stresses of the soldier's life and death situation: the strains of life in the ranks of a mass army; the pressures of daily confrontation with death—and with a rate of mortality unmatched in any American war before or since.[4]

Although the southern religious press reported scattered conversions of soldiers from the time fighting broke out, Confederates did not begin to identify what one evangelical called a "genuine and mighty work of grace" until the fall of 1862. At first confined to the Army of Northern Virginia, and always strongest there, significant religious awakenings spread to the Army of Tennessee and to the Trans-Mississippi forces in 1863 and 1864. One observer later calculated that as many as 150,000 soldiers were "born again" during the war, but even if far fewer actually converted, thousands more participated in the revival without themselves undergoing the dramatic personal experience of grace.[5]

For large numbers of men the struggle against the Yankees on the field had its parallel in the battle against Satan in the camp. Soldiers' diaries and letters make clear how widely the phenomenon extended. As one participant expressed it, "We sometimes feel more as if we were in a camp-meeting than in the army expecting to meet an enemy." A less sympathetic observer found he could not even write a peaceful letter to his wife. "It seems to me that whereever [sic] I go I can never get rid of the 'P-salm-'singers—they are in full blast with a Prayer meeting a few rods off." To many of those neither directly involved nor firmly opposed, the pattern of evangelicalism and conversion became simply a part of army routine. One captain wrote indifferently yet revealingly in his diary in mid-1863, "Today is Sunday. Nothing unusual . . . —preaching in the afternoon and evening. Many joined the church."[6]

When the timing of battle permitted, chaplains and lay preachers organized a prodigious schedule of services—sometimes as many as five or six meetings a day. During a six-week lull in the fighting in Virginia during the summer of 1864—a time when the military situation made invocation of divine help particularly appropriate—one brigade chaplain scheduled daily prayers at sunrise, an "inquiry meeting" each morning at eight, preaching at eleven, prayers for the success of the Confederate cause at four, and preaching again at night.[7]

Brigades in which the revival spirit was vigorous often constructed chapels, especially in winter quarters when the men were likely to spend several months in one place. In January 1865, for example, a Virginian reported that his brigade had erected churches every six to eight hundred yards along the lines. In summer soldiers built outdoor chapels in the woods. Split logs served as benches; a wooden platform became the altar; iron-mesh baskets held firewood to illuminate the gatherings. Even places for two thousand worshippers were often not sufficient. "The interest manifested," one soldier reported, "was so great that the seats were taken in the afternoon by such men as were not on duty. When night relieved from duty those who had been drilling, the men stood up in immense numbers around those who were seated." When observances were held indoors, the smaller number of places made competition even more intense. "Men may sometimes be seen an *hour before services* running to the house, in order that they may procure seats. They come from regiments two miles off." Men of the Army of Northern Virginia packed one brigade chapel like "herrings in a barrel."[8]

The revival spawned as well a major Confederate publishing endeavor. In spite of paper and labor shortages, nearly two hundred million pages of tracts were distributed to soldiers during the war. Several denominations also published religious newspapers for the troops, and the Confederate Bible Society, founded in 1862, hoped to supply every soldier with his own New Testament. When revivalists were unavailable, tracts served as substitutes. "These little preachers," as the *Confederate Baptist* called them, could be read over and over—in the tent, on a march, or even in the heat of battle—and were often cited as themselves responsible for conversions. The popularity of tracts and papers grew throughout the war, and Stonewall Jackson was reputed to keep a supply on hand to use as rewards for his men. One Baptist missionary thought that much of the appetite for the publications arose because "the soldiers here are *starving* for reading matter. They will read anything." But even if their appeal originated in the monotony of camp life, the tracts achieved remarkable effectiveness as an "instrument" in saving souls. Together with the exhortations of missionaries and chaplains, religious publications kept the army's revivalist fervor at a remarkably high pitch.[9]

Curiously, the evangelical fervor of the Confederate troops was not paralleled by enthusiasm at home, and, as self-righteous southerners loved to charge, "nothing like this occurred in the Yankee army."[10] Despite the widespread perception of the conflict as a holy war, southern civilians, even church members, were not experiencing God's grace in substantial numbers. The coldness of established congregations throughout the war years troubled southern clergy, who attributed their failures to the preoccupation of their flocks with the secular realities of politics and economic survival. But surely the Confederacy's soldier-converts were even more concerned with the actualities of war. For them, perhaps, the ever-present threat of death gave battle a transcendent, rather than primarily worldly, significance, or possibly the enthusiasm within the army reflected evangelicals' concerted efforts with the troops.

The comparison with soldiers' experiences in the northern army is more problematic, for revivals did occur with some frequency among Yankee troops. Most nineteenth-century observers, as well as twentieth-century scholars, have remarked, however, upon significant differences in the scale and in the intensity of army religion North and South. Abraham Lincoln himself worried that "rebel soldiers are praying with a great deal more earnestness . . . than our own troops." A number of explanations for this contrast seem plausible. The greater homogeneity of religious outlook within the overwhelmingly evangelical and Protestant southern army was certainly significant. The more profound stresses on southern soldiers, who because of shortages of manpower and materiel served for longer periods of time, with fewer furloughs, and with greater physical deprivation, undoubtedly played a role as well, for it was as the war increased in duration and intensity that revivalism began to spread.[11]

Men donning the Confederate uniform did not at first demonstrate unusual piety. At the outset the devoted found themselves very much on the defensive, for religious leaders felt obliged to combat a widespread view that godliness would undermine military effectiveness. There "is nothing in the demands of a just and defensive warfare at variance with the spirit and duties of Christianity," an oft-reprinted tract urged. "Piety will not make you effeminate or cowardly." Godly southerners at first feared that the influences might work in just the opposite direction: that battle would prove an impediment to piety. "War is the hotbed of iniquity of every kind," wrote the Reverend Charles Colcock Jones. The army had in all ages been "the greatest school of vice." History showed that men removed from the restraining, "softening" moral influences of womanhood and hearth easily succumbed to the temptations of camp life. One tract drawing soldiers' attention to the grave yawning open before them pointedly summarized the dilemma. "Men, by associating in large masses, as in camps and cities, improve their talents, but impair their virtues." The South, happily free of significant urban centers, must not now abandon her comforting moral advantage.[12]

The initial experience of camp life seemed to bear out these dire expectations. "I think the majority of the men of our Regt. are becoming very wild & contracting many bad habits," a private wrote home from Virginia in November 1861. The Sabbath brought "no preaching, no service" to counteract Satan's growing influence. "The religious destitution of the Army," a soldier confided to his diary, "is awful." By far the largest portion of the troops appeared to one tract agent as entirely godless. Of the three hundred men in three companies that he visited in the summer of 1861, only seven were "professors of religion." The army presented a moral picture that was "dark indeed."[13]

The seeming enormity of the problem inspired religious leaders to rise to meet the challenge. The large number of unconverted could certainly be regarded as a "field . . . white unto the harvest." The Baptist *Religious Herald* was not alone in viewing the evangelization of the army as the obvious *"Christian work of the day."* Ministers recognized that the very grimness of the situation they confronted contained seeds of hope. The Confederate army was young; its modal age was eighteen, almost the ideal time for conversion, as southern preachers, versed in what one modern scholar has called the "applied science" of revivalism, understood very well. "Scarcely any," the Reverend James Mc-

Gready noted in a tract entitled *An Appeal to the Young*, "are ever converted . . . after the age of twenty-five or thirty years at the farthest"; most were converted well before that time. Soldiers also provided a special opportunity for evangelical labors because they were men, those who before the war had proven "most inaccessible to pastoral influence." Now isolated from home and loved ones and confronted by the reality of death, "even the man who always repulsed the approaches of his pastor at home" might "gratefully receive the attentions of the chaplain." Perhaps in war men could be brought to feel the emotionality and vulnerability that in peacetime had been the almost exclusive domain of the other sex. "There is a foolish notion," one tract explicitly stated, "that it is unmanly to manifest any *feeling* under the pressure of bereavement or mental distress. . . . That it is womanly and childish to weep." The wartime work of the evangelist was to convince the soldier that "this is all a mistake." The availability of a large congregation, already assembled in camp, and the "contagious nature of army habits," for good as well as evil, further encouraged preachers in their task.[14]

The mobilization of the southern clergy to confront the wartime challenge paralleled the mobilization of Confederate military resources. Identifying both the hazards and the opportunities that war offered the church, ministers worked to devise a strategy for conquering army camps, and, not incidentally, for making religion—and its preachers—a central force in the creation of the new nation. With the successes of the church among the troops, a chaplain declared to a gathering of his colleagues, "The foundation for a wide religious power over the country is now lain. . . . We, then, here and now, stand at the fountain head of the nation's destiny. We lay our hands upon its throbbing heart. Never again shall we come so near having the destiny of a great nation in our own hands."[15]

But opportunity was not achievement. The role of the preacher in Confederate armies was neither clearly defined nor greatly respected. Chaplains had no official military rank, received poor pay and only a private's rations. To combat the "low repute" in which the post was held, ministers and many churches lobbied throughout the war for legislative improvement in the chaplain's situation, but their efforts met with only limited success. Most denominations supplemented meager army salaries in order to encourage qualified men to serve, but many regiments and even brigades—perhaps as many as half—never had an official minister. In June 1861 Virginia Baptists decided to augment government efforts by employing colporteurs to distribute tracts and to discuss religious subjects with the men. Several Protestant denominations also sent itinerant civilian missionaries to the troops, and these preachers usually cooperated closely with official chaplains in the effort to spread the divine word to every part of the army. Denominational differences were all but forgotten in what became an ecumenical movement to bring Christ to the camp. Baptists preached without insisting on baptism as a requirement for the forgiveness of sin; Protestant soldiers flocked to services conducted by Catholic chaplains. Evangelist J. William Jones remarked that war had brought "a truce to denominational bickerings—there are no sectarian sermons preached and no sectarian tracts circulated, but all seem to work together to make men Christians."[16]

In the fall of 1862 these religious labors began to bear fruit, as circumstances came to the aid of the southern churches. The timing of evangelical successes during the war offers important clues to the meaning of the conversion experience. By late 1862 many initial illusions had begun to disappear; after more than a year of "hard service," as one chaplain explained, "the romance of the soldier's life wore off, a more sober and serious mood seemed to prevail in the camps." Conscription had begun the previous spring, and by fall soldiers without the romantic zeal and optimism of the original volunteers had joined the ranks. Perhaps most significantly, however, revivals first broke out among troops retreating from Maryland after the Confederate loss at Antietam, which represented not only the first major southern defeat in the eastern theater but the bloodiest single battle day of American history as well. The experiences of slaughter and military failure surely had their impact in encouraging the "serious reflection and solemn resolve" that preceded evangelical commitment. There was great "eloquence" in the "din" and "carnage" of the field. "We are so much exposed," one soldier observed, as he explained why he had quit "light trashy novels" for the Bible, "we are likely to be called off at any moment."[17]

During the rest of the war the most dramatic outbursts of religious enthusiasm followed fierce and bloody battles—especially losses. The "great revival along the Rapidan" in the late summer and fall of 1863 swept through troops encamped for the first time since their retreat from Gettysburg. The pattern was clear to contemporary observers. As one army correspondent explained in 1863 to the *Confederate Baptist*,

There have been always among us, some pious men, but until that time nothing like a general revival or even seriousness. The regiment had just returned from the disastrous Pennsylvania expedition, and a few days before had the closest and most desperate encounter with the enemy that they had ever had. The minds of the men were fresh from scenes of danger and bloodshed and were forced thereby to contemplate eternity, and in many cases, to feel the necessity of preparation.

In the West, Vicksburg and Chattanooga had a similar effect. Individual experiences of grace were closely connected to the wider search for God's favor implicit in the divine gift of military victory. As one recently converted soldier wrote in a letter home, he hoped the revival in his camp would bring "a great blessing nationally as well as Spiritually."[18]

Religion thrived, however, not just on growing personal and national insecurity, not just on individual and collective fear of the Yankees, but on anxieties related to social realities within the Confederate army itself. Chaplains, missionaries, and colporteurs had begun to make clear that rather than hinder military effectiveness, they could do a great deal to enhance it. Officers previously indifferent, if not openly hostile, to religion in the camps came to encourage piety and to provide spaces and occasions for the evangelization of their troops. "It is an interesting fact," observed Baptist preacher J. J. D. Renfroe in November 1863,

> that most of our officers have undergone some change on the subject of chaplains. . . . When they first started out it made no difference with them what sort of man they had for chaplain, or whether they had any at all; but now you will not talk with an officer ten minutes about it until you will discover that he does not want a chaplain simply to "hold service," but he wants a man who will promote the religious good of his regiment. I have had irreligious officers to tell me that a good chaplain is worth more for the government of troops than any officer in a regiment.

Colonel David Lang communicated his satisfaction that his chaplain's efforts in the fall of 1863 were "making good soldiers of some very trifling material."[19]

Despite the notable and inspiring exceptions of Robert E. Lee, Stonewall Jackson, and other pious commanders, army evangelism had its greatest impact among the common soldiers. Missionaries, chaplains, and even Jackson himself complained repeatedly of the religious indifference of the officers. The rhetoric of the Confederate revival, the themes of its sermons and its tracts, suggest one obvious explanation of why so many southern leaders encouraged piety among their troops while they remained largely aloof. "Irreligious colonels," the *Religious Herald* explained, "seek the cooperation of a good chaplain in their desire to render their regiment as efficient as possible." Religion promised significant assistance in the thorny problem of governing the frequently intractable Confederate troops.[20]

From the outset the Confederate army experienced great difficulties with discipline, for the southern soldier was most often a rural youth who had every expectation of becoming—if he was not already—an independent landholding farmer. Despite the uneven distribution of wealth and particularly of slave ownership in the prewar South, the common man ordinarily had no direct experience with political or social oppression, for he lived in a democratic political and social order where decentralization minimized perceptions of sharp stratification between planters and plain folk. The prevalent ideology of republicanism had encouraged rich and poor whites alike to cherish their "independence" and autonomy, emphasizing a sharp contrast between their status and that of enslaved blacks. But the army was to demand a hierarchy and a discipline that the prewar situation had not, even if practices such as election of officers might seem to symbolize the soldier's willing contractual surrender of control over his own life. Previously masterless men were compelled in the army to accept subordination for the first time, and many recruits complained bitterly about this change in expectations and circumstances. As one young soldier wrote home in the summer of 1861, "We are not lowd to go to the Shops without a permit and we are not lowd to miss a drill without a furlo sickness or permit, we are under tite rules you dont no how tite they are I wish I coul see you and then I could tell you what I thought of campt life it is very tite rules and confinen."[21]

Religion promised considerable assistance in easing this difficult transition. Élie Halévy, E. P. Thompson, and others have described the role of Methodism in the transformation of English workers into an industrial proletariat, and more recently Anthony F. C. Wallace has explored the influence of evangelical Protestantism upon laborers in nineteenth-century Pennsylvania textile mills. In the South of the 1860s the role of religion was somewhat different, for young rural Confederates were going to war, not to the factories. But the requirements of industrialized work and industrialized warfare are alike in important ways—in their demand for new levels of discipline, regularity, and subordination. Daniel T. Rodgers has described a process of "labor commitment— . . . by which new industrial employees adjusted deeply set rural loyalties and work habits to the disrupting demands of factory labor." In their identity shift from farmers to soldiers, young southerners needed to make analogous changes in internal values and expectations. A soldier "must be trained," insisted the *Religious Herald,* "and willing to submit to thorough training. . . . There is a *moral* requirement as important as the material one—an inward man as indispensable as the outward one." Religious conversion and commitment could serve as the vehicle accelerating and facilitating this necessary personal transformation. Both southern military and religious leaders recognized that evangelicalism could contribute to internalizing discipline and enhancing the efficiency of the Confederate soldier; the church could help to mold disorganized recruits into an effective fighting force. "A spirit of subordination and a faithful discharge of duty," the *Biblical Recorder* summarized, "are [as] essential to the good soldier" as they are to the good Christian.[22]

The term "efficiency" appeared again and again in evangelical rhetoric. The Christian soldier would be an efficient soldier because he would not be afraid to die; he would be obedient and well disciplined because he would understand the divine origin of earthly duty. One army chaplain offered a striking illustration of the *"military power of religion.* In a brigade of five regiments, where there has recently been a glorious revival, two of the regiments, which had not shared in the revival, broke, while the three which had been thus blessed stood firm." A missionary of the Army of Tennessee made an even more dramatic claim. "Preaching," he asserted, had "corrected" one of "the greatest evils of our army, in a military point of view . . . —that of straggling." The servant of God, he explained, learned that he must execute all earthly as well as all spiritual obligations "conscientiously," and that meant keeping up with your regiment even if you were ill or had no shoes. A colonel of the South Carolina Volunteers emphasized the point when he congratulated a colporteur on the usefulness of his tracts, which he found "of incalculable service in encouraging the soldier to a continuation of his hard duties, and making him feel contented with his lot."[23] The Reverend R. N. Sledd no doubt won similar approval from Confederate military leaders when he insisted to a congregation of common soldiers about to depart for war that "it is . . . not only wise, but necessary to your efficiency, that for the time you surrender your will to that of your officers. . . . This lesson of submission to control is a difficult one for many to learn; but until you have completely mastered it, . . . you are not prepared to behave yourself the most valiantly and the most efficiently in the field of conflict." Significantly, religious leaders stressed the profitable management of time as well as the adoption of regular personal habits, and often chose the bourgeois language of commerce and the marketplace to emphasize the productive uses of religion. A correspondent to the *Religious Herald* suggested in 1863 that chaplains on the field make themselves easily identifiable by wearing badges emblazoned with the epigraph, "Godliness is profitable unto all." Another article reported an imaginary dialogue between an officer and a recently converted private who assured his superior, "I used to neglect your business; now I perform it diligently."[24]

But the virtues religion inculcated did not just appear on the battlefield. Evangelicalism also sought to ease the conflict over appropriate values and behavior that was disturbing many Confederate camps. Soldiers who had lived in isolated circumstances in the overwhelmingly rural South had found little necessity to adjust to the lifestyles of other groups. Many complaints in their wartime diaries and letters sound very much like the earlier reactions of genteel Yankees first confronting the squalid realities of life among the lowly in the urban North. Confederate army camps played a role analogous to that of northern cities in juxtaposing classes and cultures in what was to many a new and alarming propinquity. "One of my greatest annoyances," a Mississippian wrote to his wife, "is my proximity to one tent of the Co[mpany] next [to] me . . . in which are 9 or 10 [of] the most vile, obscene blackguards that could be raked up this side [of] the bad place, outside of a jail or penitentiary. From early morn to dewey eve there is one uninterrupted flow of the dirtiest talk I ever heard in my life. . . . Those fellows have 'had no raising.' "[25]

The nature and sources of this social conflict should not be oversimplified; the social location and meaning of southern evangelicalism is complex. Part of the controversy in army camps was a lingering hostility among some of the southern gentry toward evangelicalism, an antagonism that had persisted since the Great Awakening of the mid-eighteenth century. In 1865, for example, the Baptist *Religious Herald* referred openly and distressfully to the "causes which have tended to produce in men of taste an aversion to evangelical religion." A century before the Civil War, as Rhys Isaac has argued, the categories of class and religious identity were quite clear. The gentry overwhelmingly opposed the restrictions on their aristocratic pleasures that the pious sought to impose. But by the 1860s the class location of evangelicalism—and especially of the refined behavior that it encouraged—was more nearly reversed. As Bertram Wyatt-Brown, Donald G. Mathews, and others have contended, "the mission cause" made "good headway among the privileged ranks of southerners between 1820 and 1840." And even those of the elite who were not themselves converted often encouraged and supported the social influence of the evangelical churches. Although the controversies over lifestyle and personal behavior in southern army camps should not be seen as exclusively the effort of an upper stratum to impose its standards on a lower, this concern was certainly a significant element in the conflict. Aristocratic Confederates who themselves swore, drank, or dueled also incurred the wrath of the evangelical leaders in the army. But by far the most prominent target of reform efforts were the lower orders, the same social groups that had been the objects of intensive prewar southern missionary efforts. These were the individuals the army evangelists encouraged to behave more decorously, to wash regularly, to make prudent use of time, and, indicating the presence in this group of many illiterates, to learn to read.[26]

In the army the evangelical cause took on a new urgency because of the "great trial" imposed on numbers of refined southerners who found themselves required to tent next to "such abounding wickedness" as was represented by some of their comrades. Separated before the war by the decentralized, overwhelmingly rural nature of southern life, privileged and less privileged whites came to know each other in new and unsettling ways within the Confederate camps. And with this knowledge came not the rapprochement of different social groups so often hailed as the outcome of the English experience in the trenches of World War I. Instead, in a South that had throughout the antebellum period stressed the republican equality of all white men, this wartime experience brought an emerging awareness of class. "Cannot something be done to lessen the unnatural distance that is gradually and rapidly creeping in between officers and men?" one tract demanded. *The Soldier's Paper* worried in similar terms: "Let not our private soldiers feel that they have ceased to be men because they are soldiers. Let them not imagine that they are degraded to mere machines because they are fighting in the ranks. . . . Let them feel that they still have friends in their officers." A correspondent in the *Confederate Baptist* in 1863 was more explicit still in a discussion of the plight of the common fighting man oppressed by his superiors. "CLASSES—," he reflected. "We were struck with a remark made to us by a private in the army. He said, 'before the war, there were only white men and negroes among us; now there are white men, negroes and soldiers.'" It could not but have been chillingly symbolic for the troops marched out in June 1862 to witness the punishment of army deserters with thirty-nine lashes and branding on the cheek—a characteristic form of correction for runaway slaves throughout the antebellum period. White men previously above corporal punishment seemed as soldiers to occupy a new status in which even the most cherished distinctions between freeman and black slave were fast disappearing. As the *Confederate Baptist* protested in 1863, "That any officer in the Confederate army should inflict upon a fellow soldier, a punishment which is peculiar to slaves, is enough to make us blush for our country. Is the poor man a negro, and is he fighting only for the privilege of having a different master?"[27]

The social significance of the revival impulse is perhaps most strikingly revealed to a twentieth-century observer by the unexpected centrality and importance of the evangelical campaign against profanity, which one chaplain hailed as "*the* national sin." Although one response to such a curious claim might be admiration for the level of virtue such a minor indictment implies, evangelical preoccupation with swearing deserves fuller explanation. By the mid-nineteenth century public profanity was becoming largely a class sin, found most often, as one tract explained, among the "common" and the "ill bred." In an 1860 analysis of social classes in the South, for example, native Alabamian Daniel R. Hundley defined "low, vulgar and obscene" speech as characteristic of one particular element of the region's lower orders.[28] But what might now be regarded as the seemingly harmless "profanity of the privates" attracted enormous attention from evangelicals. Swearing, they declared repeatedly, was dangerous because it was a "useless sin." Unlike gluttony, venality, or lust, it had no rational objective. The swearer risked damnation for no purpose. "You commit the utter folly of . . . ruining your souls, for nothing at all!" To swear was "to incur guilt, without delight." In an age and within a religious movement increasingly dedicated to the advancement of utilitarian values, swearing·represented an "*irrational*," "unprofitable," inefficient vice; it simply did not "pay." In its purposeless affront to piety it seemed to carry with it a dangerous "spirit of rebellion against conscience, society and God." Swearing was "disinterested sin—sin committed only from the love of sin." It was a direct and overt attack on religion and social order rather than a sin committed out of moral weakness in the face of irresistible temptation. A quintessential embodiment of loss of control and rejection of deference, profanity became a symbolic as much as a substantive enemy of the army revivals.[29]

In writing of World War I, Eric J. Leed has argued that there occurred a "militarized proletarianization" of European soldiers. Certainly no such dramatic transformation took place in the Confederate South, for this first modern war fell far short of the 1914 conflict in its demands for hierarchy, routine, and control. Nevertheless, Leed's observation, combined with the rhetoric of Confederate army religion, cannot help but draw attention to the new work patterns warfare imposed and to the loss of autonomy and independence it implied for the average southerner. As one Virginia private tellingly observed, "A soldier in the ranks is like a piece of machinery—he moves and acts as commanded." Even though his salary was often not even paid, the Confederate soldier was in most cases undergoing his first experience as a wage laborer subordinate to the direction of his employer. When at the end of the war the *Nation* called for the North to "turn the slothful, shiftless Southern world upside down," little would editor E. L. Godkin have guessed that the leaders of the Confederate army and churches had already been acting as his unwitting allies. For four years they had struggled—albeit with uncertain success—to teach the southern soldier the very same values of training, regularity, and industry that Godkin hoped northern victory might now impose.[30]

Yet such a view of the role of Confederate religion—as manipulative and hegemonic—is partial and one-dimensional. Recent scholarly work has justly insisted that monolithic emphasis on the aspects of social control within evangelicalism must not distort its larger meaning or impugn the authenticity of revivalists' piety and sacred commitment by casting them simply as conspirators seeking to enhance their own social power. Most advocates of the order and discipline central to the revivalistic impulse sincerely believed that their goals were above all to fulfill God's design and only secondarily to serve the needs of men. The perceptions of the common Confederate soldiers who were the targets of army revivalists' efforts is less clear. Certainly the impact of the evangelical message among the troops was profound, as the large number of conversions attests. And many of these converts readily accepted the notion of a regenerate life as one of discipline and self-control, for soldiers frequently wrote home that revivals had made it impossible to find a cardplayer or a profane swearer in the regiment. It seems likely, however, that the cynicism of some reductionist twentieth-century social control historians may have been shared by at least some nineteenth-century soldiers. The suspicion and hostility toward evangelical hegemony expressed by the plain folk who participated in the antimission movement in the prewar South had not, in all probability, entirely disappeared, even though there is scant surviving evidence of its existence in the Confederate army. The revivals could not in any case have completely succeeded in transforming southern soldiers into a tightly disciplined fighting force, for complaints about insubordination continued throughout the war and even increased as the desertion rate rose dramatically in 1864 and 1865.[31]

Common soldiers may well have ignored much of the rhetoric of control in tracts and sermons to appropriate from the evangelical message truths that they found more meaningful. The notion of a disciplined and deferential Christian soldier undoubtedly had a greater appeal to religious and military leaders than to the common fighting man instructed that it was his "business . . to die." Yet evangelicalism met important needs for the soldiers themselves as well as for their military masters. Like religion among black slaves or working-class Methodists, army evangelism did what E. P. Thompson has described as a "double service," appealing in different ways both to the powerful and to the powerless. In the Old South the Christianity preached by masters to their bondsmen was quite different from that embraced by the slaves.[32]

Similarly, common Confederate soldiers used religion in their own ways, focusing on the promise of salvation from death as well as upon the reality of an evangelical community that recreated some of the ideals of a lost prewar world. The experience of conversion served as the basis for a shared equality of believers and an Arminian notion of ultimate self-determination that in profound ways replicated the antebellum republican order that military hierarchy and command had obliterated. There was, as the *Religious Herald* observed in 1863, a sense of real "homogeneity and fellow-feeling" within the brotherhood of believers.[33] The comradeship of the regenerate encouraged as well the group solidarity that modern military analysts have identified as critical to the maintenance of morale. Converts formed Christian Associations within their brigades and regiments to assume communal responsibility for evangelical discipline, and, in the words of the constitution of one such organization, "to throw as many strengthening influences around the weak . . . as it is possible to do." The associations ran Bible and reading classes, established camp libraries of tracts and religious newspapers, but, perhaps most significantly, confronted the fear of death—and of dying abandoned and alone—that haunted so many soldiers. The believers of the Seventh Virginia Infantry covenanted, for example, to "care specially for each other in all bodily or mental suffering, to show each other respect in case of death." In practice this usually meant that association members would try to identify comrades disabled on the field of battle in order to provide them either with medical care or with Christian burial.[34]

On a more individual level, evangelical religion provided psychological reassurance to southern soldiers struggling with the daily threat of personal annihilation. In its Christian promise of salvation and eternal life, conversion offered a special sort of consolation to the embattled Confederate. In striking ways accounts of camp conversions parallel descriptions of what in World Wars I and II was first known as "shell shock," then as "combat exhaustion" or "combat stress." Shaking, loss of speech, paralysis of limbs, uncontrolled weeping, and severe emotional outbursts often appeared among twentieth-century soldiers when they reached safety after military action. Similar behavior characterized many Confederate converts who found Christ in the emotion-filled revival meetings held in the intervals between Civil War battles. The fiercest encounters brought the largest harvests of souls, just as the most desperate fighting of World Wars I and II yielded the highest incidence of combat stress. These similarities in nineteenth- and twentieth-century soldiers' responses suggest that analogous psychological processes might well have been involved.[35]

Twentieth-century scholars have often commented on the seeming failure of the Civil War soldier to grapple with the emotional significance of his experience. "Much in the Civil War was to be forgotten," Marcus Cunliffe has observed. "Involvement in it was intense yet oddly superficial." Unlike World War I, which yielded its Wilfred Owen, its Siegfried Sassoon, its Ernest Hemingway, the Civil War remained in a real sense unwritten, its horrors, if not unnoticed, at least denied. Yet in their own way and in their own particular idiom, Confederate soldiers were just as expressive as their World War I counterparts. Southerners were very articulate, for example, about their *inability* to portray what they had witnessed. After his first battle in 1861 one infantryman wrote home, "I have not power to describe the scene. It beggars all description." Kate Cumming, working as a nurse in a military hospital, commented even more tellingly on the inability of all those around her to communicate their experiences: "Nothing that I had ever heard or read had given me the faintest idea of the horrors witnessed here. I do not think that words are in our vocabulary expressive enough to present to the mind the realities of that sad scene."[36]

The language of post-Freudian self-scrutiny used by World War I participants was not available to Civil War soldiers. But their silences are eloquent. Their speechlessness was part of a process of numbing, of the denial that is a widespread human response to stress. "We hurry," one soldier wrote, "through the dreadful task apparently unconscious of its demoralizing influences and destructive effects." The war, another confirmed, "is calculated to harden the softest heart." The majority came to act as "unconcerned as if it were hogs dying around them." A correspondent writing to the *Religious Herald* in 1862 understood well, however, "the true fountain" of this apparent indifference. Soldiers' unconcern, he explained, was "the result of an effort to *banish,* not to *master,* the fear of death. . . . The expedient of the ostrich [who acts] . . . as though refusing to look on a peril were to escape from it."[37]

Modern-day analysts of combat stress point out, however, that such denial has its limits, that numbness and indifference can only be retained for so long. Eventually extreme stress results in the appearance of symptoms in virtually everyone. Often denial begins to be interrupted by what psychiatrists call "intrusions," nightmares or irrepressible and unwelcome daytime visions of stress-producing events. One Confederate soldier who had previously told his wife that he had found the battle of Shiloh indescribable wrote again several weeks later, "I've had great and exciting times at night with my dreams since the battle; some of them are tragedies and frighten me more than ever the fight did when I was awake." Another soldier was obviously more profoundly affected, for, as a friend described him, he began reliving battles in his everyday life. "He became more and more alarmed, and, at last, became so powerfully excited—to use his own words—he felt as if some one was after him with a bayonet, and soon found himself almost in a run, as he moved backwards and forwards in his beat."[38]

Many psychiatrists believe that reliving stress-producing experiences in this way serves to work through and eventually to resolve material repressed in the denial phase. The appearance of intrusions, therefore, signals the emergence of overt conflict that, even though profoundly disruptive, may ultimately enable an individual to cope with and to transcend a traumatic experience. Revivals often explicitly encouraged such intrusions and exacerbated internal tension in the effort to induce the religious conversion that would dissolve all stress in the promise of divine salvation. In order to shake soldiers' personal defenses, preachers and tracts insisted, "Death stares you in the face. The next battle may be your last." The soldier, one revivalist explained, had to be "forced to feel how frail and uncertain is life." The crisis was unavoidable; numbness and denial could be no real or lasting protection. In "the GREAT CONSCRIPTION there is no discharge. . . . Are you ready to take your place with them who will have the victory? . . . Or will your place be in that vast division of death's army, which shall assemble only to be defeated, accursed and punished forever?"[39]

Significantly, the rhetoric of camp sermons was often designed to encourage a metaphorical reliving of battlefield experiences by casting religion as the equivalent of military conflict. Exhorters focused overwhelmingly on the issue of salvation and its frightening alternative, thus calling forth the feelings associated with the life-and-death struggle that soldiers actually confronted each day. Preachers manipulated already existing fear, stressing the nearness of death and its terrors for the unconverted. But at the same time that revivalists exacerbated the tension and helplessness soldiers felt in the face of battle, they emphasized that the men did retain a dimension of choice. Even amidst the

barrage of bullets, they could decide for God. As one tract demanded of
those who had not yet exercised this option, *Why Will You Die?* Death,
its author implied, was a matter of personal will and could be consciously rejected in favor of eternal life. Just as the common soldier concerned about social issues of mastery and subordination within army
life could have the symbolic comfort of electing his own captain, so he
might psychologically escape from his sense of victimization by choos-
ing Christ as the "Captain of [his] . . . salvation." He might transcend
the ultimate and profound loss of control over his destiny that battle
involved by making an existential commitment, by enlisting as a Christian soldier under the "banner of the Cross." The decision for Christ
restored the illusion of free will. And with the return of a sense of control often comes, as contemporary psychiatrists have observed, the ability once again to cope.[40]

Ultimately, revivalists insisted, this was not a war of North against
South, but one of goodness versus evil, of God against Satan. Evangelical rhetoric invited soldiers to relive the emotions of the battlefield,
to express the resulting tensions, then to resolve them in the promise of
eternal life—the only real assurance of safety from war and from the
more general inevitability of death.[41]

This process of conversion is in its general outlines remarkably similar to influential twentieth-century psychiatric notions of appropriate
therapy for combat exhaustion or other traumatic stress. During World
War II American military physicians in North Africa used drugs and
hypnosis, as Civil War revivalists used their tracts and sermons, to re-
vive "partially or completely forgotten traumatic battle episodes." As a
result of this effort "repressed battle experience was restored to consciousness, thus losing most of its previous potential to evoke anxiety."
Patients were encouraged to explore emotions that had been denied
and to release unmanageable anxiety through abreaction.[42]

Civil War conversions and twentieth-century treatments for combat
stress should not, of course, be seen as identical or interchangeable processes. The pious would object to such a rationalization of belief, while
psychologists would regard such an equation as an undue mystification
of the scientific. Undoubtedly they would point as well to the important differences in the populations under study and to their contrasting
contexts and circumstances. Yet the similarities in soldiers' responses in
the two eras are difficult to ignore, especially in the way they point to

the profound dislocation experienced by so many Civil War soldiers. Like combatants in more recent wars, Confederate soldiers found themselves personally unprepared to cope with the ways that battle threatened both their existence and their identity. Adjustment and survival required personal transformation. The cult of the Lost Cause in the postwar years and the numerous continuities between Old South and New should not lull us into forgetting that in significant ways the Civil War created new men.

Students of comparative psychiatry have emphasized that anxiety is interpreted and treated in markedly different ways in different cultural settings. What appears as an intense and debilitating conviction of sin in one era may in a more secular and rationalistic age become a case of "shell shock" or "combat exhaustion" that responds to medical treatment.[43] Within southern culture of the 1860s, religion was the obvious cultural resource for explaining and relieving such deeply felt distress. For the common soldier, therefore, evangelicalism offered a vehicle of personal reintegration and a means of dealing with the physical and psychological assaults of war upon his individual humanity—and even his continued existence. As one private reported to a sympathetic evangelist, "But for the comfort of religion, he thinks he would have lost his mind."[44] The clergy, in turn, found for themselves in war a role of enhanced secular usefulness and importance as well as authentic spiritual fulfillment in the saving of so many souls. For military leaders, revivalism promised a means of inculcating a necessary spirit of discipline and subordination in southerners not previously required to possess such virtues; it was also a way of ensuring the continued favor of the God of Battles.

But the significance of Confederate revivals transcends their meaning for the specific groups involved. Evangelical enthusiasm reflected not just religious but widespread social and cultural tensions that found expression in an evangelical idiom, a discourse that points to the wartime emergence of frictions that were to persist and to grow in the postwar South. Although religion had been at the center of traditional southern identity, it ironically and necessarily became in the army the vehicle and symbol of broader cultural innovation and change. It was religious language that demanded soldiers' adoption of values and behavior representing sharp departures from their accustomed way of life; it was religious exhortation that sought to resolve the social conflicts disrupting Confederate camps by imposing discipline on hitherto "in-dependent" farmers.

In the crucible of war, the consensus that had characterized ante-bellum white society was to break down. Demands for mobilization of men and resources created troubling wartime divisions over the opera-tion of conscription and impressment laws and over the distribution of newly scarce necessities of life. And when economic deprivation emerged as an unfamiliar reality for white southerners, social divisions that had been only intermittently visible in the prewar years intensified until they threatened the Confederacy's very survival. Individualistic southern yeomen found it difficult to adjust to the hierarchy required by war and to what many viewed as the disproportionate sacrifices ex-pected of them. These growing conflicts appeared within the context of army religion as differences of personal and cultural values over issues such as temperance, cleanliness, profanity, and self-discipline. But ulti-mately the frictions became much more overt, as they were expressed first in wartime desertions and disloyalties and later in the class-based political activity of the postbellum years.[45]

Yet evangelicalism remained central within this strife even after Appomattox. The postwar era was a time of dramatic growth for south-ern churches, for the revival spirit seemed to follow soldiers home from the camps. On the one hand, evangelicalism became, as Charles Rea-gan Wilson has argued, the language of defense for the old order and the Lost Cause. Yet at the same time the New South vision of moder-nity and industrial progress also assumed an evangelical idiom. By the 1890s the church seemed so closely allied with the business class that North Carolina Populists directly attacked religious discipline as an instrument of the class hegemony that they perceived to have grown so oppressive in the years since the close of the war. But these Populists did not reject evangelicalism entirely. Instead, like common soldiers three decades before, they too had their uses for revivalism and an alter-native vision of its significance, not so much as a form of discipline but as a means of empowerment.[46]

The broader significance of army religion may thus be the way in which it points to the importance of the experience of war itself in establishing a framework for the social and political conflicts of a New South. In the Confederate army, as in the South of the postwar years, the protean nature of the evangelical message permitted its adherents to appropriate it to satisfy very different purposes and needs. Revivalism served at once as an idiom of social strife and a context for social unity in an age of unsettling transition; it became a vehicle both for expression and resolution of conflict about fundamental transformations in the southern social order.

The identity crisis of the Confederate soldier adjusting to distressing new patterns of life and labor was but a microcosm of the wartime crisis of a South in the throes of change. Military service inaugurated for many southerners a new era characterized by a loss of autonomy and self-determination that even peace would not restore. In the postwar years a southerner was far more likely to be a tenant and far less likely to be economically self-sufficient than he had been in the antebellum period. He might even follow his experience of military wage labor with that of factory employment, as the cotton mill campaign drew thousands of white southerners into industry.[47]

But perhaps the most profound transformation for many Confederate soldiers was deeply personal. In the past decade we have been made sharply aware of the lingering effects of another lost war upon its veterans years after their return to civilian life. Irrational outbursts of violence and debilitating depression are but two characteristic symptoms of what psychiatrists have come to see as a definable "post-Vietnam" syndrome. Southerners deeply scarred by their experiences of horror in the world's first total war may have been affected in similar ways. Perhaps part of the explanation for the widespread violence of the postwar South should be psychological; Klan activity, whitecapping, and lynching may have been a legacy of soldiers' wartime stresses as well as a political response to new and displeasing social realities.[48]

In the clues that it offers to the profound impact of battle and to the social origins of a new South, revivalism is central to the Confederate experience. The Civil War challenged both the South and her fighting men to be "born again."

WOMEN

Altars of Sacrifice

Confederate Women and the Narratives of War

I t is the men, Hector tells Andromache in the sixth book of the *Iliad*, who "must see to the fighting." From ancient history to our own time, war has centered on men, for they have controlled and populated its battlefields. Even in our era of shifting gender definitions, perhaps the most assertive—and successful—defense of traditional roles has been the effort to bar women from combat. Yet war has often introduced women to unaccustomed responsibilities and unprecedented, even if temporary, enhancements of power. War has been a preeminently "gendering" activity, casting thought about sex differences into sharp relief as it has both underlined and realigned gender boundaries.[1]

Like every war before and since, the American Civil War served as an occasion for both reassertion and reconsideration of gender assumptions. Early in the conflict, Louisianian Julia Le Grand observed, "We are leading the lives which women have led since Troy fell." Yet because the Civil War was fundamentally different from those that had preceded it, the place of women in that conflict stimulated especially significant examination and discussion of women's appropriate relationship to war—and thus to society in general. Often designated the first "modern" or total war because of the involvement of entire populations in its terrible work of death, the Civil War required an extraordinary level of female participation. This was a conflict in which the "home front" had a newly important role in generating mass armies and keeping them in the field. Particularly in the South, where human and material resources were stretched to the utmost, the conflict demanded the mobilization of women, not for battle, but for civilian support services such as nursing, textile and clothing production, munitions and government office work, slave management, and even agriculture. Yet white southern women, unlike their men, were not conscripted by law. They had to be enlisted by persuasion. The resulting discourse about woman's place in Confederate society represented the rhetorical attempt to create a hegemonic ideology of female patriotism and sacrifice.[2]

Articulate southerners, male and female, crafted an exemplary narrative about the Confederate woman's Civil War, a story designed to ensure her loyalty and service. As in the tales of war enshrined in Western literature from Homer to Sir Walter Scott, its plot recounted woman's heroic self-sacrifice, casting it as indispensable to the moral, political, and military triumph of her men and her country. The historian John Keegan has compellingly described the way in which the "battle piece," the highly conventionalized and heroic account of combat, has shaped men's expectations and experiences of war. But women have been no less influenced by a genre of female "war stories," intended to socialize them through accounts of their foremothers' deeds. The conventional designation of all women as noncombatants inevitably enhances the wartime significance of gender as a social category, as well as a structure of self-definition. The focus of Confederate public discourse on a "classless" white woman reinforced the privileging of female identity. Usually cast in the homogeneous singular, the "woman" who shared with her sisters rich and poor the experience of sacrificing men to battle represented a useful rhetorical convention within a Confederate ideology struggling to minimize the class divisions that might threaten national survival. At the same time that Confederate discourse appealed to a new and recognizable commonality widely shared by white southern women—whose husbands or sons were nearly three times as likely to die as were their northern counterparts—it promoted the notion of an archetypal "Confederate woman" as a form of false consciousness obscuring social and economic differences among the new nation's female citizens. Ultimately, the focus of Confederate ideology on female self-abnegation and sacrifice as ends in themselves would alienate many women from that rendition of their interests, from the war, and in many cases, from the Confederacy itself. Ideology and its failures played a critical role in shaping the relationship of women to the southern cause and in defining Confederate viability. In recent years scholars have answered the historiographical perennial, "why the South lost the Civil War," by emphasizing deficiencies in southern morale. Almost all such arguments stress the importance of class conflict, especially growing yeoman dissent, in undermining the southern cause. Yet with a white civilian population that was overwhelmingly female and that bore an unprecedented responsibility for the war's outcome, we must not ignore gender as a factor in explaining Confederate defeat.[3]

To suggest that southern women in any way subverted the Confederate effort is to challenge a more than century-old legend of female sacrifice. The story of Confederate women's unflinching loyalty originated during the war and first found official expression in legislative resolutions offered by Confederate leaders to mark the contributions of female citizens. The Confederate Congress established the model in a declaration of gratitude passed in April 1862; the gesture was replicated in proclamations like that of the Mississippi legislature in 1863 thanking the "mothers, wives, sisters and daughters of this State" for their "ardent devotion . . . unremitting labors and sacrifices."[4] After Appomattox this hortatory narrative of female dedication was physically realized in monuments to wives and mothers of the Confederacy and incorporated into scholarly literature on women and the war as conventional historical truth. Even the titles of scholarly works, such as Mary Elizabeth Massey's *Bonnet Brigades*, published in 1966 as part of the Civil War centennial, or H. E. Sterkx's more recent *Partners in Rebellion: Alabama Women in the Civil War*, communicate the image of southern women fighting alongside their men. The same vision had a century earlier inspired Henry Timrod, poet laureate of the Confederacy, to entitle his wartime ode to Confederate ladies "Two Armies." Praising women's contributions in caring for the sick, plying the "needle and the loom," and "by a thousand peaceful deeds" supplying "a struggling nation's needs," Timrod promised women equal glory with the war's military heroes.

> When Heaven shall blow the trump of peace,
> And bid this weary warfare cease,
> Their several missions nobly done,

The triumph grasped, the freedom won,
Both armies, from their toils at rest,
Alike may claim the victor's crest.[5]

The tenacity of such a rendition of southern women's wartime role—
its survival from Confederate myth into twentieth-century historiography—is less curious than at first it seems. Confederate versions originated so early in the conflict as to have been necessarily prescriptive
rather than descriptive. This was not simply a story, but an ideology
intended to direct southern women, to outline appropriate behavior in
the abruptly altered wartime situation. The flattery, the honorific nature of this discourse, was central to its rhetorical force. And the deference to women's importance ensured the survival of the narrative and
its evolution into historical interpretation. Ironically, it fit neatly with
an emergent twentieth-century feminist historiography eager to explore women's contributions to past events previously portrayed from
an exclusively male point of view. Yet the passage of women's history
beyond its earlier celebratory phase and the adoption of more critical
and analytic approaches to female experience may enable us at last to
see the story as the fiction it largely is, to explore its development,
political origins, and rhetorical purposes and thus to understand how it
shaped Confederate women's wartime lives.[6]

With the outbreak of hostilities in early 1861, public discourse in the
Confederacy quickly acknowledged that war had a special meaning for
white females. The earliest discussions of the Confederate woman in
newspapers and periodicals sought to engage her in the war effort by
stressing the relevance of her accustomed spiritual role. The defense of
moral order, conventionally allocated to females by nineteenth-century bourgeois ideology, took on increased importance as war's social
disruptions threatened ethical and spiritual dislocations as well. "Can
you imagine," asked the magazine *Southern Field and Fireside*, "what
would be the moral condition of the Confederate army in six months"
without women's influence? What but a woman "makes the Confederate soldier a gentleman of honor, courage, virtue and truth, instead of
a cut-throat and vagabond?" "Great indeed," confirmed the *Augusta
Weekly Constitutionalist* in July 1861, "is the task assigned to woman.
Who can elevate its dignity? Not," the paper observed pointedly, "to
make laws, not to lead armies, not to govern empires; but to form those

"The House-tops in Charleston during the Bombardment of Sumter."
Reproduced from *Harper's Weekly*, May 4, 1861, New York.

by whom laws are made, armies led . . . to soften firmness into mercy, and chasten honor into refinement."[7]

But many southern women, especially those from the slave-owning classes most instrumental in bringing about secession, were to find that a meager and unsatisfactory allotment of responsibility. As one woman remarked while watching the men of her community march off to battle, "We who stay behind may find it harder than they who go. They will have new scenes and constant excitement to buoy them up and the consciousness of duty done." Another felt herself "like a pent-up volcano. I wish I had a field for my energies . . . now that there is . . . real tragedy, real romance and history weaving every day, I suffer, suffer, leading the life I do." Events once confined to books now seemed to be taking place all around them, and they were eager to act out their designated part. "The war is certainly ours as well as that of the men," one woman jealously proclaimed.[8]

In the spring and summer of 1861, many articulate middle- and upper-class women sought active means of expressing their commitment, ones that placed less emphasis than had the *Augusta Constitutionalist* on what they might not do but instead drew them into the frenzy of military preparation. As recruits drilled and bivouacked, women found outlet for their energies sewing countless flags, uniforms, and even underwear for departing units; penning patriotic songs and verse; submitting dozens of designs for the national flag to the Confederate Congress; raising money as Ladies Gunboat Societies, forming more than a thousand relief associations across the new nation; and sponsoring dramatic performances to benefit soldiers, particularly tableaux representing historic and literary themes. "I feel quite important," one lady observed with some amazement after an evening of such scenes raised a substantial amount of money for Virginia troops.[9]

That declaration of importance was in marked and self-conscious contrast to the feelings of purposelessness that appeared frequently in letters and diaries written by women of the master class. "Useless" was a dread epithet, repeatedly directed by Confederate women against themselves as they contemplated the very clear and honored role war offered men. "We young ladies are all so . . . useless," bewailed Sarah Wadley of Louisiana. "There are none so . . . useless as I," complained Amanda Chappelear of Virginia. "If only I could be of some use to our poor stricken country," wrote a young Louisiana girl to a friend in Tennessee, while Emma Holmes of Charleston sought escape from her "aimless existence." "What is the use of all these worthless women, in war times?" demanded Sarah Dawson. "I don't know how to be useful," another Virginia woman worried.[10]

Some women translated these feelings into a related, yet more striking expression of discontent. Without directly challenging women's prescribed roles, they nevertheless longed for a magical personal deliverance from gender constraints by imagining themselves men. Some few actually disguised themselves and fought in the Confederate army, but far more widespread was the wish that preceded such dramatic and atypical action. "Would God I were a man," exclaimed Elizabeth Collier. "How I wish I was a man!" seconded Emma Walton. "I do sometimes long to be a man," confessed Sallie Munford. Such speculation represented a recognition of discontent new to most Confederate women. Directed into the world of fantasy rather than toward any specific reform program, such desires affirmed the status quo, yet at the same time, they represented a potential threat to existing gender assumptions.[11]

Without directly acknowledging such frustrations, Confederate public discussion of women's roles sought to deal with this incipient dissatisfaction by specifying active contributions women might make to the southern cause and by valorizing their passive waiting and sacrifice as highly purposeful. Confederate ideology construed women's suffering, not as an incidental by-product of men's wartime activities, but as an important and honored undertaking. In a popular Confederate novel aptly entitled *The Trials of a Soldier's Wife*, the heroine explained to her husband, "Woman can only show her devotion by suffering, and though I cannot struggle with you on tne battle-field, in suffering as I have done, I feel it has been for our holy cause."[12]

Public treatments of woman's patriotism soon broadened her accepted spiritual responsibilities to encompass wartime morale. "The time has come," Leila W. wrote in the *Southern Monthly* of October 1861, "when woman should direct into the right channel the greater power which she possesses in giving tone to public sentiment and morals, and shaping national character and national destiny." Moral service to God would now be paralleled by morale service to the state. Southern women, the *Mobile Evening News* concluded, held the "principal creation and direction" of Confederate public opinion "in their hands."

The *Natchez Weekly Courier* assured the "Women of the South" that "the destinies of the Southern Confederacy" rested "in your control."[13]

Women thus became acknowledged creators and custodians of public as well as domestic culture in the wartime South, exercising their power over communal sentiment in a variety of ways. They filled the pages of newspapers and periodicals with patriotic stories and verse and, perhaps even more important, composed many of the songs that served as the central medium of public wartime expression and constituted the most substantial publishing effort of the war. With men preoccupied by military affairs, magazines such as the *Southern Literary Messenger* eagerly sought contributions from women writers and struggled to evaluate the torrents of unsolicited poetry with which patriotic ladies flooded their offices.[14]

But the escalating demand for troops after the bloody battle of Manassas in July 1861 offered women a new role to play. Here their patriotism and moral influence began to assume a more personal dimension, foreshadowing demands to be made of them as the conflict intensified. And this contribution involved women from a much wider social spectrum than had many of the earlier, largely middle- to upper-class efforts of ladies' societies and lady authors. Military manpower needs from the fall of 1861 onward required a rationalization of female sacrifice and a silencing of women's direct interest in protecting husbands and sons. The nineteenth-century creed of domesticity had long urged self-denial and service to others as central to woman's mission. But war necessitated significant alterations, even perversions, of this system of meaning; women's self-sacrifice for personally significant others—husbands, brothers, sons, family—was transformed into sacrifice *of* those individuals to an abstract and intangible "cause."

The effective redefinition of women's sacrifice from an emphasis on protection of family to a requirement for relinquishment of family was problematic enough to occupy a significant portion of Confederate discourse on gender. Songs, plays, poems, even official presidential pronouncements sought to enlist women of all classes in the work of filling the ranks. One popular theme inverted *Lysistrata*, urging young women to bestow their favors only on men in uniform. In a much-reprinted song, a male songwriter assumed a female voice to proclaim, "I want to change my name." This fictionalized heroine was searching for a husband,

Southerners preparing for war. *Equipment*, a watercolor by William
Ludwell Sheppard. Courtesy of the Eleanor S. Brockenbrough Library,
The Museum of the Confederacy, Richmond, Virginia.

But he must be a soldier
A veteran from the wars,
One who has fought for "Southern Rights"
Beneath the Bars and Stars.[15]

"None but the brave deserve the fair," a letter from "MANY LADIES" to the *Charleston Daily Courier* warned cowards and slackers in August 1861. Even Jefferson Davis addressed the question of ladies' appropriate marital choice, declaring the empty sleeve of the mutilated veteran preferable to the "muscular arm" of "him who staid at home and grew fat."[16]

One song published early in the war acknowledged the conflict between woman's traditional role and the new demands on her. From "stately hall" to "cottage fair," every woman, rich or poor, was confronted by her own "stormy battle," raging within her breast.

There Love, the true, the brave,
The beautiful, the strong,
Wrestles with Duty, gaunt and stern—
Wrestles and struggles long.[17]

But, like male songwriters who addressed that theme, the "Soldier's Wife" who had penned the lyrics was certain that women would win their own "heart victories" over themselves and in their "proudest triumphs" send their menfolk off to war. Stirring popular marches captured the very scene of parting, with men striding nobly into the horizon, while women just as nobly waved handkerchiefs and cheered their departure. "Go fight for us, we'll pray for you. / Our mothers did so before us." Popular songs and poems urged women to abandon not just interest but also sentiment, repressing their feelings lest they weaken soldiers' necessary resolve. One graphic, even gruesome, ballad entitled "The Dead" portrayed a boy "oozing blood" on the battlefield as in his dying breath he insisted,

Tell my sister and my mother
Not to weep, but learn to smother
Each sigh and loving tear.[18]

A poem published in the *Richmond Record* in September 1863 elevated such repression of emotion into woman's highest duty. "The maid who binds her warrior's sash / And smiling, all her pain dissembles," "The mother who conceals her grief" had "shed as sacred blood as e'er / was poured upon the plain of battle." Not only was she to sacrifice husband, brother, or son, woman was to give up feeling as well. As a Virginia woman diarist remarked, "we must learn the lesson which so many have to endure—to struggle against our feelings." But "tis a hard struggle for me sometimes," she admitted.[19]

Much of Confederate discourse negated the legitimacy of that emotional struggle by denying its reality altogether. Women, one newspaper proclaimed, had been offered a "glorious privilege" in the opportunity to contribute to the cause by offering up their men. Any lingering resistance, the logic of the essay implied, should be overcome by the far greater—because transcendent—satisfaction of participation in the birth of a new nation.[20]

Yet popular expressions often acknowledged women's doubts in an effort to dispel them. A newspaper poem, "I've Kissed Him and Let Him Go," was among the frankest of such treatments.

> There is some, I know, who feel a strange pride
> In giving their country their all,
> Who count it a glory that boys from their side
> In the strife are ready to fall,
> But I sitting here have no pride in my heart;
> (God forgive that this should be so!)
> For the boy that I love the tears will still start.
> Yet I've kissed him, and let him go.[21]

Best was to feel right, so dedicated to the cause that personal interest all but disappeared. Next best was to stifle lingering personal feeling. But the minimal requirement was to silence doubt and behave properly, even if right feeling proved unattainable.

There is considerable evidence that women of all social levels acted in accordance with these principles in the early months of conflict. Wartime gender prescriptions were so clear to a group of young ladies in Texas that they sent hoopskirts and bonnets to all the young men who remained at home. Other women comprehended the message well enough but, even early in the conflict, embraced it reluctantly. "Oh, how I do hate to give him up," a Louisiana woman sighed, but "I suppose I have to be a martyr during this war."[22]

And propelling men into the army was only the beginning. Once soldiers had enlisted, women were to help keep them in the ranks. The silencing of feeling and self-interest was to continue. "DON'T WRITE GLOOMY LETTERS," warned the *Huntsville Democrat*. Some women, noted an 1862 correspondent to the Georgia *Countryman*, seemed to be giving "up too easily. Some of them write very desponding letters to the soldiers. This is wrong. I am not surprised at their feeling badly; but they should not write gloomy letters," which would cause soldiers to "lose confidence in themselves."[23]

From the outset, the home front was acknowledged to exert significant control over military morale. And as the conflict wore on and desertions and disaffection increased, the connection became clearer. Women must do more than send their men to battle. When men deserted, women were to demonstrate that devotion to the cause had primacy over personal commitments to husbands or sons. The *Richmond Enquirer* appealed directly

> to the women to aid us in this crisis. None have so momentous an interest; and none, as we firmly believe, wield so much power. . . . They know those stragglers, one by one, and where they are to be found. They, the mothers and the sisters, may, if they will, be a conscript guard impossible to be evaded. They know whose furloughs are out, whose wounds are healed, who are lingering idly about . . . philandering and making love. . . . Will not the women help us, then?[24]

As the character of the war changed, so did public considerations of woman's place in it. Early discussions struggled to define some positive contribution women might make, some outlet for the patriotism that especially characterized women of the slave-owning classes. But the growing scale of the conflict transformed a rhetoric that tended to patronize women into one that implored them to make essential and increasing sacrifices for the cause. As the Reverend R. W. Barnwell emphasized in an address to the Ladies Clothing Association of Charleston, "WITHOUT YOU, THIS WAR COULD NOT HAVE BEEN CARRIED ON, FOR THE GOVERNMENT WAS NOT PREPARED TO MEET ALL THAT WAS THROWN UPON IT." Beginning with the rising toll of battle deaths, the reality of the demands on women— the reality of war itself—intruded unremittingly not just on women's

lives but on the stylized narrative created about them. Experience began to challenge the assumptions sustaining their early sacrifices.[25]

From the perspective of 1865, the first months of the conflict would
come to seem an age of innocence, a time, as one Virginia matron put
it, "when we were playing at war." Stories of military history and romance began to pall in face of the unrelenting pressures of real war. In
mid–1862 a Virginia girl answered in verse her cousin's inquiry, "If I
had found enough romance in this War":

> Yes, wild and thrilling scenes have held
> A joyous sway upon my heart,
> But what a dread romance is this,
>   To fill in life so sad a part.

> Slighter changes oft have thrilled
> My Spirit's gay and gladening song.
> But this plaug'd [plagued], horrid, awful War
>   Has *proved* to *me romance too long.*[26]

Much of the shift in women's perceptions of the war arose from the
ever-expanding dimensions of required sacrifice. The need for military
manpower was unrelenting, until by the end of the war, three-fourths of
white southern men of military age had served in the army and at least
half of those soldiers had been wounded, captured, or killed, or had
died of disease. This left almost every white woman in the South with a
close relative injured, missing, or dead. But women had to sacrifice
more than just their men. First luxuries, then necessities were to be
relinquished for the cause. "Fold away all your bright tinted dresses. . . .
No more delicate gloves, no more laces," one poem urged. Women
"take their diamonds from their breast / And their rubies from the finger, oh!" a song proclaimed. A Virginia lady later reminisced that in
the summer of 1861 she felt "intensely patriotic and self-sacrificing"
when she resolved to give up ice creams and cakes. This, she remarked
with some irony, "We called putting our tables on a war footing." By
the next year, meat and grain had begun to disappear from many plates,
and by 1864 one Confederate official informed Jefferson Davis that in
Alabama, at least, civilian "deaths from starvation have absolutely
occurred." In face of such realities, a Richmond periodical struggled to
reassure the region's women and revalidate the notion of sacrifice:

A young Mississippian and his mother. Courtesy William A. Albaugh III Collection, Tappahannock, Virginia.

But e'en if you drop down unheeded,
What matter? God's ways are the best:
You have poured out your life where 'twas needed,
And He will take care of the rest.[27]

An initial conception of wartime self-denial as an enforced separation from loved ones and the absence of cakes and ice cream had been transformed even for the most privileged women of the South into the possibility of starvation for themselves and their families and the likelihood of death or injury for a husband or child.

For women of the slave-owning classes, the departure of husbands and sons and the continuing pressures of war took on additional significance. The burden of slave management, the designated responsibility of male planters and overseers before the conflict, now often devolved on women. The isolation of many plantation women in rural areas populated overwhelmingly by blacks exacerbated white women's dismay. Unsupervised slaves began to seem an insupportable threat. "I lay down at night," Addie Harris of Alabama complained, "& do not know what hour . . . my house may [be] broken open & myself & children murdered. . . . My negroes very often get to fighting."[28]

The slave system of the American South rested upon the realities of paternalistic domination—upon the power of white males over both women and black slaves. But the ideology of paternalism always presumed reciprocal obligations between the supposedly powerful and the powerless. Both the rhetoric and the practice of white gender relations had assigned political and social control to males in return for their assumption of the duty to maintain social order, to exert effective dominance over potentially rebellious bondsmen. Protecting white women from threats posed by the slave system upon which white male power rested was an inextricable part of planters' paternalistic responsibility. Yet when masters departed for military service, the Confederate government, as collective representation of slaveholders' power, failed to provide adequate means to control plantation slaves. Under such circumstances, many Confederate mistresses felt not only terrified but also abandoned and betrayed. Slave management was a duty for which most women believed themselves unsuited; they had not understood it to be in the domain allocated them by the paternalistic social order they had long accepted as natural and right. As one woman explained, she was simply not "a fit and proper person" to supervise bondsmen; another insisted she had not the "moral courage" to govern slaves. "The idea of a lady" exercising the required corporal dominance over slaves, Alice Palmer of South Carolina noted, "has always been repugnant to me."[29]

The absence of white men accustomed to managing slaves and the disintegration of slavery under the pressures of growing black assertiveness thus placed an unanticipated and unwanted burden on plantation mistresses, most of whom had never questioned the moral or political legitimacy of the South's peculiar institution. But in the new war-born situation, Confederate women could not indulge in the luxury of considering slavery's merits "in the abstract," as its prewar defenders had urged, nor unthinkingly reap its material rewards. Slavery's meaning could not rest primarily in the detached realms of economics or politics, nor could white women any longer accept it as an unexamined personal convenience. The emotional and physical cost of the system to slaveholding white women had dramatically changed. Women now confronted all but overwhelming day-to-day responsibilities that they regarded as not rightfully theirs, as well as fears that often came to outweigh any tangible benefits they were receiving from the labor of increasingly recalcitrant and rebellious slaves.

The war's mounting death toll dictated the emergence of yet another dimension of female responsibility. While men at the front hurried their slain comrades into shallow graves, women at home endeavored to claim the bodies of dead relatives and to accord them proper ceremonies of burial. Woman's role was not simply to make sacrifices herself but also to celebrate and sanctify the martyrdom of others. In the Confederacy mourning became a significant social, cultural, and spiritual duty. Through rituals of public grief, personal loss could be redefined as transcendent communal gain. Women's tears consecrated the deaths of their men, ensuring their immortality—in southern memory as in the arms of God—and ratifying soldiers' individual martyrdom. Such deaths not only contributed to Confederate victory but also exemplified the sacred conception of Christian sacrifice with which the South had identified its nationalist effort. And in honoring men's supreme offering, women reminded themselves of the comparative insignificance of their own sacrifices. Loss of life of a beloved could not compare with loss of one's own; civilian anxiety and deprivation were as nothing in face of soldiers' contributions. "Even when a woman does her best," Kate Cumming observed of her efforts to nurse wounded soldiers, "it is a mite compared with what our men have to endure."[30]

Whatever doubts about the value of her contributions Cumming held, her labor, like that of thousands of other southern women, was essential to the Confederate social and economic order. The size of Civil War armies and the unforeseen dimensions of the conflict required civilian productivity of an unprecedented scale. And since women constituted such a large proportion of white southern civilians, the production of goods and services became in large measure their responsibility. "We must go to work, too," as a DAUGHTER OF 'OLD VIRGINIA' wrote in the Richmond Enquirer. The exigencies of war thus weakened the role prescriptions that had denied white women remunerative labor outside the home and had directed that only black women should work the land. Public ideology now needed to redefine such activities as valued while limiting the potential shift in gender expectations implicit in the altered behavior.

The debate within the Confederacy about nursing exemplifies the complexity of such wartime attitudes toward change. From the earliest months of the conflict, many journalists and editors urged that women be permitted—in fact, encouraged—to nurse wounded soldiers in military hospitals. Yet even these advocates of nursing reform were well aware of the dangers implicit in their proposals. Women, the Confederate Baptist observed, might prove "most valuable auxiliaries" within the hospital, as long as they remained "in their proper sphere" and did not seek to "direct or control the physician." Nursing would be acceptable as another dimension of women's service and sacrifice, but it must not be transformed into female empowerment.[31]

Many women showed themselves eager to make such contributions regardless of the ideological terms in which their actions were construed: they volunteered to help overworked army physicians and began to establish "wayside hospitals" to care for traveling soldiers at depot towns throughout the South. But the entry of women volunteers into hospital settings provoked outbursts of protest from those who believed nursing "would be injurious to the delicacy and refinement of a lady." In the eyes of many southerners, both male and female, hospital work was simply "not considered respectable."[32]

By the fall of 1862, however, the Confederacy's need for nurses had yielded legislation providing that women be recruited and remunerated for hospital labor. Yet resistance lingered, especially among male physicians. Phoebe Pember, a matron at Chimborazo Hospital in Richmond, encountered widespread resentment from doctors that greatly increased the difficulty of her job, and Cumming transferred from one hospital because of a senior physician's opposition to female nurses. There was, she summarized, a "good deal of trouble about the ladies in some of the hospitals of this department."[33]

Many women shared the aversion to female nursing. Ladies who dedicated themselves to ward work, such as Pember, Cumming, and Louisa McCord, were subjects of gossip and speculation. Women working in hospitals seemed in the eyes of many southerners to display curiously masculine strengths and abilities. Clara MacLean confided to her diary that her neighbor Eliza McKee, recently departed for Virginia as a nurse, had always possessed such strength as to seem "almost masculine—Indeed I used to tell her I never felt easy in her society if discussing *delicate* subjects; I could scarcely persuade myself she was not in disguise." And Mary Chesnut, the famed South Carolina diarist, felt much the same about the intimidating strength of her friend McCord, who seemed to possess "the intellect of a man." Nurses were not truly women, but in some sense men in drag.[34]

Such attitudes enabled southerners to blunt the impact and significance of women's changed behavior by framing it within existing ideological categories. These beliefs permitted some women to become nurses, excused others—who lacked the requisite "masculine" traits—from doing so, and at the same time discouraged any permanent expansion in the boundaries of the female role: nursing continued to be regarded as deviant, requiring behaviors inconsistent with prevailing class and gender expectations.

Public discussion of women's wartime entry into teaching demonstrates a similar effort to employ ideology to limit the impact of war-born behavioral change. Although a feminization of teaching had occurred in the North in the antebellum era, southerners had not encouraged women's assumption of classroom responsibilities. But, as the *Augusta Daily Constitutionalist* remarked in May 1863, the war had "swallow[ed] up" the men preparing to be teachers. "We are left no resource then but to have female teachers. . . . Women are peculiarly fitted, naturally and morally, for teachers of the young."[35] The report of the superintendent of common schools of North Carolina for 1862 reminded the people of his state that there was no employment in which ladies rendered needy by circumstances of war might labor more usefully than "in the business of forming the hearts and minds of the young." The State Education Association of North Carolina offered a prize in November 1861 for the best essay on the subject of the "propriety and importance of employing more female teachers in our common schools," thus inviting the general public to help redefine the ideological consensus the association hoped to foster.[36]

Confederate educators gave significant attention to training women as teachers. To some degree the shift was self-interested, for in the absence of young men, professors' livelihoods depended on recruiting other minds for instruction. Trinity College in North Carolina began in 1864 to fill its depleted classrooms with women, and many women's colleges thrived during the war. Wytheville Female College in Virginia reported its population "but very slightly diminished"; Baptist Female College of Southwest Georgia grew steadily, even though it had to move into the president's house and relinquish its main building to a soldiers' hospital. Hollins College in Virginia worked to establish a system of scholarships for future teachers, and the Statesville North Carolina Female College created a new teaching department.[37]

But southerners by no means uniformly embraced this new departure. Emma Holmes of South Carolina reported in 1862 the opposition a friend confronted from her family when she took over the village school, and Holmes herself faced stubborn family resistance to her desire to become a schoolmistress. Elizabeth Grimball's mother was "terribly mortified" by her daughter's insistence on teaching, and as late as mid-1863, the Convention of Teachers of the Confederate States pointedly restricted membership to "any male citizen" of the new nation. Yet, as the president of Davidson College in North Carolina baldly declared to an 1864 graduating class of women, *Our females must engage in the work of teaching; for there is no other alternative.*"[38]

Discussions of gender appeared in almost every public mode of communication within the Confederacy—in sermons, newspapers, poetry, song, the new Confederate drama, even painting—and in personal documents such as diaries and letters.[39] But the comprehensive narrative of Confederate women and the war evolved in the course of the conflict and, while comprising a largely coherent whole, usually appeared piecemeal rather than as a complete story. In 1864, however, an Alabamian named Augusta Jane Evans published a novel that might justly be regarded as the most systematic elaboration, and in many ways the culmination, of the discussion that had preceded it. As a novel, it was quite literally a narrative, a story of woman and the war entitled *Macaria; or, Altars of Sacrifice.* Evans had written it as she sat at the bedsides of wounded soldiers, and she dedicated it to the Confederate army. *Macaria* became a wartime best-seller, read widely not just by women, for whom novel reading had become such an important and pleasurable pastime, but by men in the intervals between battles or during periods of hospital convalescence.[40]

Like the mythological figure in her title, who sacrificed herself on the altar of the gods in order to save Athens in time of war, Evans's heroine Irene is "ambitious of martyrdom." The novel is structured as her pilgrimage toward "Womanly Usefulness," which she ultimately realizes in the Confederate war effort. Here, at last, after the long struggles that constitute the bulk of the story, Irene finds her lifework, giving her father and her beloved beau Russell up to die on the battlefield and dedicating herself to the highest possible existence, laboring in "God's great vineyard."[41] But even as Augusta Evans wrote, even as thousands of southern women eagerly read her paean to self-sacrifice, they had begun emphatically to dissent from the roles and scenarios composed for them. A pseudonymous woman wrote revealingly to the *Montgomery Daily Advertiser* in June 1864. At first, she observed, women had rivaled "the other sex in patriotic devotion," but

> Oh what a falling off is there! . . . A change and such a change, has come over the spirit of their dream. The Aid Societies have died away; they are a name and nothing more. The self-sacrifice has vanished; wives and maidens now labor only to exempt husbands and lovers from the perils of service. . . . Never were parties more numerous. . . . Never were the theatres and places of public amusement so resorted to. . . . The love of dress, the display of jewelry and costly attire, the extravagance and folly are all the greater for the brief abstinence which has been observed.[42]

The effort to define sacrifice as purposeful was failing. As a New Orleans Creole woman wrote her soldier son, "Je ne vois que des sacri-

fices, des victimes, la ruine, la misère, rien de gagné." Women's willingness to be disinterested, to embrace the needs of the nation as prior to
their own, had begun to disappear. As one woman facing the conscription of her last son explained, "I know my country needs all her children and I had thought I could submit to her requisitions. I have given
her cause my prayers, my time, my means and my children but now the
last lamb of the fold is to be taken, the mother and helpless woman
triumph over the patriot."[43]

White southern women, socialized from an early age in the doctrines
of paternalism with their implicit promises of reciprocal obligation,
expected that their sacrifices would be recompensed. At all class levels,
women had retained the sense of a moral economy of gender in which
they traded female self-abnegation for care and protection. The "helpless woman" held an implicit power of requisition within her very assumption of helplessness. By the later years of the war, however, the
ability of southern men to meet requirements for care and protection,
to ensure the physical safety—and even the subsistence—of the civilian
population had broken down. In response, many women began to demonstrate the conditional nature of their patriotism; there were clear
limits to their willingness to sacrifice. Concerns about personal loss
and personal survival—both physical and psychological—had eroded
commitment to the cause. The romance of the "battle piece" had disappeared before the pressing realities of war. Unable any longer to
imagine herself one of the legendary "Spartan women," Lizzie Hardin
confided to her diary,

> Perhaps there are few of us who in reading stories of ancient heroism
> or the romance of modern war have not had some idle thoughts of the
> role we might have played in similar circumstances. How often have I
> dropped the book while my fancy kept time to the warlike trumpet or
> languished in some prison cell or sent up Te Deums from the bloody
> field of victory. But how different the picture when you view it in a
> nearer light.

On a tour of the battlefield at Seven Pines in search of her wounded
cousin, Constance Cary (later Harrison) reported seeing men "in every
stage of mutilation" and proclaimed herself "permanently convinced
that nothing is worth war!" Margaret Junkin Preston greeted the news

of the death of her stepson and several of his friends by protesting, "Who thinks or cares for victory now!" Sarah Jane Sams proclaimed herself "sick and tired of trying to endure these privations to which we are all subjected," and as early as 1862, Julia Le Grand had come to feel that "nothing is worth such sacrifice." For the most part, women's satiety with war remained personal. Yet even if growing dissatisfaction with the day-to-day management of Confederate affairs did not shade over into explicit criticisms of southern war aims, women were becoming increasingly alienated from the new nation and resentful of its demands on them. "What do I care for patriotism," one woman pointedly demanded. "My husband is my country. What is country to me if he be killed?" "The Confederacy!" Emily Harris complained to her diary late in 1864, "I almost hate the word."[44]

Wartime experiences rendered some women almost incapable of functioning. Modern psychology might define such women as in the grip of traumatic stress reactions or severe depression, but Confederates used quite effective descriptive language of their own. Lila Chunn explained to her soldier husband in the spring of 1863, "I experience such constant dread and anxiety that I feel all the time weary and depressed." Another woman described many wives and mothers she knew as "stunned and stupefied . . . forever" by grief, and a resident of Lynchburg, Virginia, believed that her poverty and suffering had driven her "almost upon the borders of crazziness." Cornelia McDonald, struggling to care for a family of seven children in embattled Winchester, Virginia, clearly understood the relationship between her debilitated physical condition and her emotions. Emaciated and weakened by hunger, she found that by 1863 she had become "faint-hearted" as well. "My feelings were beyond control. . . . I had lost the power of resistance and all my self-command." Her depression was so intense she felt she "could willingly say 'good night' to the world and all in it." A mother writing to a son captured by the Yankees and imprisoned in the North may perhaps have put it most simply and eloquently: "I would wrote before now but I was Clean out of hart."[45]

But many Confederate women retained hope that their sufferings would be relieved. Within the framework of paternalistic assumptions to which they clung, hardships were defined as injustices worthy of attention and intervention by rulers of the Confederate state. As an "unassuming girl" from Alabama explained to the secretary of war in requesting a furlough for her brother, "I feel there is yet justice & *mercy* in the land, to *you* therefore I present my humble petition." Women thus began to regard their difficulties as a test of the moral as well as the bureaucratic and military effectiveness of the new nation and tied their patriotism to the competency of the state's performance in these matters of personal concern. Women penned anguished letters to President Jefferson Davis and a succession of secretaries of war seeking assistance in return for their sacrifices. Miranda Sutton of North Carolina was unable to sign her name, but she dictated a petition asking that one of her sons be released from the military to help provide her with food. Six of her sons had served in the army; two, in addition to her husband, had died. She professed certainty that the moral economy of sacrifice would bring favorable attention to her request. "Your petitioner humbly concieves that having made such sacrifices for the southern cause her claims humble though she be will not be overlooked." Sixty-year-old Harriet Stephenson of North Carolina was perhaps even more direct. With five sons in the army, she informed Secretary of War James Seddon, "I think I have did enough to you for you to take sum intrust in what I so mutch desrie of You"—the discharge of one of her sons to provide her support. Nancy Williams of Mississippi made a similar request of Davis: "I think I have done well for our cause, give up all of my sons, one of which was only fifteen. . . . Please answer my letter immediately." When he did not, she wrote again, still expressing faith that her expectations would be fulfilled. "I ask this favor from the government, hoping and believeing that it will be granted." Frances Brightwell of Louisa County, Virginia, appealed directly to Davis's paternalism in asking the discharge of her husband after her father's death had left her an "orfrint child." "My heart is broken I have no one to take care of me oh I think it will kill me Please try and doo sumthing for me. . . . I know a good gentlemond like yourself feals for a tinder female."[46]

Some bolder—or perhaps only less calculating—women seemed less to implore Confederate officials than to threaten them. "One of the anxious widowed mothers of Alabama" was unwilling to sign her letter of complaint to the president. But she promised him that the unjustified conscription of her son guaranteed that "a day of retribution will surely come" to the South. Another female correspondent who believed her son had been unfairly taken by the army informed Davis, "I

suspect that our confederacy must fall where such injustice reigns."
Almira Acors wrote Davis, describing her desperate poverty and the
failure of her neighbors to aid her, a failure suggestive of a more general
breakdown of paternalism throughout southern society:

> It is a folly for a poor mother to call on the rich people about here
> there hearts are of steel they would sooner thow what they have to
> spare to their dogs than give it to a starving child. . . . I do not see
> how God can give the South a victory when the cries of so many
> suffering mothers and little children are constantly ascending up to
> him. . . . If I and my little children . . . die while there Father is in
> service I invoke God Almighty that our blood rest upon the South.

A War Department official marked the outside of the letter "File"; Almira Acors did not even receive a reply.[47]

For all their intended audacity, these women offered only a limited
challenge to Confederate power and legitimacy. They threatened Davis
and his government by invoking a higher, divine paternalism, rather
than by assaulting the larger assumptions of paternalism itself. God,
they warned, would punish the Confederacy because it had not lived up
to its own ideals—particularly its obligations to the women and children that its social assumptions had defined as powerless and dependent. Within such a framework of criticism, women still regarded
themselves as largely passive—even if increasingly angry. God, not they
themselves, would avenge their wrongs. If Davis and his secretary of
war would not protect them, they would summon a yet more powerful
father figure to the task.[48]

But by 1863, at least some Confederate women had become more
aggressive in their expressions of discontent. In the case of women from
yeoman families particularly, oppressions of class and gender reinforced
one another, impelling numbers of the aggrieved toward overt action
against the war effort. Destitute female petitioners warned Confederate
officials they would urge their husbands and sons to desert if their basic
needs for family subsistence were not met. As Nancy Mangum explained to Governor Zebulon Vance of North Carolina, prices must be
lowered or "we wimen will write for our husbans to come . . . home and
help us we cant stand it." Other wives and mothers did not bother with
warnings. Martha Revis informed her husband after news reached her
of southern defeats at Gettysburg and Vicksburg, "I want you to come

home as soon as you can after you get this letter." One mother, whose willingness to sacrifice had reached its limit, wrote her son, a Confederate captain and prisoner of war, "I hope, when you get exchanged, you will think, the time past has sufficed for *public* service, & that your own family require yr protection & help—as others are deciding." As the desertion rate rose steadily in the southern army throughout 1864, Confederate officials acknowledged the significant role needy wives and mothers played in encouraging soldiers to abandon their posts. As one North Carolinian bluntly explained, "Desertion takes place because desertion is encouraged. . . . And though the ladies may not be willing to concede the fact, they are nevertheless responsible . . . for the desertion in the army and the dissipation in the country."[49] And women undertook a kind of desertion of their own, many from the northern tier of Confederate states fleeing to friends and relatives in the North because of what a Confederate provost marshal described as their inability "to support themselves here."[50]

As the emotional and physical deprivation of southern white women escalated, the Confederate ideology of sacrifice began to lose its meaning and efficacy. Hardship and loss were no longer sacred, no longer to be celebrated, but instead came to seem causes for grievance. Late in 1862 an article in the *Children's Friend,* a religious periodical for boys and girls, found in what might earlier have been labeled a dedicated wartime "sacrifice" only deplorable "Oppression." "Many women," the paper reported, "especially in large cities, have to work hard, and receive very little for it. Many of them sew with their needles all day long, making garments for others, and get so little for it that they have neither food enough, nor clothes, nor fire to make their children comfortable and warm. There are many such now in Richmond working hard, and almost for nothing."[51] Southerners had defined the purpose of secession as the guarantee of personal independence and republican liberty to the citizens and households of the South. Yet the women of the Confederacy found themselves by the late years of the war presiding over the disintegration of those households and the destruction of that vaunted independence. Most white southern women had long accepted female subordination as natural and just, but growing hardships and women's changed perception of their situation transformed subordination, understood as a justifiable structural reality, into oppression, defined as a relationship of illegitimate power.

The erosion of the sacredness of sacrifice was also evident in the changed attitudes toward death that appeared among Confederate civilians by the last months of the war. As one Virginia woman explained, "I hear now of acres of dead and . . . wounded with less sensibility than was at first occasioned by hearing of the loss of half a dozen men in a skirmish." This shift in perception was reflected in altered mourning customs. As Kate Stone explained in the spring of 1864, "People do not mourn their dead as they used to." Constance Cary was shocked by the seemingly cavalier and uncaring manner in which military hospitals treated the deceased, dropping six or seven coffins in "one yawning pit . . . hurriedly covered in, all that a grateful country could render in return for precious lives."[52] The immediate and tangible needs of the living had become more pressing than any abstract notion of obligation to the dead.

The urgency of those needs yielded a sense of grievance that by 1863 became sufficiently compelling and widespread to erupt into bread riots in communities across the South. In Savannah, Georgia, Mobile, Alabama, High Point, North Carolina, Petersburg, Virginia, Milledgeville, Georgia, Columbus, Georgia, and in the capital city of Richmond itself, crowds of women banded together to seize bread and other provisions they believed their due. Their actions so controverted prevailing ideology about women that Confederate officials in Richmond requested the press not to report the disturbance at all, thus silencing this expression of female dissent. In the newspapers, at least, reality would not be permitted to subvert the woman's war story that editors had worked so assiduously to develop and propagate. A Savannah police court charged with disciplining that city's offenders similarly demonstrated the incompatibility of such female behavior with the accepted fiction about southern women's wartime lives. "When women become rioters," the judge declared baldly, "they cease to be women." Yet in resorting to violence, these women were in a sense insisting on telling—and acting—their own war story. One Savannah rioter cared enough about the meaning of her narrative to print up and distribute cards explaining her participation in the disturbance. "Necessity has no law & poverty is the mother of invention. These shall be the principles on which we will stand. If fair words will not do, we will try to see what virtue there is in stones."[53]

Upper-class women did not usually take to the streets, but they too expressed their objections to the prescriptions of wartime ideology. And, like their lower-class counterparts, they focused much of their protest on issues of consumption and deprivation. The combination of symbolism and instrumentalism in the bread riots was paralleled in the extravagance to which many Confederate ladies turned. In important ways, reckless indulgence represented resistance to the ideology of sacrifice. Mary Chesnut's husband James found her "dissipated" and repeatedly criticized her refusal to abandon parties and frivolity. In February 1864 the *Richmond Enquirer* declared the city to be a "carnival of unhallowed pleasure" and assailed the "shameful displays of indifference to national calamity." Richmond's preeminent hostess was reported to have spent more than thirty thousand dollars on food and entertainment during the last winter of the war. Even a council of Presbyterian elders in Alabama felt compelled in 1865 to "deplore the presence, and we fear, the growing prevalence of a spirit of gaity, especially among the female members of some of our congregations." And instead of resorting to riots, numbers of more respectable Richmond ladies subverted ideals of wartime sacrifice and female virtue by turning to shoplifting, which a Richmond paper reported to be "epidemick" in the city, especially among women of the better sort. Women, one observer noted in 1865, seemed to be "seeking nothing but their own pleasure while others are baring their bosoms to the storms of war."[54]

The traditional narrative of war had come to seem meaningless to many women; the Confederacy offered them no acceptable terms in which to cast their experience. Women had consented to subordination and had embraced the attendant ideology of sacrifice as part of a larger scheme of paternalistic assumptions. But the system of reciprocity central to this understanding of social power had been violated by the wartime failure of white southern males to provide the services and support understood as requisite to their dominance. And many southern women would not assent indefinitely to the increasing sacrifice and self-denial the Civil War came to require. By the late years of the conflict, sacrifice no longer sufficed as a purpose. By early 1865, countless women of all classes had in effect deserted the ranks. Refusing to accept the economic deprivation further military struggle would have required, resisting additional military service by their husbands and sons, no longer consecrating the dead, but dancing while ambulances rolled by, southern women undermined both objective and ideological foundations for the Confederate effort; they directly subverted the South's military and economic effectiveness as well as civilian morale. "I have said many a time," wrote Kate Cumming in her diary, "that, if we did not succeed, the women of the South would be responsible." In ways she did not even realize, Cumming was all too right. It seems not insignificant that in wording his statement of surrender, Robert E. Lee chose terms central to women's perceptions of themselves and the war. The Confederate effort, he stated at Appomattox, had become "useless sacrifice." Confederate ideology about women had been structured to keep those terms separated by interpreting sacrifice as a means of overcoming uselessness, by rendering sacrifice itself supremely purposeful. But the war story offered Confederate women at the outset of conflict had been internally flawed and contradictory and finally proved too much at odds with external circumstance; it was an ideology designed to silence, rather than address, the fundamental interests of women in preservation of self and family. As Julia Le Grand explained, it was an ideology that left women with "no language, but a cry," with no means of self-expression but subversion. In gradually refusing to accept this war story as relevant to their own lives, women undermined both the narrative presented to them and the Confederate cause itself. And without the logistical and ideological support of the home front, the southern military effort was doomed to fail.[55]

Historians have wondered in recent years why the Confederacy did not endure longer. In considerable measure, I would suggest, it was because so many women did not want it to. The way in which their interests in the war were publicly defined—in a very real sense denied—gave women little reason to sustain the commitment modern war required. It may well have been because of its women that the South lost the Civil War.

In Search of the Real Mary Chesnut

———————————

Mary Chesnut recorded one civil war. Now, nearly a hundred years after her death, she appears to be contributing to another. When Kenneth Lynn attacked C. Vann Woodward's new edition of Chesnut's journals as a "fraud" and a "hoax," scholars seemed temporarily to abandon a long-standing interest in the historical figure behind these remarkable wartime reflections. Instead, attention turned first to this unaccustomed display of public acrimony and then to a new critical scrutiny of the text in question. Now that William R. Taylor, William Styron, Steven M. Stowe, and others have vindicated Woodward's meticulous editing of *Mary Chesnut's Civil War*, it may at last be possible to look beyond the document that has caused such dispute to the woman and the society that created it. The publication of Elisabeth Muhlenfeld's *Mary Boykin Chesnut: A Biography* encourages such a focus, for it is the first full-scale treatment of Chesnut's life before and after the dramatic years portrayed in her journal. "And just as the journal illuminates her world for the twentieth-century reader," Muhlenfeld argues, "so her life—compelling and indomitable—informs and illuminates her work."[1]

Woodward and Muhlenfeld cooperated closely on their projects, and each expresses gratitude and admiration for the other. The senior scholar has written a laudatory preface to Muhlenfeld's biography and declares her aid to have been "indispensable" to his own efforts, while she in turn offers him effusive thanks in her preface. Despite these testimonies to collaboration, the two historians' interpretations of Chesnut are quite different. Muhlenfeld's predominant interest seems to be Chesnut's postwar writings, perhaps because these literary manuscripts make up such a large proportion of her surviving personal papers. Woodward's introduction and editorial notes for *Mary Chesnut's Civil War* show him

less taken with her art than with her politics. More narrowly concerned with the years between 1861 and 1865, he hails Chesnut as a
feminist and a near-abolitionist, a brilliant and clear-sighted individual
who saw beyond her time to the wisdom of our own.

Even in the bowdlerized earlier editions of A Diary from Dixie by Isa-
bella Martin and Myrna Lockett Avary (1905), who omitted half the
original manuscript, and by Ben Ames Williams (1949), who cut one
hundred thousand words from the journals and altered countless others, the charm of Mary Chesnut was irresistible. For mid-twentieth-
century readers who have lived through the civil rights and women's
movements, her impassioned complaints about slavery and the patriarchal structure of southern society have only intensified her appeal.
With Woodward's essentially complete version of the revised journal of
the 1880s and his careful explanation of the relationship of this manuscript to the notes and jottings of the Civil War period itself, we can at
last be confident that our view of the era is genuinely Chesnut's and
not one imposed by subsequent editorial intervention.

Yet the Mary Chesnut that Woodward's painstaking edition of the
journals reveals is not quite the same woman his introductory remarks
describe. Certainly the impression of her intelligence, wit, and insight
is only reinforced by this expanded version of her reminiscences. Clearly,
too, she is dissatisfied with much of her life in the South and with the
peculiar institution of her section. But to characterize her attitudes as
"abolitionist leanings" and "militant feminism" is to place her in opposition to fundamental usages and assumptions of a society she loved.
While men marched off to battle to save the South, Mary Chesnut
struggled in her own way to preserve the existing southern social order.

Chesnut's own sense of futility and frustration arose as much from
her inability to fill the traditional women's roles of mother and home-
maker as from her dissatisfaction with such delineations of male and
female spheres. Her childlessness weighed heavily upon her because
she accepted the prevailing view that "women need maternity to bring
out their best and true loveliness" (105). She chafed, too, at not having
her own household, and her most bitter complaints about her lot appeared during the times she was compelled to live, almost as a guest, in
her father-in-law's home, Mulberry, near Camden, South Carolina.

In spite of her protests against male domination—"There is no slave,
after all," she wrote, "like a wife" (59)—Mary Chesnut's emotional

Mary Chesnut. Courtesy South Caroliniana Library,
Columbia, South Carolina.

satisfaction derived largely from the attentions of men—the flirtatious interest of John Manning, the knowing satisfaction in her uncanny "power to make myself loved" (32). It was a male world with which Chesnut identified; men imparted status and meaning to social interaction and provided Chesnut with necessary affirmation of her self-worth. When she spoke, as she often did, of her "personal ambition," she referred without thinking to her husband's political advancement; his identity subsumed her own.

Chesnut's dissatisfactions with southern patriarchy were embryonic. They did not become the kind of articulate criticisms of existing relations between the sexes that would warrant the designation of "militant feminism," for part of Chesnut still accepted the notion that in crucial areas of life, men truly were superior. Mary Chesnut, who took such pride in her own intellect, meant to pay her friend Louisa McCord the highest imaginable compliment when she declared her to have "the brains and energy of a man" (304).

In fact, many of Chesnut's actions during the war were directed more toward maintaining the status quo than toward launching an attack upon it. She personally took little advantage of wartime upheaval to bring about change in her own position. When Louisa McCord accomplished so much for the soldiers' hospital in Columbia, Chesnut was overwhelmed by the level of "personal responsibility" her undertaking represented. Chesnut could not imagine herself in such a role, nor was she able until the very last months of the war even to serve as an effective hospital volunteer. The "failure, illnesses, and fainting fits" brought on by the sight of suffering kept Chesnut from aiding her friend's worthy project until at last in August 1864 shame overcame her, and she offered her services in the "feeding department." Yet she retained lingering uncertainties about hospital work, especially about the propriety of exposing her younger women friends to the suggestive remarks of lonely injured soldiers.

The entry of women into other new fields filled her with even greater alarm. She greeted with scorn those "Department women" forced by financial straits to work in government bureaus. Together with Mrs. John Smith Preston, she vowed that "come what will, survive or perish—we will not go into one of the departments. . . . We will live at home with our families and starve in a body. Any homework will do. Any menial service—under the shadow of our own rooftree. Department—never!" (350).

Instead, Mary Chesnut assumed two other roles. When isolated at

Mulberry, she retreated from what she viewed as intolerable reality into books, particularly the fantasy world of novels, or into illness and the opium she took to cure it. In Richmond and Columbia, by contrast, she delighted in society and in her position as hostess and *maitresse de salon:* "at my house it is *a party,* day and night" (549). Her husband repeatedly accused her of "too much levity," especially when the dire news of the last months of war made her festive gatherings all the more discordant. But James Chesnut did not understand the wider social purpose of what he viewed as women's gossip and extravagance. Anthropologists have frequently noted the function of gossip in underlining and maintaining existing norms and standards. In very much the same way as male dueling, gossip served for southern women as a means of enforcing conformity, of censuring irregular behavior by designating it scandalous. During this period of confusion and change, Mary Chesnut worked to uphold social and sexual mores, condemning lovers kissing on a train, disdaining women who were too forward, department girls who had learned "to misbehave," or widows who began courting too soon. Socialized in the belief that the ideal woman should possess a "soft, low and sweet voice" and "graceful, gracious ways," Mary Chesnut was incapable of direct challenge to southern patriarchy, for she shared too many of its values and assumptions.

Similarly, Chesnut's criticisms of slavery hardly amounted to abolitionism. Like Thomas Jefferson, she continued to benefit from the system while enjoying the luxury of abhorring it. She reacted with no little annoyance when disruptions at the end of the war left her without the usual assemblage of personal servants. Undertaking unaccustomed household tasks, Chesnut could only think "how dreadful it would be . . . *if I should have to do it all*" (733). As a woman, her choices in regard to slavery were certainly limited, for she herself owned no slave property to free. But even her attitudes seem to reveal more of uncertainty and ambivalence than of the kind of implacable opposition abolitionism implies. "Reading Mrs. Stowe," she wrote, "one feels utterly confounded at the atrocity of African slavery. . . . At home we see them, the idlest, laziest, fattest, most comfortably contented peasantry that ever cumbered the earth—and we forget there is any wrong in slavery at all. I daresay the truth lies between the two extremes" (428). Unlike Sarah and Angelina Grimke, fellow South Carolinians who became genuinely outspoken abolitionists, Mary Chesnut was devoted above

all to the South and her husband's advancement within it. Her enthusiastic support for the Confederacy served as but the clearest testimony
to her ultimate loyalties.

Yet because Mary Chesnut was neither militant feminist nor abolitionist, her journal is all the more valuable. She was a woman who
criticized, yet remained part of, her world, and her writing therefore
reveals both the strengths and weaknesses of her society. She was not so
alienated as to be an entirely unreliable observer, nor was she so enamored of the South and its peculiar institutions as to become simply a
regional apologist. In her ambivalence lies the power of her appeal.

The defeat of the South she loved destroyed Chesnut's familiar world.
Cling as she might to the past, Mary Chesnut was compelled by Confederate surrender to lead a new sort of life, an existence in which survival demanded that she become a different sort of person. The years
between the end of the war and Chesnut's death in 1886 occupy nearly
half of *Mary Boykin Chesnut: A Biography*. Unfortunately, Elisabeth
Muhlenfeld has been unable to locate extensive manuscript sources
detailing Chesnut's early life. Only a few childhood letters supplement
memoirs written when she was well into adulthood. After her marriage
to James in 1840, the record becomes somewhat richer, and Muhlenfeld
is able to trace the young wife's growing "despondency," her unhap-
piness with her "useless existence" at Mulberry, and her grief as she
gradually realized she would never bear a child. And Muhlenfeld shows
well the way in which Chesnut's "own sense of worth became increasingly identified" with her husband's success; despite her rhetorical discontent, in practice Chesnut largely accepted her wifely role.

While Muhlenfeld underlines every possible evidence of antislavery
sentiments in Chesnut's early life, the biographer is more cautious than
Woodward about the extent and import of Chesnut's opposition to the
peculiar institution. Far from leaning toward abolitionism, Chesnut, as
Muhlenfeld quotes her in an 1850 letter to her husband, declared her
hatred of these anti-slavery extremists because of their "*cant* & abuse of
us . . . & worse than all their using this vexed question as a political
engine & so retarding beyond all doubt the gradual freeing of our states"
(59). Yet Muhlenfeld describes as well how Chesnut's hopes for an even-
tual end to slavery were coupled with a love of the luxuries human
bondage made possible and with a racism that led her to regard blacks
as "dirty—slatternly—idle—ill smelling by nature" (109). At one point

Muhlenfeld suggests that Chesnut's "outspoken detestation of slavery" may have served as a serious handicap in Camden society. But the biographer provides no evidence of Chesnut publicly airing her views. Her oft-quoted statements deploring human bondage all come from private journals and from letters to her husband. No surviving data suggest that South Carolinians were generally aware of her sentiments. The documentation Muhlenfeld presents reveals Chesnut as a critic of slavery unable, indeed unwilling, overtly to challenge the system.

With the destruction of the peculiar institution and the wealth upon which southern patriarchy was based, Chesnut's flirtations and frivolities, her lively social whirl, became impossible. Careful attention to every penny was now a necessity, and Mary Chesnut's butter-and-egg business grew to be nearly as important to the family as James's devalued patrimony of land and emancipated slaves. Under these circumstances, Chesnut lost her sense of uselessness, for she was contributing to her own and her husband's survival. And she knew she possessed as well a store of notes and memories about a period of enormous historic importance; this consciousness liberated her ambition and gave her the courage to write. Despite the difficult conditions of life in postwar South Carolina, Chesnut seemed to manifest little of the "despondency" that had characterized her prewar outlook. In fictional and autobiographical works and in the revision of her Civil War journals undertaken in the 1880s, Mary Chesnut, as Muhlenfeld describes her, found a vocation at last.

Yet Chesnut succeeded in selling only one newspaper sketch for ten very needed dollars; her fiction, in Muhlenfeld's view, was promising but unrealized; her journals remained unpublished at her death. Mary Chesnut never knew her own worth. She continued to derive her fundamental identity from her husband and his achievements. When he became ill in 1884, she promptly abandoned her own literary endeavors to aid him in arranging his papers and autobiographical reflections, regarding them as far more important than her own scribblings. When she died at the age of sixty-three with the revisions of her journal unfinished, she could have had little notion of the importance it would one day assume as a window into her beloved South and the role of women within it. And how surprised she would be to think that the twentieth century would remember James Chesnut, senator, Confederate general, and statesman, primarily as Mary Chesnut's spouse.

Race, Gender, and Confederate Nationalism

William D. Washington's *Burial of Latané*

With remarkably few exceptions, American intellectual historians have ignored iconographical evidence. In the study of southern thought and belief, this tendency has perhaps been even more marked. Historians have routinely privileged the written word over pictorial or sculptural representation, and those examining the South have been reinforced in this proclivity by the assumption that the region has never been an important locus of achievement in the visual arts. Until recently, it has been difficult even to locate prints or photographs of southern works, which have been largely excluded from the teaching of both American art and American history. Yet whether or not individual examples of southern art are ultimately judged worthy of inclusion in the northern-dominated artistic canon, they still constitute significant cultural artifacts that offer important insights into the civilization that produced them.[1]

This task of connecting iconographic works with wider cultural realities, however, is far from simple. The relationship of most artistic creations to broader patterns of intellectual or social life can rarely be directly traced. And if one hopes to break out of the elite circles that almost always circumscribe both the producers and consumers of painting and sculpture in order to speculate about broader public relevance, the problem of evidence often proves daunting.

Sometimes, however, data survives to aid historians in reconstructing the relationship of particular works of art to past mentalities. Just such evidence, in the form of details concerning origins, reception, and response, makes *The Burial of Latané* a promising object for scholarly attention. Painted in 1864 by Virginian William D. Washington, the 36-by-46-inch canvas first hung in a small Richmond studio where it attracted such "throngs of visitors" that it was moved to the Confederate capitol. There a bucket was placed beneath it for contributions to the Confederate cause. After the South's defeat Washington arranged for engravings of the painting, which were widely distributed in a promotional effort undertaken by the *Southern Magazine*. These prints became a standard decorative item in late nineteenth- and early twentieth-century southern homes, and what historian Frank Vandiver called its "fantastic popularity" has led scholars to recognize the engraving as a central symbol of the Lost Cause.[2]

Yet William Washington's original painting was not designed as a commemoration of defeat and destruction. Like the money deposited beneath it in the Richmond capitol building, the work was instead intended to represent a contribution to southern victory. *The Burial of Latané* was created as an icon of Confederate nationalism. Through its many allusions to stylistic conventions as well as in its own narrative, the painting defines the terms of the southern effort in a manner intended as much to be prescriptive of public loyalties as it was descriptive of actual events of the war itself. The canvas, as contrasted with the later copies derived from it, was a product of the Confederate moment and offers significant insights into the particular meaning of the South's experience in the years between 1861 and 1865.

The Burial of Latané portrays the funeral of a young lieutenant, killed during the legendary ride by Jeb Stuart's cavalry around McClellan's army prior to the Seven Days Campaign in June 1862. William Latané, the only Confederate casualty of the expedition, was left among strangers, southern civilians surrounded by enemy forces and thus unable to summon either his family or a minister to perform the last rites. Slaves built his coffin and dug his grave, and a white Virginia matron read the burial service. The women attending the makeshift funeral were all of some prominence, and the story soon became known in nearby Richmond. In July a correspondent calling herself "Lucy Ashton" after a heroine of Sir Walter Scott wrote pseudonymously to John Thompson, a former editor of the *Southern Literary Messenger* and a poet already well known for his popular nationalist verse. Describing the circumstances of Latané's interment and claiming close friendship with the dead lieutenant, Lucy Ashton urged Thompson to offer "homage and

The Burial of Latané by William D. Washington. Courtesy Judge
John DeHardit, Gloucester, Virginia.

celebrity" to the slain soldier. Before the end of the year, Thompson
had complied, publishing in broadside a poem that drew directly on
Lucy Ashton's depiction of the scene. While she had described a
child scattering roses "not whiter" than Latané's "soul, or purer than
his heart," Thompson took poetic license to elevate these into "pale
roses not more stainless than his soul, / Nor yet more fragrant than his
life sincere." As Lucy Ashton had hoped, Latané's death had begun
in Thompson's hands to assume the language and status of romantic
legend.[3]

   As wartime residents of Richmond, Thompson and William Washington both participated regularly in the activities of a group called the
Mosaic Club, where Thompson frequently offered readings of his latest

poetic works. The artist may well have learned the details of the Latané incident at just such a gathering. In the summer of 1864, he assembled models for his painting from friends and acquaintances in the circles of well-connected Virginia families to which his Washington blood had given him access. The ladies involved perhaps regarded their effort as the equivalent of participation in the popular theatrical tableaux sponsored by women all over the South to commemorate stirring scenes of literature and history. In performing the Latané story in this manner, the models not only rendered the painting's creation a quasi-public event, but made their own contribution to transforming William Latané into heroic legend.

Washington himself probably reflected less upon parallels with ladies' wartime theatricals than on the place of his work within the stylistic traditions of Western painting. A student of Emanuel Leutze, he was thoroughly educated in the idioms of romantic art, and his canvas is a representative example of the genre of late eighteenth- and early nineteenth-century "grand style" history paintings. Drawing its inspiration from works like Benjamin West's *Death of General Wolfe* and Leutze's own *Washington Crossing the Delaware*, *The Burial of Latané* operates both as narrative and as social and political allegory. William Washington was creating for the new Confederate nation a patriotic symbol fashioned after those his artistic predecessors had earlier offered the people of Britain and the United States. Just as Wolfe in 1758 at Quebec and Washington in 1776 at Trenton had guaranteed national triumph, so too, the painter promised in his invocation of these images, Latané's sacrifice must ensure southern independence. Personal heroism appears as both the essence and the exemplification of national greatness.[4]

The portrayal of martyrdom in *Latané*, as in *Wolfe*, invokes Christian iconography to extend a religious dimension to the nationalist endeavor. The painting becomes a kind of visual counterpart to the transcendent language of the era's self-consciously nationalist rhetoric. In the terms of Confederate self-definition, the identification of the nation with God was especially intense, for southerners frequently cited their greater godliness as a central rationalization for secession and independence. The United States Constitution, they noted, was a "Godless instrument," whereas Confederates pointedly invoked divine aid in their fundamental law. Discussions in the Confederate Congress that led to the selection of "Deo Vindice" as the motto for the national seal revealed a religious as well as political consensus: southerners were God's chosen people. Nationalism was not just manipulating the language and power of religion; nationalism and religion had by 1864 already become inseparable.[5]

In the context of such all-pervasive rhetoric appearing in sermons, political orations, schoolbooks, newspaper editorials, and even popular song, the Christian symbolism of *The Burial of Latané* assumed a direct political relevance. The ethereal light from the heavens shines upon and selects the uplifted face of the woman who as preacher has become God's chosen instrument. Open prayer book in hand, she, like the scene more generally, represents the illuminating power of God's favor, which is allegorically promised here to the whole South. The drape of blood red that covers Latané's bier is echoed across the painting in the red kerchief of the woman slave and the gown of the sobbing white matron, as it appears in diluted manner in the pink dress of the little girl on the extreme right. The color encoded in Western artistic tradition as that of sacrifice thus extends from the hero across the diversity of his mourners, incorporating whites and blacks, women, and even children into a social as well as chromatic unity with him in ultimate devotion to the cause. The roses described by Lucy Ashton and memorialized by Thompson are transformed into the traditional martyr's garland, which here seems shaped strikingly like a crown—of thorns as well as flowers. The women, "strangers, yet sisters," in the words of Thompson's poem, have come, like Mary, to entomb the victim of the supreme sacrifice. The canvas thus represents not just the genre of history painting but alludes as well to the hallowed artistic theme of lamentations over the dead Christ, to such works as Giotto's fourteenth-century frescoes or Van Dyck's perhaps even better-known seventeenth-century rendition of the same subject. As surely as any of the innumerable wartime sermons stressing the South's divine mission, *The Burial of Latané* affirmed that God, like the dead lieutenant, was a Confederate, and that the slain hero had as Confederate become a surrogate for Christ.

Many of the southerners who thronged to see the painting on display in Richmond would in all probability not have known how to read the conventions and symbols of artistic tradition Washington utilized so pointedly. But even the most unsophisticated among the audience of viewers would have brought to it assumptions that would have structured and explicated what they saw. Familiarity with Thompson's poem, with its own references to the Virgin Mary and to heroic immortality and sacrifice, would have prepared many to receive a Christian message, just as effectively as would any explicit knowledge of Giotto or Van Dyck. For others, especially among the city's elite, recognizing the faces of well-known Richmond figures, of Pages and Dabneys, would have encouraged emotional identification with the scene, and no doubt many would also have known the Latané family, prominent residents of the nearby Virginia Tidewater. This was a highly personalized history and allegory, to which numbers of southerners, from "Lucy Ashton" to John Thompson to the painters' models, had already contributed. In very concrete ways, the canvas was not the creation of a single artist, but of a community.

By the time of the painting's completion in 1864, southerners of nearly every social rank would have been well acquainted with a public rhetoric defining the war's legitimating goals and purposes. Reflecting his understanding of the ideological context within which the work would be received, Washington did not dissolve the political specificity of his narrative into the generalizations of allegory. For all its encoded symbols, its invocation of painterly genres and traditions, *The Burial of Latané* addresses as well the particular realities of the southern experience. In a sharp departure from the conventions of Christian iconography and of history painting, the canvas uses its narrative power to make significant statements about both race and gender, issues of fundamental concern within southern wartime discourse. The story the painting tells thus embodies central themes specific to the ideology of Confederate nationalism.

As anthropologist Margaret Mead once noted, war is an invention. She might have gone on to say that it is, moreover, a narrative invention, for only a story of purpose and legitimation can transform random violence into what human convention has designated as war. War-born ideology thus inevitably tells a story describing the effort of the protagonists to achieve some legitimate goal in face of opposing—and illegitimate—enemy efforts. At the same time, this discourse prescribes the sorts of behavior necessary to achieve the desired resolution of the plot. Ideology strives quite literally to cast individuals into the roles its narrative has written for them.[6]

History painting before *The Burial of Latané* chiefly concerned itself with the behavior appropriate to male heroes—soldiers like those with Wolfe in Quebec or Washington on the Delaware. But the Civil War marked a departure in the nature of military conflict, the appearance of a new intensity in combat that involved whole populations in war's terrible work of death. The enormous and unanticipated size of Civil War armies, the introduction of conscription by both North and South, the unprecedentedly high death rates, and the mobilization of civilian resources to support this extraordinary military endeavor gave the home front a significance it had not possessed in previous wars. The nationalist ideology of the Confederacy was thus directed as much at securing essential civilian support for the war effort as at motivating soldiers to fight. William Washington's revision of the conventional history painting to portray women and black slaves was a significant ratification of these changed realities. Unlike Leutze's George Washington or even West's moribund General Wolfe, the only white male in *The Burial of Latané* is already quite dead.

A considerable proportion of nationalist discourse addressed the problem of home-front loyalty and support so critical to Confederate success. From the earliest days of the war, widespread fear of black uprising disturbed both the white women left at home among largely unsupervised populations of slaves and men off at the front who worried about the safety of their families. After Lincoln issued the Emancipation Proclamation in 1862, fears of black insurrection became even more pointed. Overtly revolutionary action by slaves against the system and its masters was in fact not widespread. But slaves were far from consistently loyal to the South. When Union troops approached, bondspeople fled to northern lines, and nearly one hundred thousand ex-slaves became soldiers in the Union army. Even those slaves who remained on their plantations resisted and challenged the system of human bondage in a variety of ways, from simple disobedience, to organized work slowdowns and stoppages, and even, in some cases, to direct violence against their masters. Yet slave owners needed to regard slavery as a benevolent institution, appreciated by blacks as well as whites, in order to justify their struggle for a nation state committed to human bondage. Nationalist ideology acknowledged the centrality of slavery to Confederate purposes and identified the conversion and "remedial advancement" of heathen Africans as God's special mission for His chosen southern nation.[7]

In face of the reality of slavery's disintegration all around them, Confederate nationalists articulated a story of black loyalty and contentment designed to assist whites in preserving both their peace of mind and their self-image as benevolent Christian masters. One of the most striking renditions of this tale was perhaps "Dixie," the emblematic Confederate song supposedly delivered by a black affirming his preference for the "land ob cotton." Confederate ideology cast slaves themselves as defenders of the peculiar institution. Equivalent narratives appeared in a variety of other forms, from sketches in the era's increasingly popular minstrel shows, to newspaper poetry, to the numberless "faithful servant" stories describing slaves hiding the family silver and defending the white womenfolk in order to save both from the Yankee invader.[8]

The Burial of Latané offered a visual rendering of this theme. Slaves leaning on their shovels here bury not the family silver, but a nation's spiritual treasure. And the Confederacy's mission of converting the African is advanced by this graphic enactment before slave onlookers of the drama of Christian sacrifice and redemption, with a white southern man in the inspirational role. Washington's work thus forcefully emphasizes this central aspect of southern national purpose. Whites and blacks together affirm their commitment to God and nation in a ritual of community worship.

Yet the painting depicts hierarchy as well as unity. It is, after all, the white man who has attained Christian martyrdom and the white women and children who are favored by God's light, while blacks remain in literal as well as spiritual shadow. Working together, the races are at the same time kept carefully apart, with the slaves segregated on the left side of the painting. Physically linking them is a blond child, a representation of southern innocence and purity, who evokes, in a kind of play on symbols, the many popular prewar illustrations of Harriet Beecher Stowe's Little Eva. Although in *Uncle Tom's Cabin* Eva dies to redeem the South from the sin of slavery, here she lives to affirm the moral legitimacy of the southern nation's peculiar institution. It is the northern army, not slavery, that bears responsibility for the death this painting illustrates.

In *The Burial of Latané* not only blacks but white women affirm the righteousness of the southern cause in a ritual at once religious and political, a ritual that by 1864 had become far too familiar to nearly all of them. For Confederate women, mourning emerged as a responsibility of considerable social and cultural as well as spiritual significance. When their men marched off to battle in 1861, white women were left uncertain about their roles in the new wartime situation. Many expressed frustration at the seeming lack of purpose in their lives, especially in comparison with the opportunities for heroic achievement now offered their male counterparts. Finding outlets for their pent-up energies in sewing flags and uniforms, raising money as Ladies Gunboat Societies, sponsoring dramatic performances and concerts to benefit soldiers, women struggled in the early months of conflict to overcome the feelings of uselessness that so many of their diaries and letters describe.[9]

Confederate ideology readily acknowledged the need to make an honored place for women in the war effort. On one level, women themselves became a purpose of the war, serving Confederate needs in a manner not wholly unlike that of the slaves; just war rhetoric urged soldiers to protect their wives and firesides from Yankee invaders in the same way that nationalist discourse insisted on the importance of saving both slaves and slavery from northern assaults. Since more white southern men in fact had wives than bondsmen, and since virtually all had female relatives of some sort, this appeal provided a powerful rationale for southern fighting men. But women longed for a less symbolic, more active means of assisting in the Confederate cause. Public discussion of women's roles in the wartime South sought to deal with this incipient female dissatisfaction both by specifying active contributions women might make to the southern cause and by valorizing their waiting and sacrifice as an achievement in its own right.

Ideological pronouncements could not change the objective realities of deprivation women faced as the southern economy began to disintegrate under the pressures of total war. But ideology could transform deprivation into sacrifice by imposing on it a meaning that gave it transcendence and purpose. The same narrative that remade violence into war offered women legitimation of their suffering. And one of the primary means through which this transubstantiation of suffering took place was mourning, for in the rituals of public grief an immediate personal loss could be redefined into a larger individual and communal gain. Without survivors, without mourners, a death is without impact; it is simply nothingness. Only those who remain behind define its meaning by constructing its relationship to the living. Christianity, of course, offers just such a construction in its promise that death is in fact eternal life for those who believe. Women's tears and grief consecrated the deaths of their men to assure them spiritual and political immortality, ratifying each casualty as a positive contribution not only to Confederate victory, but to a more sacred and abstract notion of Christian martyrdom with which the cause had become confounded. And in honoring soldiers' supreme offering, women at the same time reminded themselves of the comparative meagerness of their own sacrifices. Loss of life of a beloved could not compare with loss of one's own life; civilian anxiety and deprivation were as nothing in face of the toll of men's lives demanded by the war. The activity of mourning gave women a sense of purpose at the same time it encouraged their continuing submission to both the will of God and of the Confederate state.

The Burial of Latané embodies the larger Confederate discourse about gender by illustrating its exemplary ritual. Women here enact their roles in Christian sacrifice and celebration; the burial is at once a holy and a political communion. Even the clothes of the white ladies emphasize the conjoint religious and political significance of the narrative—two dressed in the black of Christian mourning, the others in the colors of the Confederate flag. And as strangers to the dead Latané, they generalize the particularity of the event to embrace a broader affirmation of Christian and national unity. Latané, like Christ, died for us all.

Like women in a variety of wartime situations—from nursing, to factory or office work, to agricultural management—the matron serving as preacher has in one sense been significantly empowered through her assumption of a position previously reserved to men. Yet her purposes are reassuringly traditional. John Thompson's poem pointedly described her voice as "soft and low," but Washington does not show her speaking at all. Instead, her eyes are cast heavenward; in the absence of terrestrial masters, she seeks her guidance from a divine father; the structures of patriarchy remain. The women in the painting, like the slaves, have chosen to use their autonomy, their new-found independence of direct white male control, to affirm rather than challenge the status quo. The matron-preacher is the instrument through which a male God and a male-authored Book of Common Prayer may speak; the voice she has gained as a result of wartime circumstance is not truly her own. Like

Confederate discourse that urged women to serve dutifully as nurses without questioning the authority of male doctors, or to fill classroom vacancies without expecting to match the intellectual capabilities of their male predecessors, *The Burial of Latané* casts necessary alterations in gender roles into the service of continuity.

But, as in its portrayal of slaves, *The Burial of Latané* represented by the time of its completion in 1864 less a model of than a model for women's behavior. Observers described Richmond in that last fall and winter of the war as a frantic round of parties and balls, of self-indulgence and excess that made mockery of the ideal of sacrifice. The city's most fashionable hostess was reputed to have spent more than thirty thousand dollars on food and entertainment while soldiers starved in the trenches nearby. Women, one diarist noted, danced on oblivious to the unremitting wail of ambulances outside their windows. Some of the very ladies Washington used as models were undoubtedly guests at these extravagant affairs.

Women of lesser social standing had by 1864 demonstrated even more striking dissent from the ideals of loyalty and sacrifice *The Burial of Latané* enshrined. Beginning in the spring of 1863, women across the South responded to mounting food shortages by taking to the streets in what came to be known as "bread riots." Women, like the hundreds of men daily fleeing Lee's army or the slaves escaping to Union lines, were deserting the Confederate cause.

The divergence between the realities of southern civilian life in 1864 and the ideal portrayed by William Washington is both dramatic and significant. In the years after Appomattox, adherents of the Lost Cause came to view the popular engravings of the Latané scene as a touching rendition of the virtues of loyalty and sacrifice the war had called forth. William Washington knew better. His painting was designed as nationalist rhetoric, as a persuasive rationale for continued struggle in face of the erosion of Confederate loyalty all around him. Instead of a paean, it was a plea. Curiously, however, it ultimately became a promise. The postwar engraving of Latané achieved its enormous popularity because it assured a defeated people that the South, like the dead lieutenant, could rise again.

The appropriation of *The Burial of Latané* as a vehicle for this conservative message has all but obscured its innovative impact—as both an artistic and political force. For all its efforts to cast women and blacks into traditional roles, the painting subverts its own agenda. By including blacks and women in history painting, William Washington in an important sense admits them into history; he acknowledges them as significant political actors. In representation lay both a source and a reflection of this emerging reality. But it would remain for women and blacks to struggle to redefine that participation in their own terms. Perhaps for some white women in the postwar South, the engraving of Latané prompted genuinely subversive memories of their Confederate years. At least one southern gentleman growing up in the 1890s believed that women had never recovered from their wartime taste of autonomy, "nor could they forget how pleasant life had been when all the men were gone." For some women, *The Burial of Latané* may have represented a lament for their own lost independence as much as for that of the Confederate nation.[10]

A War Story for Confederate Women

Augusta Jane Evans's *Macaria*

arfare, anthropologist Margaret Mead once noted, is an invention. Only human imagination can transform brute violence into the structures and conventions of war; only a story of purpose and legitimation can redefine killing into culturally sanctioned enterprise. In one of its essential aspects, war, therefore, is not just an invention, but, more particularly, a narrative construction. Telling war stories is a central component in the definition and in the waging of war itself. Inevitably, war-born ideology comprises a narrative describing the effort of combatants to achieve some just goal in face of illegitimate opposition. At the same time, these war stories prescribe the sorts of individual roles and actions necessary for the desired plot resolution. Discursive strategies both define and elicit wartime behavior.[1]

War stories have functioned as a central part of boys' play and of the definition of male gender roles from Hector and Achilles to Rambo. Indeed, as historian John Keegan has described, these images and the identities they define may take on a reality that is larger—or at least more compelling—than life, for men have often shown themselves ready to die in emulation of their fabled heroes. The romanticized "battle piece," the highly conventionalized and heroic account of combat, Keegan argues, has shaped—indeed warped—men's expectations and experiences of war.[2]

Although war has traditionally been seen, to borrow Margaret Mitchell's phrase from *Gone with the Wind*, as "men's business, not ladies'" women too have been told war stories designed to socialize them through accounts of their forebears' deeds. Describing and pre-scribing a variety of home front activities—from silent "Spartan" suf-fering, to ritualized mourning, to supportive sacrifice—such tales have for centuries instructed and inspired women to accept and even cham-pion the martial adventures of their men. As Julia Le Grand of Loui-siana explained in the midst of the American Civil War, "We are lead-ing the lives which women have led since Troy fell."[3]

Yet for all Le Grand's sense of continuity, her life and indeed the lives of all Confederate women differed significantly from those of women touched by earlier conflicts. And these changed realities would give war stories and women themselves a new and newly important role. Often designated the first "modern" or total war because of its involve-ment of entire populations, the Civil War required an unprecedented level of female participation. This was a conflict in which the home front was to have dramatically increased responsibility in generating mass armies and keeping them in the field. Particularly in the South, where human and material resources were stretched to the utmost, the conflict would demand the mobilization of white women, not for bat-tle, but for civilian support services that had heretofore been the al-most exclusive province of males, such as military nursing, munitions and government office work, teaching, slave management, and even agriculture.

But Confederate women, unlike their men, would not be conscripted by law. They had to be enlisted by persuasion. Out of this necessity grew an exemplary narrative, crafted by articulate southerners both male and female, about the Confederate woman's Civil War. Like tales enshrined in Western literature from Homer to Sir Walter Scott, this plot was designed to ensure woman's loyalty and sacrifice by casting her at once as heroic and as indispensable to the moral, political, and mili-tary triumph of her men and her country. Yet at the same time that it invoked legendary women from the past, the Trojans, the Spartans, even the women of the American Revolution, the Confederate wom-en's war story necessarily embraced new departures born of profoundly changed social and cultural realities. It had to confront the empower-ment of women that had arisen from the centrality of their home front responsibilities to the waging of modern warfare. And it was shaped as well by its emergence in an era when other sorts of women's stories had begun to appear in increasing numbers. In the mid-nineteenth century,

dozens of "scribbling women" were asserting by the very act of authorship woman's right to create her own narratives, to shape the choices
and define the meaning within her life.

Augusta Jane Evans's novel *Macaria*, published in Richmond in
1864, stands at the point of intersection of these two cultural imperatives: the needs of an embattled new nation and the agenda of the
literary woman. Author of the 1859 best-seller *Beulah*, Evans was among
the most successful of the prewar authors of woman's fiction. As an avid
Confederate and a wartime hospital volunteer, she at the same time
fully embraced the opportunities for both service and sacrifice the war
offered.[4]

By 1864, public and private discussion of gender had already engaged
Confederates for three years. In sermons, newspapers, poetry, song,
drama, and painting, not to mention countless diaries and letters, white
southerners had explored the implications of the war and of national
independence for gender definitions. Reflecting Evans's own wartime
experience as well as that of the southern nation more generally, *Macaria* might well be regarded as the most systematic elaboration, and in
many ways culmination, of the discussion that had preceded it. Much
of the earlier public consideration of women's wartime roles had appeared piecemeal—in brief editorial pronouncements, or in popular
songs like "Our Mothers Did So Before Us" or newspaper poems like
"I've Kissed Him and Let Him Go." But *Macaria* was a full-scale novel,
quite literally a narrative of women and the war. In its reproduction of
ideas and themes already familiar in Confederate discourse, in its almost formulaic renderings of experiences identical to those recounted
in innumerable actual southern women's diaries and correspondence,
Macaria became the quintessential war story for Confederate women.
Yet in its merger of the characteristic form of woman's fiction with that
of the male war story, *Macaria* transgressed the bounds of both genres.
Evans created a work filled with contradiction, a work that in the service of Confederate nationhood subverted the agenda of the domestic
novel that had given *Macaria* its overt form.[5]

The purpose of literature, Evans had stated quite explicitly in an
1859 series of articles in the *Mobile Daily Advertiser*, was to provide
moral instruction. *Macaria* would offer southern women the language
and the context in which to imagine their own wartime lives; they
would see themselves, as Evans clearly regarded herself, in the lives of

the novel's two Confederate heroines. And, just as Evans hoped, their consequently enhanced patriotism did in fact inspire at least some women to act on this new understanding of their centrality to the Confederate cause. No doubt Ella Gertrude Clanton Thomas of Augusta was not alone when she responded to her reading of *Macaria* by the very next evening becoming a hospital volunteer. In the tradition of the prewar domestic novels Jane Tompkins has described, the "cultural work" of *Macaria* would be to "reorganize" the Confederate war effort "from the woman's point of view."[6]

To effect this identification between her readers and her fiction, Evans drew directly on her own experiences in the initial years of war, even transcribing entire paragraphs from her personal correspondence into the mouths of the book's characters. An enthusiastic Confederate from the outset, the twenty-six-year-old novelist had rushed from her home in Mobile to the state capitol at Montgomery to celebrate Alabama's positive vote on secession. In the early months of conflict, she, like many Confederate women, eagerly sought ways of contributing to the war effort. She mobilized ladies to sew sandbags for community defense, delivered patriotic addresses to departing military companies, organized the establishment of a hospital in a vacant lot near her home, sponsored an Orphan Asylum for children bereaved by the war, and, over the objections of her brothers, began regular work as a hospital nurse.[7]

Yet, like the many other Confederate women who bemoaned their uselessness in diaries and letters, Evans continued to feel marginal to the war effort. In a letter to General P. G. T. Beauregard in mid-1862 she overtly complained about the minor role allotted to women. But quickly silencing her dissent, she consoled both herself and the illustrious general in language she would later give to the heroine of *Macaria*. "Woman's sphere of influence might," she mused, "be . . . 'one of which the centre is everywhere, the circumference nowhere.' . . . Though debarred from the 'tented field,' the cause of our beloved, struggling Confederacy may yet be advanced through the agency of its daughters." As part of her own search for a wartime role and in response to similar feelings of frustration shared by women around her, Evans created *Macaria*, the story of two southern women's journey toward ultimate self-realization in their Confederate wartime services. Evans intended the novel both as her own contribution to Confederate

Augusta Jane Evans. Courtesy Alabama Department of
Archives and History, Montgomery.

nationalism and as a narrative that would provide women with models for emulation in their search for "agency" within the Confederate cause. Evans composed the book on scraps of paper as she sat at the bedsides of wounded soldiers, and she dedicated it to the Confederate army. *Macaria* became a wartime best-seller, hailed as the most popular book in the Confederacy, with more than twenty thousand copies in circulation in the print-starved South before war's end.[8]

The title of the novel itself alludes both to Evans's design to make the work her own sacrificial offering and to the long tradition of women's war stories within which she intended to place her effort. In classical times, Macaria had saved Athens from invasion by giving herself as a sacrifice on the altar of the gods. Like the mythological figure of the title, the book's main character, Irene, is herself "ambitious of martyrdom" (116). But her progress toward that goal, the discovery of her "life-work" as a laborer in "God's great vineyard" (183), is achieved only in the face of enormous obstacles. She must resist the insistent courtship of Hugh, the cousin her father has chosen to be her husband, as well as her father's threats to disinherit her if she does not bow to his will. Yet far more difficult than rejecting a loveless marriage, she must because of an old family feud hide her devotion from her true love, Russell, until the very moment he marches off to battle and to death. Ultimately, she must sacrifice both Russell and her father to the Confederate cause.

Like many nineteenth-century women novelists, Evans employs paired heroines. Although somewhat less prominent and less arresting a character, Electra follows much the same life trajectory as her friend Irene. Imbued with imagination and artistic creativity to parallel Irene's rational and intellectual powers, Electra too resists a loveless match and ultimately consecrates herself to the Confederate effort, even carrying dispatches through the Union blockade in what Evans intended as a thrilling depiction of female heroism.

Irene's struggles parallel the essential conflict within the structure of the book more generally. Carolyn Heilbrun has recently distinguished between plot structures customarily found in men's and women's fiction, arguing that conventionally, men's stories are "quest" narratives, in which activity in the world takes precedence over adventures of the heart. In contrast, women's novels trace the path of the heroine toward romantic fulfillment, which in nineteenth-century fiction is translated into domestic wedded bliss. In *Macaria,* however, war gives Irene the unprecedented choice of whether to live her life as a "quest" plot or a "romance" plot, just as Evans herself confronts the possibility of an alternative narrative structure for her novel. The fundamental struggle within *Macaria* is between these two plot resolutions and definitions. Will Irene and Electra hold to their insistence never to marry? Will Evans resist the romantic formula that the contradictions of her earlier novel *Beulah* seemed to show her struggling futilely to defy? As Anne Goodwyn Jones has suggested, Evans had achieved the conventional domestic denouement of *Beulah* only by "wrenching her heroine out of character." Evans does no such disservice to Electra or Irene. When Russell begs at the moment of his departure for war that he at least be permitted to correspond with her, Irene rejects both romance and the romantic narrative out of hand. "I want neither your usefulness or mine impaired by continual weak repining" (145). In a striking departure from usual male fictional roles, Russell has found that his "ambition dims . . . in comparison with . . . your love" (143). But Evans will not permit him to lapse into acceptance of romantic goals. In an inversion of the conventional identification of males with worldly achievement and women with love, Evans has Irene insist that both she and Russell dedicate themselves to their particular quests.[9]

Throughout the novel, which opens nearly a decade before the outbreak of war, Irene and her alter ego Electra struggle for their independence. Motherless in the tradition of romantic heroines, both work to earn their financial as well as ultimate emotional autonomy. Even as a young child, Irene declines to permit a slave to carry her school books. "I don't choose," she declares, "to be petted like a baby or made a wax-doll of. . . . I am strong enough to carry my own books" (9). Electra too insists on her own strength, rejecting monetary support from her cousin Russell—"I must depend on myself" (34)—as well as a newly discovered inheritance—"I am young and strong, and I expect to earn my living" (49). Both women speak of themselves in the language of bourgeois individualism, stressing their rights of self-ownership and self-determination. To her cousin Hugh, who insists, "You belong to me and you know it," Irene responds, "No! I belong to God and myself" (13). In face of her father's explicit order that she marry, Irene weighs duty to him against duty to herself and her Maker. "I am responsible for no acts but my own. . . . I am a free-born American. . . . I, only, can give myself away" (90). Having declared her independence, Irene is overcome by a "thrill of joy; she had burst the fetters; she was free" (91). But at the same time she celebrates personal independence, Evans denounces the "selfishness" (40) that arises from entirely unchecked individualism, and her reservations constitute a sharp critique of the philosophy of bourgeois individualism as it was evolving in mid-nineteenth-century America. Evans's own notion of self-fulfillment remains closely tied to the organic connectedness so often seen as its opposite. Self-realization, Evans acknowledges, necessarily involves being true to oneself, just as Irene successfully "grew up what nature intended her to be" (21). Yet the self-fulfillment that is true freedom cannot be achieved independent of a social community to which one is connected by ties of duty and belonging. Irene deplores the "parasitic clinging" (81) of dependence but recognizes as well the lessons of her friend and mentor, the minister Harvey Young, who counsels that "people are too isolated, too much wrapped up in their individual rights, interests or enjoyments. I, Me, Mine, is the God of the age. . . . We ought to live more for others than we do" (40).[10]

Irene's declaration of independence thus only begins her struggle for self-realization. Despite her private scholarly pursuits, despite the abstruse astronomical researches she undertakes while her father and household sleep, she feels purposeless, and finds the fashionable life of southern society empty of meaning. "Everybody ought to be of some use in this world, but I feel like a bunch of mistletoe, growing on somebody else, and doing nothing." All who truly seek happiness, she recognizes, "should be employed in some way" (25). Electra voices almost identical sentiments, indicating her commitment to following a quest plot in her own life. "I want to accomplish some work," she declares, "looking upon which my fellow creatures will proclaim; 'That woman has not lived in vain; the world is better and happier because she came and labored in it.'" Electra is unreservedly ambitious, desiring her name carved upon "the living, throbbing heart of my age" (95).

In the context of Irene's persistent cry, "I want to be useful" (141), a cry that echoes sentiments expressed in nearly every surviving Confederate woman's diary, the war comes as a fortuitous solution. In Confederate independence, Irene and Electra find both true personal independence and fulfillment; through war, they discover the path to the ultimate spiritual peace represented by Irene's given name. Women, Evans suggests, thus need not simply endure the war but might justly celebrate its unprecedented opportunities for self-realization. In an allegorical canvas she entitles a "Modern Macaria," Electra depicts two symbolic female figures, Independence and Peace, one "athrob with national pride," the other "serene and holy," the two together representing not only Electra and Irene, but the two poles of Evans's conception of personal as well as southern national fulfillment (182). Through Confederate nationalism, these women thus may truly find themselves.

In 1864, with nearly half the white male population of the South wounded or killed, the single life was for many inevitable. Evans felt she could dare to make it seem desirable. Necessity became not so much the mother, as the legitimator of fictional invention. *Macaria*, the word itself meaning "blessed" in Greek, ends with a celebration of single blessedness. A woman who "dares to live alone," Irene confirms, is certainly "braver and nobler, and better" than one who consents to a "loveless marriage" (182–83). More important, however, is the unmarried woman's potential for vocation, for service, for achievement. Even though a married woman may be superficially happier, Evans concedes, the single woman is unquestionably more useful "because she belongs exclusively to no one, her heart expands to all her suffering fellow creatures" (182). Like Evans herself, Irene recognizes that "upon the purity, the devotion, and the patriotism of the women of our land, not less than upon the heroism of our armies, depends our national salvation" (183). And like Evans herself, Irene devotes her time to nursing wounded and establishing an orphan asylum. Electra, whose Greek name means "unwedded," has similarly embraced spinsterhood and dedicates her life to creating artistic forms for southern national greatness. With Irene's financial backing, she will direct a School of Design for aspiring women artists cast upon their own resources by the exigencies of war. Strikingly, Evans presents a version of the late twentieth-century notion of comparable worth to argue for an enlargement of woman's role. The "remuneration of the peculiar employments of women," she notes, "is always far below that of employments of equal skill carried on by men. . . . Hence in improving the condition of women, it is advisable to give them the readiest access to independent industrial pursuits, and extend the circle of their appropriate occupations." She concludes her novel with a poetic call for women to assume their newly elevated station:

Rise, woman, rise!
To thy peculiar and best altitudes. . . .
The sanctified devotion and full work
To which thou art elect for evermore.
                                         (183)

Evans has in *Macaria* significantly undermined the restrictiveness and
transformed the meaning of female sphere by excusing women from
exclusive domesticity and providing them a critical role in the public
life of the new nation.[11]

Nevertheless, Electra has no illusions but that women's hands remain significantly "tied; and they walk but a short narrow path, from
hearthstone to threshold, and back again" (163). Evans's call to women
in fact invokes the notion of "peculiar" female "altitudes" to which a
woman is "elect for evermore," of a limited set of "appropriate occupations." *Macaria* makes no direct attack upon these persisting constraints.
Instead, the novel reaffirms prevailing notions of women's proper sphere
and explicitly decries "Brook Farm" socialism, northern feminism, and
woman's suffrage. "Southern women," Irene assures the novel's readers, "have no desire to usurp legislative reins; their appropriate work
consists in moulding the manners and morals of the nation" (163). Men
are "at home with state papers, machine shops, navies, armies, political
economy, and agricultural chemistry," while women "have a knack"
for "embroidery on the coarse grey serge of stern, practical everyday
life" (82).

Despite her use of the language of liberal individualism, Evans remains committed, in her novel as in her private correspondence, to a
hierarchical view of the social order in which race, class, and gender all
play a part in assigning individuals their designated social roles. She
sees no apparent contradiction between Irene's proud claims to ownership of her person and the bondage of the slaves who serve as background characters throughout the book. Imperatives of duty, as Russell
explains, mean "we are all in bondage more or less" (99). And at the
same time Irene professes to "despise . . . ridiculous nonsense about
aristocracy of family" (9), she, like Evans herself, firmly opposes the
"demagoguery" of universal suffrage. Irene's individualism, the principles of personal independence she and Electra insist upon throughout
the book, rest uneasily with the assumptions of hierarchy *Macaria* si-

multaneously espouses. Evans's war-born subversion of the domestic
novel, her adoption of a male quest plot for female fiction exacerbates
the contradictions already inherent in her views about woman's role as
well as in the structures of the woman's novel. Ironically, these contradictions were rendered all the more forceful by Evans's southernness.
Her social location within the plantation patriarchy and her highly
positive fictional portrayal of the slaveocracy rendered her adoption of
bourgeois liberal language all the more discordant. At the same time,
the special demands of war upon women within the invaded South
were posing the most dramatic challenge to conventional gender roles
in the very region where traditional notions of women's proper place
had been most assiduously defended.

Macaria does not leave these contradictions unattended; Evans
struggles to contain her subversion within acceptable boundaries by
turning to religion for resolution of the paradoxes she and her heroines
confront. Evans redefines the work that is at the center of both Irene
and Electra's self-fulfillment as but a special form of divine worship.
"Laborare est orare," she insists. For the painter Electra, "Aesthetics is
a heavenly ladder, where pure thoughts and holy aspirations come from
and go to God" (159). And Irene's astronomical observations serve
above all to remind her of the "immeasurable heights and depths, the
infinitude, the grandeur, and the glory of the universe—and there, as
nowhere else, I can bow myself down, and say, humbly and truly, 'Not
my will, oh God! but thine!'" (167) The self-assertion implicit in the
pursuit of artistic or intellectual goals is thus subsumed within the
larger context of religious submission.

Although the theme of martyrdom central to the title and the book
is on the one hand undermined by the recurrent language of individual
realization, the invocation of Christ as a deus-ex-machina ultimately
valorizes the concept of sacrifice and resolves the contradictions of the
plot. Irene, Electra, even Russell on his deathbed are all converted to
evangelical religion, finding in doing God's will at once the perfect
fulfillment and abnegation of their own. In divine thrall, each character discovers perfect freedom while Evans identifies a means of having it both ways. Once, Electra explains, artistic "fame was all that I
cared to attain" (183). Now, she continues, she hopes to spend her years
as a painter in pursuit of spiritual as well as earthly immortality. Her
worldly achievements are no longer directed toward crass ambition, but

divine service. Her quest, like Irene's, has become a pilgrimage. "Thus," Evans writes, "by different, by devious thorny paths, two sorrowing women emerged upon the broad highway of Duty, and, clasping hands, pressed forward to the divinely-appointed goal—Womanly Usefulness" (168). God has in a very real sense taken the place of a man in these women's lives; single they might be, but their independence, asserted throughout most of the book, is by the conclusion once again safely contained. Evans in the final analysis subverts her own subversion.

But her initial apostasy did not pass unnoticed. For all its popularity, *Macaria* received some highly critical notices from reviewers objecting to Evans's abandonment of the domestic plot. A lengthy essay in the Richmond *Age* complained, for example, that the novelist had "done no inconsiderable violence to our just expectations." In fact, the reviewer asserted, *Macaria* was only a "quasi-novel—a new experiment in the art of book-making called forth by the times through which we, the citizens of the Southern Confederacy, are now passing," for "although love forms the great staple of the work, yet it is introduced with the special design of making it subservient to what are regarded as the higher dictates of patriotism." The reviewer objected to Irene puzzling over the heavens when she should have been entertaining her father's guests, domiciling herself in a hospital filled with men, abandoning her opportunities for motherhood, and, worst of all, adopting the "mistaken idea" that the single state is anything but one of "isolation and discomfort." Miss Evans may be "skilful in sketching character," the reviewer concluded, "but not in casting a plot." Irene's life choices seemed all too "improbable."[12]

A lady of Oxford, Mississippi, calling herself FIDELIA composed an essay on Macaria for her local literary society that the *Mobile Evening News* published as a review. No Southern maiden, FIDELIA insisted, would have rejected "the dark and glorious Russell." The reviewer professed to love "the peerless Irene," but, she continued revealingly, "much as some . . . loved Fanny Kemble; we want but one Fanny Kemble." If many heroines like Irene should appear, "the world will need the new classification of men, women and Irenes." FIDELIA explicitly associated Irene with the outspoken critic of the South, the English actress Fanny Kemble, who in her divorce from Georgian Pierce Butler had become a notorious symbol of the dangers of women's independence.[13]

Augusta Jane Evans regarded herself as anything but a feminist. Yet readers charged the author of *Macaria* with so violating gender conventions as to have created an androgynous heroine, to have denaturalized and denatured their southern social world by introducing a new and anomalous gender category. Scholars of nineteenth-century women's novels have vigorously debated how radical domestic fiction really was or was intended by its authors to be. *Macaria* demonstrates one such writer self-consciously taking advantage of war-born opportunity to extend the limits of the possible, of the imaginable—in her fiction as in her own life. But the response of at least some of her reviewers suggests that Evans may have tried to extend those boundaries too far. *Macaria* clearly appeared as a "new experiment," but one that seriously violated many "just expectations."

Wars have always had a special relationship to constructions of gender, refining and redefining accepted male and female roles. Evans's actions as an author, her movement to transform in significant ways the assumptions on which her fiction was based, might be seen as a literary act directly parallel to the social actions of middle-class women who like herself as hospital nurse moved into a variety of previously male roles. In her depiction of Irene, she was creating not just a new gender, as FIDELIA charged, but a new genre as well. Yet Evans demonstrates for us both the persistence of social conservatism about gender and the limited radicalism of many of these women pioneers themselves. Even in *Macaria*, Evans ultimately offered a sharply conflicted message, stepping back from a celebration of genuine female autonomy.

In her own postwar life and writing, Evans might be said to have made the same retreat. Her immediate and highly ambitious project after Appomattox was to write another war story. But this time Evans planned not to restrict herself to woman's sphere. Instead, she intended to claim the whole of Confederate experience as her own literary domain. Evans hoped to compose the definitive history of the South in the Civil War, to herself define the terms in which the Confederacy would live into posterity.

She would never realize her goal, and in 1867 she wrote her old friend Beauregard explaining why. Her extraordinary letter exemplifies the fate of female ambition in the South—its transformation into coexisting docility and assertiveness, compliance and repressed rage. Evans had abandoned her intention to write a Confederate history in deference to former Vice-President Alexander Stephens, who planned one of his own. "I humbly put my fingers on the throat of my ambitious daring design of becoming the Confederate Xenophon and strangled it. . . . I confess it cost me a severe struggle to relinquish the fond dream . . . but abler hands snatched it from my weak womanly fingers and waved me to humbler paths of labor."[14]

Evans's ambition is crushed—"strangled" only indirectly by male prerogative; the actual murder takes place at her own hand. Evans immolated herself on the very altars of sacrifice at which she herself had worshiped; she became the final victim of her own paradoxes. In 1867 she published *St. Elmo*, a warmly reviewed and enormously popular domestic novel with a heroine whose life and story culminate in conventional wedded bliss. In 1868 Evans herself, at age thirty-three, married a man twenty-seven years her senior. The war, *Macaria*, and single blessedness were over.

"Trying to Do a Man's Business"

Gender, Violence, and Slave Management in Civil War Texas

Between 1861 and 1865, three-fourths of white southern men of military age entered the army of the Confederacy, removing from communities across the American South those very individuals whose unceasing exercise of power and vigilance had maintained order in the region's slave society. With their departure, the social relations of the Old South were necessarily and abruptly transformed. The threat—and often the reality—of physical force, together with the almost equally coercive manipulations of planter paternalism, had served as fundamental instruments of oppression and thus of race control. The white South had justified its "peculiar institution" as a beneficent system of reciprocal obligations between master and slave and had defined slave labor as a legitimate return for masters' protection and support. But in the very notion of mutual duties, the ideology of paternalism conceded the essential humanity of the bondspeople, who turned paternalism to their own uses, manipulating it as an empowering doctrine of rights.

Desiring to see themselves as decent Christian men, most southern slaveholders of the antebellum years preferred the negotiated power of reciprocity to the almost unchecked exercise of force that was in fact permitted them by law. In the paternalistic ideal, whipping was regarded as a last, not a first resort, as a breakdown in a control that was most properly exerted over minds, rather than bodies. Yet violence was implicit in the system, and both planters' records and slaves' reminiscences demonstrate how often it was explicit as well. The ideal of racial

174

reciprocity, of hegemonic paternalistic domination was just that: an ideal articulated more often in proslavery tracts, plantation manuals, or agricultural journals than in the day-to-day experience of plantation life. Violence was in fact never far from the minds of either blacks or whites, for overseers carried whips, slaves bore scars of past punishment, and almost everyone had personally witnessed masters' physical coercion of slaves.[1]

In the antebellum years, white men had assumed the overwhelming responsibility for slavery's daily management and perpetuation. Just as paternalism was founded in a belief in the dominance of men within the family and household, so violence was similarly gendered as male within the ideology of the Old South. When the Civil War removed thousands of white men from households across the region, it became unclear how the slave system would be maintained. Called to fight for slavery on the battlefield, Confederate masters could not simultaneously defend it on the home front.

In many ways, the daily struggle over coercion and control taking place on hundreds of farms and plantations was just as crucial as any military contest to defense of the southern way of life. Slavery was, as Confederate Vice-President Alexander Stephens explained, the "cornerstone" of the region's social, economic, and political order. Yet slavery's survival depended less on sweeping dictates of public policy than on tens of thousands of individual acts of personal domination exercised by particular masters over particular slaves. The nineteenth-century southerner's designation of slavery as the "domestic institution" thus becomes in retrospect curious and even ironic, for such a term might be seen to imply a contrast with the public or the political. But the very domesticity of slavery in the Old South, its imbeddedness in the social relations of the plantation or yeoman household, made those households central to the most public, most political aspects of regional life. The direct exercise of control over slaves was the most fundamental and essential political act in the Old South. With the departure of white men, this transcendent public responsibility fell to Confederate women.[2]

Although white southerners—both male and female—might insist that politics was not, even in the changed circumstances of wartime, an appropriate part of woman's sphere, the female slave manager necessarily served as a foundation of the South's political order. White women's actions as slave mistresses were critical to Confederate destinies, for the viability of the southern agricultural economy, the stability of the social order, as well as the continuing loyalty of the civilian population all depended upon successful slave control. On a microcosmic level, the daily interactions of particular women slaveholders with specific slaves yield a striking vision of the master-slave relationship in a new wartime guise, of war-born redefinitions of social power and social roles, and of a society in turmoil.

This essay will examine the experience of one woman in order to explore how the dynamics of war, slavery, gender, and mastery played themselves out within a single richly documented context. Lizzie Scott Neblett lived in Texas, far from any direct threat of Union troops. Hers was a situation in which the forces and the internal logic of southern society operated in comparative freedom from the most direct intrusions of war. As a recent historian of Texas slavery has written, "The Peculiar Institution remained less disturbed in Texas than in any other Confederate state." Yet even without a Union military presence, the absence of white men would itself change the system profoundly and transform the white women and black slaves who, like Lizzie Neblett and her human property, became caught up in slavery's wartime disintegration.[3]

Slave management was not an opportunity white southern women eagerly sought. As one Georgia plantation mistress put it, a woman was simply not a "fit and proper person" to govern slaves. But like men conscripted into battle, Confederate women of the slave-owning classes often found they had little choice. When Will Neblett enlisted in the Twentieth Texas Infantry in March of 1863, his wife, Lizzie, explained that her impending service as agricultural and slave manager was "a coercive one." But, she vowed, she would be "faithful and conscientious in its discharge."[4]

Already thirty-seven years old, Will Neblett was in poor health— "Rheumatism, Neuralgia and Bronchial Affections, as well as General physical delicacy of organization," his service record described it. Designated as "unable to perform active field service," Neblett was assigned to the Quartermaster Corps and spent most of the two years remaining in the war stationed in Galveston on the Texas coast. Because the likelihood of losing her husband to Yankee fire was considerably less than that confronting many Confederate wives, the concerns

Lizzie Neblett. Courtesy Eugene C. Barker Texas History Center,
Center for American History, University of Texas, Austin.

Lizzie expressed about the difficulties of her own situation may have been proportionately increased. At age thirty she found herself in circumstances very unlike those she had envisioned as an idealistic girl, publishing romantic outpourings in local Texas publications, dreaming of literary reputation, and maintaining an intense and intellectual correspondence with a circle of former schoolmates. Marriage and motherhood had compelled a change in her aspirations. Ambition, she explained to her diary soon after her wedding in 1852, now must focus on her husband. "I am ambitious for *him*. . . . I can never gain worldly honors. Fame can never be mine." Even her hopes of teaching proved impossible, as Lizzie became caught up in a cycle of pregnancies, childhood diseases, and family demands. When Will left home in the spring of 1863, Lizzie was awaiting her unwelcome fifth confinement. She was already mother of a ten-year-old daughter and three sons, ages eight, six, and four. The much resented baby Bettie would arrive in May.[5]

Born in Mississippi, Will and Lizzie were both children of slave-owning families who had migrated to the rich cotton lands of Grimes County, some fifty miles northwest of Houston, during the late 1830s. Will's father was a physician, and Lizzie's had been a circuit judge, as well as the master of more than seventy-five slaves, a holding large enough to place him in the top 1 percent of Texas slaveholders. When the war broke out, Will had been practicing law for well over a decade and had just resigned after a year of service as editor of the *Navarro Express*, a staunchly secessionist Democratic paper. In addition, the Nebletts owned eleven slaves, who in 1860 had cultivated the ninety-two improved acres of a nearly 6,000-acre farm to produce 15¼ bales of ginned cotton and 500 bushels of corn. With this force, which they had received from Judge Scott, Will and Lizzie ranked among the top quarter of Texas slaveholders in 1860 but well below the upper 3 percent of the population who possessed more than twenty slaves and thus qualified as plantation owners. Nevertheless, with real estate valued at $12,500 and personal property worth $14,500 in 1860, the Nebletts stood well above the state mean, even among the 27 percent of Texas families who held slaves and averaged $7,000 in real and $12,500 in personal property. Lizzie clearly had little right to her complaint that the neighbors were unjust in accusing her of being rich.[6]

Lizzie set about the task before her in the spring of 1863 committed to "doing my best" but apprehensive both about her ignorance of agriculture and the behavior she might anticipate from the slaves. Their initial response to her direction, however, seemed promising. "The negros," she wrote Will in late April, "seem to be mightily stirred up now, about making a good crop." Before his departure, Will had arranged to swap slave work with a neighbor in exchange for his assumption of a general supervisory eye over Lizzie and her slaves. Mr. Rivers seemed to Lizzie, however, to be taking advantage of the situation from the outset, using her slaves chiefly to his own profit. And, in her advanced state of pregnancy, dealing with outsiders was more trying than dealing with her own laborers. "I look so unsightly & feel that I do so sensibly that a man is a horror to me." Above all else, however, Lizzie was disgusted by Rivers's lack of shame in acknowledging his own slave children, and she was convinced that if the war did not end she must make different management arrangements after the current crop year.[7]

Anxious about her confinement and then overwhelmed by a difficult and demanding infant, "cursed like her mother with the female sex," Lizzie wrote little of her agricultural dilemmas until the harvest season had nearly arrived. And by this time her initial optimism about the blacks' behavior had disappeared. A matching of Lizzie's scattered letter and diary references with the 1860 census count makes possible a rough re-creation of the Neblett slaves and their family ties. But because Lizzie often borrowed slaves from other members of her family, it is difficult to achieve an exact congruence between those individuals regularly mentioned as part of her household and those officially listed as belonging to the Nebletts in the public record. Although the 1860 census enumerator noted that the eleven Neblett slaves occupied two houses, they did not comprise two distinct family groups. Thornton and Nance, who had married in the mid-1850s, were in their late twenties or early thirties and parents of Lee, born in 1857, Henry, born in 1860, and Harrison, an infant when Will departed in 1863. Sarah, who worked chiefly in the house, was in her midforties, and Lizzie's records make no mention of her family ties. Sam, the oldest male on the place, was of a similar age, and, like many slaves on such small holdings, had a wife belonging to another owner. Joe, probably in his thirties, also had an "abroad" wife and children, and Will's inability to meet Joe's request that he purchase them was in all likelihood the source of Joe's "propensity for running about at night and on Sundays." Tom, Randall, Bill, and Kate were all in their midteens, as was Polly, a house servant on loan from Lizzie's brother in the army. Anticipating the impressment of Randall for hospital detail in Brenham, about fifty miles away, Lizzie reckoned she would have five laborers to cultivate and harvest the corn and cotton crops.[8]

But persuading them to actually work was another matter. "The negros are doing nothing," Lizzie wrote Will at the height of first picking in mid-August. "But ours are not doing that job alone nearly all the negros around here are at it, some of them are getting so high in anticipation of their glorious freedom by the Yankees I suppose, that they resist a whipping." Many slave owners, she noted, had become "actually affraid to whip the negros." Lizzie harbored few doubts about the long-term loyalty of her own black family. "I don't think we have one who will stay with us."[9]

Under these difficult conditions, Lizzie reported a cotton crop of eight bales, an achievement well below the 1860 average of 2.5 bales per slave for Texas farms of her size and only a bit more than half of what the Nebletts themselves had realized three years before. In the same letter in which she informed Will of these troubling realities, Lizzie announced her new arrangements for slave and crop management. She had, as she described it, "insisted" that another neighbor come to her aid. For $400 of Confederate money—the equivalent, she estimated, of $80 of "good money"—Mr. Meyers would spend a half day with her slaves three times a week. "He will be right tight on the negroes I think, but they need it, they never feared Rivers one single bit." And, she implied, they did not fear her either. "Meyers," she continued, "will lay down the law and enforce it." But Lizzie emphasized that she would not permit cruelty or abuse. She was sure he would not "have to whip but one or two before the others will take the hint."[10]

But controlling Meyers would prove in some ways more difficult than controlling the slaves. His second day on the plantation Meyers whipped all three teenage boys for idleness, and on his next visit, as Lizzie put it, "he undertook old Sam." Gossip had spread among slaves in the neighborhood—and from them to their masters—that Sam intended to take a whipping from no man. Will Neblett had, in fact, not been a harsh disciplinarian, tending more to threatening and grumbling than whipping. Lizzie anticipated, however, that Sam might well prove a problem for Meyers, and her ten-year-old daughter, Mary, passed this concern along to Sam himself. Sam assured Mary and her eight-year-old brother,

Will and Lizzie Neblett. Courtesy Eugene C. Barker Texas History Center, Center for American History, University of Texas, Austin.

Bob, that he would run away rather than submit to Meyers's lash: "He shant whip me." For Meyers, this very challenge was quite "enough." On his next visit to the farm, Meyers called Sam down from atop a wagon of fence stakes. Sam refused to come, saying he had done nothing to deserve a whipping. When Sam began edging away from Meyers, the white man ordered him to stop, then began shooting at him. Sam ran but was soon cornered. At first he threatened to kill anyone who laid a hand on him, but when Meyers countered by waving his gun, Sam surrendered. Enraged, Meyers beat Sam so severely that Lizzie feared he might die. She anxiously called the doctor, who assured her Sam had no internal injuries and that he had seen many slaves beaten far worse.[11]

Lizzie was torn about how to respond—to Meyers or to Sam. "Tho I pity the poor wretch," she confided to Will, "I don't want him to know it." To the other slaves she insisted, "Meyers would not have whipped him if he had not deserved it," and to Will she defensively maintained, "Somebody must take them in hand they grow worse all the time I could not begin to write you . . . how little they mind me." She saw Meyers's actions as part of a plan to establish control at the outset: "He lets them know what he is, when he first starts, & then has no more trouble." But Lizzie's very insistence and defensiveness suggest that this was not, even in her mind, slave management in its ideal form, and the criticisms from her rejected neighbor Rivers—"a damed shame the way Sam was whipped"—stung all the worse when she was told of them indirectly by her own slaves, eager to report this fissure in white solidarity.[12]

Over the next few days, Lizzie's doubts about Meyers and his course of action grew. Instead of eliminating trouble at the outset, as he had intended, the incident seemed to have created an uproar. Sarah, a cook and house slave, reported to Lizzie that Sam suspected the whipping had been his mistress's idea, and that when well enough, he would run away till Will came home. Perhaps this meant, Lizzie worried, that Sam was planning some act of vengeance against her.[13]

To resolve the volatile situation and to salvage her reputation as slave mistress, Lizzie now enlisted another man, Coleman, to talk reasonably with Sam. Coleman had been her father's overseer and continued to manage her mother's property. In the absence of Will and of Lizzie's brothers, he was an obvious family deputy, and he had undoubtedly known Sam since the slave's days as the property of Judge Scott. Coleman readily agreed to "try to show Sam the error he had been guilty of." At last Sam spoke the words Coleman sought, admitting he had done wrong, promising "he would let Meyers whip him, one more time," as long as it was not so severe. But Coleman suggested an even more desirable survival strategy, promising him that "if only he would be humble & submissive . . . Meyers would never whip him so again."[14]

Two weeks after the incident, Lizzie and Sam finally had a direct and, in Lizzie's view at least, comforting exchange. Meyers had ordered Sam back to work, but Lizzie interceded in response to Sam's complaints of persisting weakness. Taking his cue from Lizzie's conciliatory gesture and acting as well in accordance with Coleman's advice, Sam apologized for disappointing Lizzie's expectations, acknowledging that as the oldest slave he had special responsibilities in Will's absence. Henceforth, he promised Lizzie, he was "going to do his work faithfully & be of as much service to me as he could. I could not help," Lizzie confessed to Will, "feeling sorry for the old fellow. . . . He talked so humbly & seemed so hurt that I should have had him whipped so."[15]

Sam's adroit transformation from rebel into Sambo helped resolve Lizzie's uncertainties about the appropriate course of slave management. Abandoning her defense of Meyers's severity, even interceding on Sam's behalf against her own manager, Lizzie assured Sam she had not been responsible for his punishment, had indeed been "astonished" by it. Meyers, she reported to Will with newfound assurance, "did wrong" and "knows nothing" about the management of slaves. He "don't," she noted revealingly, "treat them as moral beings but manages by brute force." Henceforth, Lizzie concluded, she would not feel impelled by her sense of helplessness to countenance extreme severity. Instead, she promised Sam, if he remained "humble and submissive," she would ensure "he would not get another lick."[16]

The incident of Sam's whipping served as the occasion for an extended negotiation between Lizzie and her slaves about the terms of her power. In calling upon Meyers and Coleman, she demonstrated that despite appearances, she was not in fact a woman alone, dependent entirely on her own resources. Although the ultimate responsibility might be hers, slave management was a community concern. Pushed toward sanctioning Meyers's cruelty by a fear of her own impotence, Lizzie then stepped back from the extreme position in which Meyers had placed her. But at the same time that she dissociated herself from Meyers's action, she also reaped its benefit: Sam's abandonment of a posture of overt defiance for one of apparent submission. Sam and Lizzie were ultimately able to join forces in an agreement that Meyers must be at once deplored and tolerated as a necessary evil whom both mistress and slave would strive ceaselessly to manipulate. Abandoning their brief tryouts as Simon Legree and Nat Turner, Lizzie and Sam returned to the more accustomed and comfortable roles of concerned paternalist and loyal slave. And each recognized at last that his or her own performance depended in large measure upon a complementary performance by the other.

The lines of communication in this negotiating process are likewise revealing of the wider social structure of farm and neighborhood. Lizzie and Sam communicated repeatedly through intermediaries: first her young children, whom Sam perhaps regarded as a means of blunting the impact of the defiance toward which he felt himself propelled; then through Sarah, a black woman to serve as translator between a white woman and a black man; then Coleman, a white man experienced in the language and manipulations of paternalism, who reminded Sam of his appropriate and, in this situation, most wisely calculated role. Slave management here involved not just master or mistress and slave, but, in the phraseology of the Old South, all the "family white and black," as well as much of the surrounding neighborhood.[17]

Meyers's actions, explicitly cited by Sam's physician as entirely within the law, were nevertheless quietly or overtly criticized by those for whom the paternalistic scenario of slavery remained, even in wartime exigency, far preferable to the harsh realities of physical domination. Rivers was gloating perhaps when he decried Sam's treatment as a "damed shame," but he also provided an opportunity for Lizzie's slaves to pressure their mistress to rebuke Meyers and offer Sam an opening for compromise. Eager for her to hear Rivers's disapproval directly, the slaves took the initiative to inform Lizzie that Rivers wished to speak with her, thus demonstrating the part slaves played as communicators and negotiators not just within individual farms or plantations, but across neighborhoods. Yet Rivers, father of his own slave children, could hardly play the virtuous and upstanding paternalist. That role remained to Coleman, who as Scott family retainer and as Sam's former overseer stood midway between Lizzie and her defiant slave. Symbolizing both Sam's and his own long-standing ties with the Scott family, Coleman invoked the class language of paternalism to remind Sam of his place within these traditions of social order and obligation.

Lizzie's behavior throughout the crisis demonstrated as well the essential part gender identities and assumptions played in master-slave relationships. As a female slave manager, Lizzie exploited her apparently close ties to the woman house slave Sarah to secure information about the remainder of her force. "Sarah is worth a team of negro's with her tongue," Lizzie reported to Will. Yet Lizzie's gender more often represented a constraint than an opportunity. Just before the confrontation between Meyers and Sam, Lizzie had written revealingly to Will about the physical coercion of slaves. Acknowledging Will's reluctance to whip, she confessed to feeling the aversion even more forcefully than he. "It has got to be such a disagreeable matter with me to whip, that I haven't even dressed Kate but once since you left, & then only a few cuts—I am too troubled in mind to get stirred up enough to whip. I made Thornton whip Tom once." Accustomed to occasional strikes against female slaves, Lizzie called upon a male slave to whip the adolescent Tom, then, later, a white male neighbor to dominate the venerable Sam. Yet even this structured hierarchy of violence was becoming increasingly "disagreeable" to her as she acted out her new wartime role as "chief of affairs." Lizzie knew she was objectively physically weaker than both black and white men around her, and she feared that wartime disruptions of established patterns of white male authority might encourage slaves to resist physical punishments—especially if inflicted by their new—and weaker—female managers. But she confessed as well to a "troubled . . . mind," to uncertainties about her appropriate relationship to the ultimate exertion of force upon which slavery rested. As wartime pressures weakened the foundations for the "moral" management that Lizzie preferred, what she referred to as "brute force" became simultaneously more necessary and more impossible as an instrument of coercion.[18]

The resolution of the crisis concerning Sam hardly brought permanent peace to the Neblett farm. Even as she struggled with the aftermath of conflict, Lizzie found herself faced with unceasing demands from other slaves. When Thornton was gored in the hand by a wild pig, it was to Lizzie that he came for help. He seemed almost scared to death, but Lizzie remained calm, even though she saw his finger was almost severed. Calling upon her experience in domestic needlework, she took "two stitches through the flesh and tied it, to bring the cut together," then covered the wound with sugar and turpentine. It was, she reported, the "hardest sewing I ever done."[19]

Lizzie's medical skills would be taxed more thoroughly, however, by the extended illness of six-year-old Lee, who in December of 1863 was seized by a flux. Lizzie sat with him for days and nights on end and administered a veritable pharmacopeia of remedies: mustard plasters, rhubarb, soda, peppermint leaves, cinnamon bark. Removing him from his parents, Nance and Thornton, who, Lizzie complained, "don't take care of their children," Lizzie installed the boy in a room in her own house. Although she took "every precaution," she assured Will, to prevent spread of the disease and tried to keep her own children out of Lee's room, she still worried that she herself, who had "spared neither hands nor nose," would contract the disease. Confident in her own course of therapeutics, Lizzie did not send for a doctor for almost two weeks, and then was gratified to have him entirely approve her course of treatment.[20]

Yet at the same time Lizzie recognized and performed all the duties expected of the benevolent slave mistress, she reported to Will the halfheartedness she felt in executing her role. "I have nursed him closely," she assured her husband, "& done as much for him as if he was my own child, but have not of course felt the anxiety about him, that I would one of my own." "If it was not for the humanity of the thing I had much rather let him lay in his mothers house & died than to run the risk of myself & all the children taking it. . . . I have had a great deal of trouble with him, more than he is worth." But the "humanity of the thing," especially in the case of a child, still had a firm if grudging hold on Lizzie Neblett.[21]

It was much harder to feel that benevolence toward Joe. In the fall of 1863, Lizzie's difficulties in managing Joe combined with fears that he would be seized by Confederate soldiers for military labor and prompted the Nebletts to send Joe to Will in Galveston. But Will found his camp services of little use and hired him out in Houston. Slave hiring was widespread in Texas and seems to have become even more common during the Civil War when many families found they preferred reaping profit from their unfree property without bearing the responsibility for their direct supervision. And as Lizzie became increasingly exasperated with slave management, she would ever more strongly urge such a course on Will. Joe's contract, however, was brief and at Christmas he was to be returned to Lizzie in Grimes County. But the New Year of 1864 arrived with no sign of Joe, and Lizzie was not at all sure what had become of him. Perhaps, she feared, he had run away or had been seized for government service. By the middle of January, however, Joe appeared with a lengthy and, Lizzie thought, "plausible tale" to account for his delay: flooding en route, fear of impressment officers, an injury from being kicked by a horse. A letter from Will, who had spoken with Joe's boss, told another story—of Joe's eagerness to be rehired for another year, of his reluctance to return to Grimes, of his improvidence and his delay in departing. Lizzie should, Will urged, make Joe pay her in cash for the work days he had missed. Lizzie mocked Will's suggestion. "You seem to think I can do more with Joe than you can. You know I cant get money or work out of him."[22]

Joe perfectly embodied the independence that southern critics of the hiring system feared as its inevitable outcome. Not only did Joe possess a keen sense of independence from the Nebletts' power, he had also acquired property and skills in transacting business that had made him into an energetic entrepreneur. Lizzie, far less experienced in such matters than he, found herself at a complete loss to control him. When Joe returned to Grimes County, he brought with him a mule, which he used to visit his wife and family. He began feeding the animal with Lizzie's corn and soon took the girth and stirrup leathers from Will's saddle to put his own "in riding order." "I expect him to take all hands soon," Lizzie wryly remarked, "& build himself a stable." When Lizzie wanted to use the girth for her own animals, she found Nance had locked it up in one of the slave houses. Meanwhile, Joe had begun negotiations to acquire a better mount from another slave in the neighborhood. By May, he had gained possession of a horse. He "is now too proud to ride his old mule," Lizzie reported.[23]

Lizzie acknowledged to Will that the situation must seem on the face of it unthinkable. But, she explained resignedly, "necessity compels me to do many things I rebel at, when they first present themselves." She considered killing Joe's steed but recognized that would just make the slave run away or cease work altogether. And yet Joe's influence threatened to transform the rest of her slave force into small businessmen. Tom had sold her hens to an "old negro" in the neighborhood and was discovered cutting down trees to market to the neighbors as firewood.[24]

Meyers sought to enforce control over both Tom and Joe exactly as he had Sam months before. He gave Tom an unprovoked whipping and succeeded in beating his back raw before Lizzie discovered that the young black had in response run away. When Meyers threatened Joe, however, the slave escaped through the woods and appeared in front of Lizzie before Meyers could lay a hand on him. Lizzie interceded. "I told him not to whip Joe, as long as he done his work well & that he must not shoot at him, that he might run away & we might never get him & if he never done me any good he might my children." Slavery in the present had become unworkable. Lizzie could only hope for its future. The balance of power between mistress and bondsmen seemed to have been reversed. "Joe, is doing very bad—it is his day now certainly, but whether my day will ever arrive or not is . . . exceedingly doubtful." Freedom had not yet officially come to Texas, but in Lizzie's despairing eyes the bottom rail seemed already firmly situated on top.[25]

Forbidden the physical severity that served as the fundamental prop of his system of slave management, Meyers requested to be released from his contract with Lizzie at the end of the crop year. Early on, Meyers had told Lizzie that he could "conquer" her slaves, "but may have to kill some one of them." It remained with Lizzie, he explained, to make the decision. In her moments of greatest exasperation, Lizzie was ready to consent to such extreme measures. "I say do it." But with calm reflection, tempered by Will's measured advice, considerations of humanity inevitably reasserted their claim. Repeatedly she interceded between Meyers and the slaves—protecting them from whippings or condemning Meyers when he disobeyed her orders and punished them severely. Yet despite her difficulties in managing Meyers himself, and despite her belief that he was "deficient in judgment," Lizzie recognized her dependence upon him and upon the threat of physical coercion that he represented. She was determined to "hold him on as long as I can." If he quit and the slaves found that no one was coming to replace him, she wrote revealingly, "the jig will be up." The game, the trick, the sham of her slave management would be over. Without a man—or part of a man for three half days a week—without the possibility of recourse to violence that Meyers embodied, slavery was impossible. The velvet glove of paternalism required its iron hand.[26]

The dependence of slavery upon violence and the Old South's gendering of physical force as male made women regard themselves as ineffective managers. "I am so sick," Lizzie wrote Will, "of trying to do a man's business when I am nothing but, a poor contemptible piece of multiplying human flesh tied to the house by a crying young one, looked upon as belonging to a race of inferior beings." Her angry frustration seemed pointless and only provoked the slaves to "meriment," so Lizzie resorted to private tears as a consolation for her "entire inability to help myself." Never had her dependence seemed greater than in this wartime situation of apparent independence and responsibility.[27]

Central to Lizzie's dilemma were her ambivalence and confusion about the role of physical coercion in social relations. In the Old South, violence was anything but the monopoly of the state. Instead, recourse to physical violence in support of male honor and white supremacy was regarded as the right, even the responsibility, of each white man—within his household, on his plantation, in his community. The outbreak of Civil War, the South's resort to the organized, regionwide violence of military conflict, simply underscored the legitimacy of force in social relations. In battle, white southerners embraced violence as a desirable, heroic means of resolving issues of power. But like the Old South's code of honor, military violence was to be fundamentally male; women were, in the words of one female Confederate, "barred from the tented field."[28]

Yet, as men moved in increasing numbers from the South's households to its battlefields, women of the region's plantation-owning elite would be left as the custodians of social order and would find themselves confronting the dependence of their slave society upon the implicit threat, if not explicit use, of force. Throughout the history of the peculiar institution, slave mistresses had hit, slapped, even brutally whipped their slaves—particularly slave women. But their relationship to this exercise of physical power was significantly different from that of their men. No gendered code of honor celebrated their physical power or dominance. A contrasting, yet parallel ideology extolled their female sensitivity, weakness, and docility. In the prewar years, exercise of the violence that was fundamental to slavery was overwhelmingly the responsibility and prerogative of white men. A white woman disciplined and punished as the master's subordinate and surrogate. Rationalized, systematic, autonomous, instrumental use of violence belonged to men.[29]

As a wartime slave manager, Lizzie soon discovered that she could live neither with violence nor without it. The manipulations of paternalism's velvet glove were growing progressively less effective as means of control, yet unrestrained terror, however appealing at times, was, Lizzie recognized, inhumane. Perhaps it had even become dangerous, threatening to provoke restive slaves themselves to act upon southern society's lessons about the primacy of force. Lizzie in fact worried about violence from her slaves—and especially feared retaliation for Meyers's cruelties. And she wondered too about the origins of mysterious fires that burned her mother's house, her father-in-law's gin, and the Nebletts' own property now rented out in Navarro County, for she knew arson to be widely acknowledged as a characteristic slave "crime."

Violence seemed to permeate the white family as well. Lizzie's ill-behaved children were nearly as exasperating as her slaves and perhaps even more out of control. Bob mistreated the horses; Walter used a cowhide to beat the cat; all the children's faces bore the permanent scars of Billy's fingernails; and infant Bettie cried ceaselessly. Here Lizzie felt empowered to act in a way she dared not with her slaves. Here, with her own young children, a woman need not fear the use of physical force—even if considerations of humanity prompted doubt. Lizzie threatened she would whip Billy every day if necessary "& I do it well when I begin." "I can't get him to do anything unless I get the cowhide in hand." And Bob, she complained, just "don't mind me as well as he once did." By the time Bettie reached ten months, Lizzie confessed to Will, "I have whipped her several times." Reporting her aunt's stern disapproval of beating such a small child, Lizzie admitted she was surprised when Will did not scold her as well. As she restrained herself from abusing her slaves, Lizzie turned to abusing her children.[30]

Frustrated by feelings of powerlessness and incompetence as both slave manager and parent, Lizzie turned to brute force. Will's regime of "grumbling and threatening" slave management was replaced by the counterpoint of Meyers's cruelty and Lizzie's paternalism; Lizzie and Will's socialization of their children devolved into Lizzie's threats and punishments and the children's own resort to violence with their inferiors—younger siblings and animals.

Historians and social scientists exploring "family violence" have concentrated upon its appearances in urban settings, particularly in the industrial North. But the phenomenon, with its invaluable perspective on fundamental issues of social power, deserves historical attention in the South as well. Within slaveholding society, domestic violence took on a distinctive shape and meaning, one that suggests it would most usefully be examined not just in terms of biological family, but within the context of the wider household—the "family white and black" in which expressions of physical force were structured and influenced by intimate relationships of race as well as age and gender.

The South's social hierarchies created a spectrum of legitimate access to violence, so that social empowerment was inextricably bound up with the right to use physical force. Violence was all but required of white men of all classes and forbidden to black slaves, except within their own communities where the dominant society regarded it as essentially invisible. White women stood upon an ill-defined middle ground where behavior and ideology often diverged. The Civil War exacerbated this very tension, disrupting the broader structures of social order by removing a sizeable portion of the white men and thus compelling women in slave-owning households to become the reluctant agents of a power they could not embrace as rightfully their own. The centrality of violence in the Old South had reflected and reinforced white women's inferior status in that society. Within the Confederacy, it threatened to make women like Lizzie feel growing contempt for their identity as females trying, unsuccessfully, "to do a man's business." In their eyes, a man's business it would—and should—remain.[31]

Violence was the ultimate foundation of power in the slave South, but gender prescriptions carefully barred white women—especially those elite women most likely to find themselves responsible for controlling slaves—from purposeful exercise of such authority. Even when circumstances had shifted to make female authority socially desirable, it remained for many plantation mistresses personally impossible. Lizzie's struggle with her attraction to violence and simultaneous abhorrence of it embodied the contradictions that the necessary wartime paradox of female slave management imposed on her individual life. Ultimately and tragically, she embraced violence by exercising power over the most helpless being of all. Lizzie turned in frustration and, I would suggest, self-loathing, to the beating of an infant child—a child who happened to be not just speechless and helpless, but named for Lizzie herself and "cursed like her mother with the female sex."

The role of female slave manager was within the gender assumptions of the Old South a contradiction in terms that left Lizzie longing only for escape: she wished repeatedly to die; to be a man; or to give up the slaves altogether—except, tellingly, for one to wait on her in the house. White women had reaped slavery's benefits throughout its existence in the colonial and antebellum South. But they could not be its managers without ceasing to be what they understood as women. In the absence of men, a society based in the violence of slavery could not stand.

If he would not hire out his slaves and free her from their management, Lizzie begged Will in the spring of 1864, "give your negros away and I'll . . . work with my hands, as hard as I can, but my mind will rest." A year later Lizzie would have to trouble her mind about slave management no longer. With war's end, Will returned safely from the coast and took up farming once again. By the time of the 1870 census, he was annually paying out $100 in wages to farm workers and raising 4 bales of cotton, as well as 200 bushels of corn. The value of his real estate had fallen 60 percent during the decade, and his personal property, with the freeing of his slaves, to just 5½ percent of its former value. Lizzie later described "seven years of struggle together after the war closed," for in the spring of 1871, Will died of pneumonia, leaving his wife five months pregnant with a third daughter.

A widow at thirty-eight, Lizzie had lived less than half her life. She would survive until 1917, returning to her early literary ambitions as a temperance columnist in the 1880s and emerging by the end of the century as matriarch of a growing clan of descendants. Ironically, she would pass the last decades of her life in the Austin household of her second daughter, the unwelcome war baby Bettie. Lizzie Neblett's scattered postbellum letters and papers cannot provide the vivid portrait of a woman's experience that emerges from her Civil War writings. We can never know whether the end of war and its responsibilities had indeed brought her sad and tormented mind to "rest."[32]

Notes

Abbreviations

Duke   William R. Perkins Library, Duke University, Durham, North Carolina

LC   Library of Congress, Washington, D.C.

NA   National Archives, Washington, D.C.

SCL   South Caroliniana Library, University of South Carolina–Columbia

SHC   Southern Historical Collection, University of North Carolina–Chapel Hill

VHS   Virginia Historical Society, Richmond, Virginia

Introduction

1. Carolyn Heilbrun, *Writing a Woman's Life* (New York: Norton, 1988), 37.

2. For a collection that reveals some of the major influences in the revivi-fication of intellectual history, see Dominick LaCapra and Steven L. Kaplan, eds., *Modern European Intellectual History: Reappraisals and New Perspectives* (Ithaca: Cornell University Press, 1982). See also John Higham and Paul K. Conkin, eds., *New Directions in American Intellectual History* (Baltimore: Johns Hopkins University Press, 1979), and David A. Hollinger, *In the American Province: Studies in the History and Historiography of Ideas* (Bloomington: Indiana University Press, 1985).

3. Eugene D. Genovese, *Roll, Jordan, Roll: The World the Slaves Made* (New York: Pantheon, 1974), and *The World the Slaveholders Made: Two Essays in Interpretation* (New York: Random House, 1969). For a discussion of Genovese's influence on the historiography of the Old South, see Drew Gilpin Faust, "The Peculiar South Revisited: White Society, Culture and Politics in the Antebellum Period, 1800–1860," in *Interpreting Southern History: Historiographical Essays in Honor of Sanford W. Higginbotham,* ed. John B. Boles and Evelyn Thomas Nolen (Baton Rouge: Louisiana State University Press, 1987).

On more southern intellectual history, see Michael O'Brien, *Rethinking the South: Essays in Intellectual History* (Baltimore: Johns Hopkins University Press, 1988), and Michael O'Brien and David Moltke-Hansen, eds., *Intellectual Life in Antebellum Charleston* (Knoxville: University of Tennessee Press, 1986).

4. Clifford Geertz, *The Interpretation of Cultures* (New York: Basic Books, 1973). See also Ronald G. Walters, "Signs of the Times: Clifford Geertz and Historians," *Social Research* 47 (Autumn 1980): 537–56. For a recent critique of Geertz and his influences on historians see Aletta Biersack, "Local Knowledge, Local History: Geertz and Beyond," in *The New Cultural History*, ed. Lynn Hunt (Berkeley: University of California Press, 1989), 72–96.

5. Geertz, *Interpretation of Cultures*, 118. I find this position consistent with Pierre Bourdieu's more recent and currently influential formulation of "habitus" as created by the social world and simultaneously constructive of it, although Geertz and Bourdieu differ significantly on other matters. See Bourdieu, *Distinction: A Social Critique of the Judgment of Taste* (Cambridge: Harvard University Press, 1984).

6. Edmund Rhett, "Agricultural Address—Entitled 'Who is the Producer?',", *Southern Cabinet* 1 (December 1840): 714. On speech acts see references to Part 1, Chapter 2 below. For a helpful presentation of the materiality of ideas see Raymond Williams, *Marxism and Literature* (Oxford: Oxford University Press, 1977).

7. See Drew Gilpin Faust, *The Creation of Confederate Nationalism: Ideology and Identity in the Civil War South* (Baton Rouge: Louisiana State University Press, 1988). For a very brief, yet useful summary of poststructuralism, see Jane Tompkins, "A Short Course in Poststructuralism," *College English* 50 (November 1988): 733–47. For a discussion of the history of ideology as a subject of scholarly inquiry and for a pointed and sensible critique of poststructuralism see Terry Eagleton, *Ideology: An Introduction* (London: Verso, 1991).

8. For a cogent and sophisticated argument that reality and history are more than language or discourse, see Gabrielle M. Spiegel, who addresses the implications of postmodernism for history and vice versa in "History, Historicism, and the Social Logic of the Middle Ages," *Speculum* 65 (1990): 59–86. She calls for renewed appreciation for the historical enterprise and the materiality of history and for refocused attention upon power, human agency, and social experience.

9. David F. Jamison, *Annual Address Before the State Agricultural Society of South Carolina* (n.p., 1856), 353.

10. Elizabeth Fox-Genovese and Eugene Genovese, *Fruits of Merchant Capital: Slavery and Bourgeois Property in the Rise and Expansion of Capitalism* (New York: Oxford University Press, 1983).

11. On Hammond, in addition to Part 1, Chapter 3 below, see Drew Gilpin

Faust, *James Henry Hammond and the Old South: A Design for Mastery* (Baton Rouge: Louisiana State University Press, 1982). On Chesnut, in addition to Part 2, Chapter 2 below, see C. Vann Woodward, *Mary Chesnut's Civil War* (New Haven: Yale University Press, 1981).

12. A number of social and cultural studies of the war have recently begun to appear. One among several new considerations of soldiers' lives is Reid Mitchell, *Civil War Soldiers: Their Expectations and Their Experiences* (New York: Viking, 1988). Community studies represent another genre within this new social history of the war. See, for two southern examples, Wayne K. Durrill, *War of Another Kind: A Southern Community in the Great Rebellion* (New York: Oxford University Press, 1990), and Stephen V. Ash, *Middle Tennessee Society Transformed, 1860–1870: War and Peace in the Upper South* (Baton Rouge: Louisiana State University Press, 1988). Studies of the disintegration of slavery are also a part of this new historiography. For one example among many such studies, see Clarence L. Mohr, *On the Threshold of Freedom: Masters and Slaves in Civil War Georgia* (Athens: University of Georgia Press, 1986). New interest in civilian life has included new interest in women particularly. See, for example, George Rable, *Civil Wars: Women and the Crisis of Southern Nationalism* (Urbana: University of Illinois Press, 1989). Catherine Clinton and Nina Silber are editing a volume on gender and the war that will be published by Oxford University Press. Maris Vinovskis has edited a collection with the promising title *Toward a Social History of the American Civil War: Exploratory Essays* (New York: Cambridge University Press, 1990), but, disappointingly, it deals exclusively with the North. See also three recent historiographical essays on these new directions in Civil War studies: Joseph T. Glathaar, "The 'New' Civil War History: An Overview," *Pennsylvania Magazine of History and Biography* 115 (July 1991): 339–70; Gary W. Gallagher, "Home Front and Battlefield: Some Recent Literature Relating to Virginia and the Confederacy," *Virginia Magazine of History and Biography* 98 (April 1990): 135–68; Richard Slotkin, " 'What Shall Men Remember?': Recent Work on the Civil War," *American Literary History* 3 (Spring 1991): 120–35. While military history needs to be supplemented by more work in social history, social and cultural historians need, in my view, to pay more attention to military historians as well.

Evangelicalism and the Proslavery Argument: The Reverend Thornton Stringfellow of Virginia

1. Donald G. Mathews, "Religion in the Old South: Speculation on Methodology," *South Atlantic Quarterly* 73 (1974): 34. Several recent studies have begun to explore the nature and influence of evangelicalism in the South. See

Bertram Wyatt-Brown, "The Antimission Movement in the Jacksonian South: A Study in Regional Folk Culture," *Journal of Southern History* 36 (1970): 501–29, and James Brewer Stewart, "Evangelicalism and the Radical Strain in Southern Antislavery Thought during the 1820s," *Journal of Southern History* 39 (1973): 379–96. I would like to thank Richard R. Beeman and John J. Green for critical readings and Charles E. Rosenberg for his patient and invaluable assistance throughout the preparation of this paper.

2. E. N. Elliott, ed., *Cotton is King and Pro-slavery Arguments* (Augusta, 1860); Thornton Stringfellow, *A Brief Examination of Scripture Testimony on the Institution of Slavery* (Washington, 1850); *Scriptural and Statistical Views in Favor of Slavery*, 4th ed. (Richmond, 1856); *Slavery: Its Origin, Nature and History . . . Considered in the Light of Bible Teachings, Moral Justice, and Political Wisdom* (Alexandria, 1860; New York, 1861).

3. Letter to William Gilmore Simms from James Henry Hammond, June 11, 1852, Hammond Papers, LC.

4. Some modern historians have recognized Stringfellow's importance but have not produced any information on him beyond that contained in his pamphlets. See Eric L. McKitrick, *Slavery Defended: The Views of the Old South* (Englewood Cliffs, N.J.: Prentice Hall, 1963); William Sumner Jenkins, *Pro-slavery Thought in the Old South* (Chapel Hill: University of North Carolina Press, 1935); more recently, H. Shelton Smith, *In His Image, But . . . : Racism in Southern Religion, 1780–1910* (Durham: Duke University Press, 1972); and W. Harrison Daniel, "Virginia Baptists and the Negro in the Ante-bellum Era," *Journal of Negro History* 56 (1971): 1–16.

5. Clifford S. Griffin, *Their Brothers' Keepers: Moral Stewardship in the United States, 1800–1865* (New Brunswick: Rutgers University Press, 1960).

6. Ibid. See also Charles Foster, *An Errand of Mercy: The Evangelical United Front, 1790–1837* (Chapel Hill: University of North Carolina Press, 1960), and John R. Bodo, *The Protestant Clergy and Public Issues, 1812–1848* (Princeton: Princeton University Press, 1954).

7. Will of Robert Stringfellow, Fauquier County, Virginia, Will Book 6, p. 98.

8. *Religious Herald*, March 18, 1869 and September 19, 1844.

9. Ibid., March 3, 1864. Will of Thornton Stringfellow, Culpeper County, Virginia, Will Book, Volume W, p. 123.

10. Obituary of Thornton Stringfellow, *Minutes of the Shiloh Baptist Association* (Alexandria, 1870), 12.

11. On the Baptists in this period see Robert Baylor Semple, *A History of the Rise and Progress of the Baptists in Virginia*, revised and extended by Rev. G. W. Beale (Richmond, 1894); Benjamin F. Riley, *A History of the Baptists in the Southern States East of the Mississippi* (Philadelphia, 1898); W. W. Barnes, *The Southern Baptist Convention, 1845–1953* (Nashville: Broadman Press, 1954);

Mary Burham Putnam, *The Baptists and Slavery, 1840–1845* (Ann Arbor: G. Wahr, 1913).

12. In a recent article, Lois W. Banner has pointed out how the desire of social reformers to inculcate morality led them to promote institutions and arrangements which had much broader educational effects. Although in certain instances, as for example that of the Cumberland Presbyterians, evangelicalism was antieducational, when it was connected with social reform movements, it often produced educational advances. Banner documents some of these in "Religious Benevolence as Social Control: A Critique of an Interpretation," *Journal of American History* 60 (1973): 31–41.

13. Obituary, *Minutes of the Shiloh Baptist Association*, 14.

14. Ibid.

15. Records of Stevensburg, Virginia Baptist Church, Shiloh Association, 1833–1927, Virginia Baptist Historical Society, University of Richmond.

16. Stringfellow, *Slavery: Its Origin, Nature and History* (New York, 1861), 48.

17. *Religious Herald*, October 6, 1842 and December 29, 1842. For record of Stringfellow's temperance activity see also Providence Church Minutes, 1833–1850, Potomac Association, Virginia Baptist Historical Society.

18. John R. Bodo sees two groups within northern reform: a clerical, social-control oriented faction that rejected the legitimacy accorded the individual conscience by the other group, which included such men as Garrison. Stringfellow would clearly fit in with his colleagues in the northern clergy on this as on many other issues (*Protestant Clergy and Public Issues*, 29–30).

19. *Religious Herald*, October 6, 1842.

20. Ibid., June 6 and July 3, 1851; April 29, 1852; May 5, 1855.

21. Ibid., August 22, 1850.

22. Ibid.

23. It is interesting to note in light of Stringfellow's concern with physical health the analogous involvement of northern mission workers in public health activities in northern cities. Carroll Smith-Rosenberg suggests in *Religion and the Rise of the American City* (Ithaca: Cornell University Press, 1971) the existence of an identity in the reformers' minds between spiritual and physical health (199).

24. Again see Griffin, Foster, and Bodo.

25. In his portrayal of social-control oriented reformist clergy in the North, John R. Bodo identifies this anti-individualism as one of their salient characteristics. Bodo contrasts the individualism of such men as Channing, Garrison, and Theodore Parker with the dedication of many clergy to establishing an "American theocracy" through the instrument of benevolent associations. It is interesting that he mentions the Anti-Mission Baptists, a group that Stringfellow opposed from the earliest days of his ministry, as one of the groups

most devoted to this concept of individualism (*Protestant Clergy and Public Issues*, 26–27).

26. Stringfellow, *Scriptural and Statistical Views*, 6.

27. *Religious Herald*, February 25, 1841.

28. Stevensburg Minutes, July 1, 1844.

29. Ibid., July 1851.

30. Carroll Smith-Rosenberg draws this distinction neatly in her consideration of social control. "Men deeply committed to the need for universal salvation could not but assume that a secular by-product of this spiritual change would be universal thriftiness, temperance, prudence—and hence social stability. These reformers desired both to save souls and to control social stress—but saw the two goals as essentially the same. Emphasis by historians on the religious benevolence of the period as a form of social control thus creates an artificial distinction, a misinterpretation of the Jacksonian world view, by assuming a nonexistent distinction between the realms of the secular and the spiritual, and thus, by a kind of necessary extension, seeing as conspiratorial design a common vision of the good society" (8–9).

31. Stringfellow, *Slavery: Its Origin, Nature and History*, 48.

32. Stringfellow, *Scriptural and Statistical Views*, 144.

33. Ibid., 105.

34. Stringfellow, *A Brief Examination*, 18.

35. Ibid., 17.

36. Letter from George F. Stringfellow to Rev. C. W. Brooks, July 28, 1933, Virginia Baptist Historical Society.

37. Records of Stevensburg Baptist Church, Virginia Baptist Historical Society, list two slaves of a George Fitzhugh as members of Stringfellow's congregation, although it is not certain that this was the same Fitzhugh.

38. Ralph E. Morrow has suggested that the proslavery argument was directed chiefly toward southerners ambivalent about their peculiar institution. A review of Stringfellow's *Slavery, Statistical and Scriptural* that appeared in the New Orleans *Delta* and was republished in the *Religious Herald* indicates that this was the purpose seen by Stringfellow's contemporaries. "The true use of such a book at this time is to dissipate the doubts of that apologetic class of people in the South who are in the habit of weakening the cause of the South by a weak defense and illogical support of her vital institution of slavery. This class is really as dangerous to the South as her open assailants" ("The Proslavery Argument Revisited," *Mississippi Valley Historical Review* 48 [1961]: 79–94; *Religious Herald*, November 6, 1856).

39. A number of historians have asserted that the involvement of northern clergy in public issues and benevolent activities was in one sense an attempt to promote and cement the sense of American nationhood. Stringfellow's par-

ticipation in similar activities combined with his expression of a belief in a special destiny for the South could plausibly be viewed as evidence of a concern with a nascent southern nationalism analogous to the Americanism of the group others have described (Bodo, *Protestant Clergy and Public Issues*, 6; Perry Miller, *The Life of the Mind in America* [New York: Harcourt, Brace & World, 1965]).

40. *Religious Herald*, April 7, 1845.

41. This manuscript diary, kept intermittently between 1845 and 1863, is in the possession of Dr. James Stringfellow of Culpeper, Virginia. I am grateful to Mrs. Thornton Stringfellow and her daughter Patty for permitting me to use it and for providing me with the information that they had about the Reverend Thornton Stringfellow.

42. Diary, July 5, 1863.

43. Ibid., September 19, 1863.

44. Ibid., September 25, 1863.

45. Ibid., October 5, 1863.

46. Ibid., October 6, 1863.

47. Ibid.

48. Ibid., December 2, 1863.

49. Ibid., December 24, 1863.

50. Ibid., December 31, 1863.

51. *Religious Herald*, September 29, 1870.

52. Will of Thornton Stringfellow.

The Rhetoric and Ritual of Agriculture in Antebellum South Carolina

1. I. A. Richards, *The Philosophy of Rhetoric* (New York: Oxford University Press, 1936), 134; Kenneth Burke, especially his discussion of "Terministic Screens" in *Language as Symbolic Action: Essays in Life, Literature, and Method* (Berkeley and Los Angeles: The University of California Press, 1968), 44–62, and his discussion of "dramatism" in *A Grammar of Motives* (New York: Prentice Hall, 1945), xv–xviii, and *A Rhetoric of Motives* (New York: Prentice Hall, 1950). "The things of the world," he summarizes, "become material exemplars of the values which the tribal idiom has placed upon them" (*Language as Symbolic Action*, 361). I would like to thank Richard R. Beeman, Dan Ben-Amos, Sacvan Bercovitch, Harold J. Bershady, Henry H. Glassie III, Rhys Isaac, Bruce Kuklick, Robert C. McMath, Jr., George C. Rogers, Jr., Charles E. Rosenberg, Allen H. Stokes, Harry S. Stout, Janet A. Tighe, Anthony F. C. Wallace, Peter H. Wood, and the Ethnohistory Workshop of the University of

Pennsylvania for criticisms and comments on earlier versions of this paper. An original, much briefer version was presented at a conference on language and culture in South Carolina sponsored by the Department of Anthropology, University of South Carolina, in March 1977.

2. Humphrey Moore, *An Address Delivered at Hopkinton, Before the Hillsborough Society . . . October 17, 1821* (Amherst, N.H., 1822), 13.

3. For specific discussion of the meaning of these changes to the South see Drew Gilpin Faust, *A Sacred Circle: The Dilemma of the Intellectual in the Old South, 1840–1860* (Baltimore: Johns Hopkins University Press, 1977).

4. The approach taken in this paper has been greatly influenced by Dell Hymes's formulations of the methodology of "the ethnography of speaking" in *Foundations in Sociolinguistics: An Ethnographic Approach* (Philadelphia: University of Pennsylvania Press, 1974). See also Richard Bauman and Joel Sherzer, eds., *Explorations in the Ethnography of Speaking* (Cambridge: Cambridge University Press, 1975). On genre see Dan Ben-Amos, "Analytic Categories and Ethnic Genres," *Genre* 2 (September 1969): 275–301; Roger D. Abrahams, "The Complex Relations of Simple Forms," *Genre* 2 (June 1969): 104–28; and Abrahams, "Introductory Remarks to a Rhetorical Theory of Folklore," *Journal of American Folklore* 81 (April–June 1968): 143–58. See also Maurice Bloch, ed., *Political Language and Oratory in Traditional Society* (London: Academic Press, 1975); J. L. Austin, *How to Do Things with Words* (Cambridge: Cambridge University Press, 1962); S. J. Tambiah, "The Magical Power of Words," *Man* 3 (June 1968): 175–208; John R. Searle, *Speech Acts: An Essay in the Philosophy of Language* (London: Cambridge University Press, 1969); Michelle Rosaldo, "I Have Nothing to Hide: The Language of Ilongot Oratory," *Language in Society* 2 (October 1973): 193–223; Peter Seitel, "Haya Metaphors for Speech," *Language in Society* 3 (April 1974): 51–67; Max Black, *Models and Metaphors: Studies in Language and Philosophy* (Ithaca: Cornell University Press, 1962); Stephen C. Pepper, *World Hypotheses: A Study in Evidence* (Berkeley and Los Angeles: The University of California Press, 1942); and the following six works by James W. Fernandez: "Unbelievably Subtle Words: Representation and Integration in the Sermons of an African Reformative Cult," *History of Religions* 6 (August 1966): 43–69; "Poetry in Motion: Being Moved by Amusement, by Mockery and by Mortality in the Asturian Countryside," *New Literary History* 8 (Spring 1977): 459–80; "Symbolic Consensus in a Fang Reformative Cult," *American Anthropologist* 67 (August 1965): 902–29; "The Mission of Metaphor in Expressive Culture," *Current Anthropology* 15 (June 1974): 119–45; "Persuasions and Performances: Of the Beast in Every Body . . . and the Metaphors of Everyman," in Clifford Geertz, ed., *Myth, Symbol and Culture* (New York: Norton, 1974), 39–60; and "The Performance of Ritual Metaphors," in J. David Sapir and J. Christopher Crocker, eds., *The Social Use*

of Metaphor (Philadelphia: University of Pennsylvania Press, 1977). A historian who has employed this approach in the study of texts is Quentin Skinner. See his "Motives, Intentions and the Interpretation of Texts," *New Literary History* 3 (Winter 1972): 393–408, and "Some Problems in the Analysis of Political Thought and Action," *Political Theory* 2 (August 1974): 277–303.

5. I am much indebted to Clifford Geertz for the "model of/model for" conceptualization of the way belief systems operate. See Geertz, *The Interpretation of Cultures: Selected Essays* (New York: Basic Books, 1973), 118. On the jeremiad see Sacvan Bercovitch, "Horologicals to Chronometricals: The Rhetoric of the Jeremiad," *Literary Monographs* 3 (1970): 33; Bercovitch, *The American Jeremiad* (Madison: University of Wisconsin Press, 1978); and Perry Miller, *The New England Mind: From Colony to Province* (Cambridge: Harvard University Press, 1953): 29–52. I do not intend to indicate an exact identity between the Puritan jeremiad and the Carolina agricultural address. The Puritan "plain style" was in structure and expression quite different from the Classical rhetoric that influenced the Carolinians. Rather, I see a more general similarity, a parallel in modes of perception much like what Bercovitch has referred to as "the Puritan origins of the American self." See Bercovitch, *The Puritan Origins of the American Self* (New Haven: Yale University Press, 1975), and David Minter, "The Puritan Jeremiad as a Literary Form," in Bercovitch, ed., *The American Puritan Imagination: Essays in Revaluation* (London: Cambridge University Press, 1974), 44–55.

6. On the recurrent crises within South Carolina see William W. Freehling, *Prelude to Civil War: The Nullification Controversy in South Carolina, 1816–1836* (New York: Harper and Row, 1965), and Steven A. Channing, *Crisis of Fear: Secession in South Carolina* (New York: Norton, 1970).

7. On the economic situation in South Carolina in this period see Alfred G. Smith, Jr., *Economic Readjustment of an Old Cotton State: South Carolina, 1820–1860* (Columbia: University of South Carolina Press, 1958); Marjorie S. Mendenhall, "A History of Agriculture in South Carolina, 1790 to 1860: An Economic and Social Study" (Ph.D. diss., University of North Carolina, 1940); and Arthur R. Hall, *The Story of Soil Conservation in the South Carolina Piedmont, 1800–1860* (Washington: U. S. Department of Agriculture, *Miscellaneous Publication* No. 407, 1940). I have not discussed rice production here. Rice prices remained steadier than cotton, but rice lands were beginning to suffer from neglect as well. See Mendenhall, "A History of Agriculture," 338; and Black Oak Agricultural Society Minutes, 1842–1844, South Carolina Historical Society, Charleston, S.C. There is a vigorous debate at present about the dimensions and reality of "decline" in the southern economy. For a discussion of this see Faust, *A Sacred Circle*, 156 n. 19. Carolinians unquestionably perceived a decline in comparison with past prosperity.

8. W. A. G., "On Manures," *Southern Agriculturist* 6 (March 1833): 122.

9. Agricola, "Observations on the Present Condition of the Southern States," *Southern Agriculturist* 7 (June 1834): 287; James Henry Hammond, "Anniversary Oration of the State Agricultural Society of South Carolina . . . 25th November, 1841," in *The Proceedings of the Agricultural Convention and of the State Agricultural Society of South Carolina from 1839 to 1845 Inclusive* (Columbia, 1846), 182. The preceding volume will be cited hereafter as *Proceedings*.

10. "Proceedings of the South-Carolina Agricultural Society," *Southern Agriculturist* 3 (August 1842): 397; "Agricultural Convention, Monticello, Fairfield District, July 5, 1843," clipping in Private Diary of Edmund Ruffin, State Agricultural Surveyor of South Carolina, 1843, Edmund Ruffin Papers, VHS.

11. For statistics on population decline see Mendenhall, "A History of Agriculture," 195, and Smith, *Economic Readjustment*, 19–44.

12. Diary entries, 107, 117, Private Diary, Edmund Ruffin Papers, VHS; "Claims of the Agricultural Interests to Legislative Aid," *Farmer and Planter* 1 (November 1850): 138. See also Hall, *The Story of Soil Conservation*.

13. "Suggestions for Southern Planters," *Southern Agriculturist* (June 1845): 201. This is a process Kenneth Burke calls *entitlement*. The definition of a situation encompasses within it a strategy for dealing with the reality so defined. See Burke, "What Are the Signs of What? A Theory of Entitlement," in *Language as Symbolic Action*, 359–79.

14. "Introduction," *Southern Agriculturist* 9 (January 1836): i–ii.

15. "Southern Agriculture," *Magnolia* 4 (March 1842): 129; "Culture and Preparation of Indigo for Market," *Southern Agriculturist* 4 (May 1844): 186. See also William Gilmore Simms, "The Good Farmer," *Ladies Companion* 15 (August 1841): 156.

16. Simms, "The Good Farmer," 154.

17. "Southern Agriculture," 135–36.

18. Basil Manly, "An Address on Agriculture," *Southern Agriculturist* 2 (July 1842): 344; William H. Wigg, "Address on the Anniversary of the Agricultural Society of St. Luke's Parish . . . 13th May, 1836," *Southern Agriculturist* 6 (July 1846): 257–58.

19. Edmund Rhett, "Agricultural Address—Entitled 'Who is the Producer?' . . . August 1840," *Southern Cabinet* 1 (December 1840): 714. This study is based on the approximately ninety complete agricultural addresses from South Carolina that I have been able to locate for this period and thirty northern addresses analyzed for comparison. Every educated South Carolinian was given at least some training in classical rhetoric, a staple of both school and college curricula. See, for example, Daniel W. Hollis, *University of South Carolina*, 2 vols. (Columbia: University of South Carolina Press, 1951–1956), 1:31–32.

20. James Fernandez refers to this process as moving ideas through "quality space." See Fernandez, "Poetry in Motion," 475. For a description of this device in a text used widely in nineteenth-century South Carolina see Richard Whately, *Elements of Rhetoric* (Boston, 1839), 192.

21. James M. Banner, Jr., "The Problem of South Carolina," in Stanley M. Elkins and Eric L. McKitrick, eds., *The Hofstadter Aegis: A Memorial* (New York: Alfred A. Knopf, 1974), 91.

22. Joel Roberts Poinsett, "A Discourse," *Southern Agriculturist* 4 (December 1844): 452.

23. Edward R. Laurens, "An Address Delivered Before the Agricultural Society of South Carolina, September 18, 1832," *Southern Agriculturist* 5 (November 1832): 562; Daniel K. Whitaker, "An Address Delivered Before the Agricultural Society of South Carolina, August 20th, 1833," *Southern Agriculturist* 6 (October 1833): 505. See similar remarks by Henry Colman, "An Address Before the Hampshire, Franklin, and Hampden Agricultural Society, Greenfield, Mass., October 23, 1833," *Southern Agriculturist* 7 (March 1834): 139–41.

24. M. P. Crawford, *An Address Delivered Before the Lancaster Agricultural Society* (Lancaster, S.C., 1854), 5.

25. Angus Patterson, *An Address to the Farmers' Society of Barnwell District, Second Day of January, 1826* (Charleston, 1826), 4. The textbook of rhetoric used in South Carolina College explained: "One of the objects most frequently proposed in an Introduction, is, to shew that the subject in question is *important* . . . and worthy of attention" (Whately, *Elements of Rhetoric*, 113–14).

26. Manly, "An Address on Agriculture," 338.

27. Andrew P. Calhoun, "Address Delivered Before the Pendleton Farmers' Society, October 13, 1855," *Farmer and Planter* 6 (December 1855): 269; O. R. Broyles, "An Address Delivered Before the Anderson District Farmers Society, 21st November 1849," *Farmer and Planter* 1 (May 1850): 34.

28. J. Jenkins Mikell, "Address Delivered Before the Agricultural Society of St. John's, Colleton," *Southern Agriculturist* 5 (January 1845): 19; J. M. Verdier, "Address Delivered Before the Agricultural Society of Beaufort," *Southern Agriculturist* 12 (September 1839): 461–62. On the use of religious terminology note rhetorician Whately's remark that it "has been supposed to carry with it an air of appropriate dignity and sanctity, which greatly adds to the force of what is said" (*Elements of Rhetoric*, 206). Agricultural jeremiads abound with expressions of anxiety about growing materialism. See for example John B. O'Neall, "An Agricultural Address Delivered Before the State Agricultural Society, 29th December, 1842," in *Proceedings*, 196–97.

29. Whitemarsh Benjamin Seabrook, *An Address Delivered at the First Anni-*

versary Meeting of the United Agricultural Society of South Carolina, 6th December 1827 (Charleston, 1828), 3.

30. Victor Turner, *The Forest of Symbols: Aspects of Ndembu Ritual* (Ithaca: Cornell University Press, 1967), 30; Hammond, "Anniversary Oration," 182; James Hamilton, "An Address on the Agriculture and Husbandry of the South," *Southern Agriculturist* 4 (August 1844): 304, 310–11.

31. This establishment of general frameworks of meaning uniting tradition and progress also characterizes the first portion of most northern agricultural addresses. It is in the second section, where specific applications of the principles were addressed, that the differences become striking.

32. Legaré is quoted in Freehling, *Prelude to Civil War,* 5.

33. Henry William Ravenel, *Anniversary Address Delivered Before the Black Oak Agricultural Society, April 1852* (Charleston, 1852), 9; Mikell, "Address," 14. Such an understanding of nature is what Mary Douglas calls "natural symbols," the perception of nature in terms of social categories. See her *Natural Symbols: Explorations in Cosmology* (New York: Pantheon, 1973).

34. William Elliott, *The Anniversary Address of the State Agricultural Society of South Carolina . . . November 30, 1848* (Columbia, 1848), 4; Frederick A. Porcher, "An Address," *Southern Agriculturist* 5 (January 1845): 2.

35. Ravenel, *Anniversary Address,* 6.

36. "Proceedings of the State Agricultural Society of South-Carolina," *Southern Agriculturist* 5 (November 1845): 413.

37. John B. O'Neall, "An Address Delivered Before the State Agricultural Society . . . 11th September 1844," in *Proceedings,* 217; R. A. Maxwell, "An Agricultural Address at the Anniversary Meeting of the Pendleton Farmers' Society, October 1844," *Carolina Planter* 1 (June 1845): 265; William Taylor, "Anniversary Address, Delivered Before the State Agricultural Society . . . 30th of November 1843," in *Proceedings,* 206–7; Colleton, "Some of the Causes of the Decline and Fall of Most of the Agricultural Societies of South Carolina," *Southern Agriculturist* 8 (March 1835): 114.

38. Maxwell, "An Agricultural Address," 265; Andrew P. Calhoun, "Address Delivered Before the State Agricultural Society . . . November 11th, 1856," *Farmer and Planter* 8 (January 1857): 4.

39. Joseph E. Jenkins, "An Address Delivered Before the Agricultural Society of St. John's, Colleton," *Southern Agriculturist* 11 (August 1838): 404; Elliott, *The Anniversary Address,* 34; Seabrook, "From an Address Delivered . . . 6th December 1827," *Southern Agriculturist* 9 (March 1836): 126.

40. Whitemarsh Benjamin Seabrook, *A Concise View of the Critical Situation and Future Prospects of the Slave-Holding States* (Charleston, 1825), 3; and Seabrook, *An Essay on the Agricultural Capabilities of S. Carolina* (Columbia, 1848).

21; O'Neall, "An Address Delivered at Greenville, 11th September 1844," in *Proceedings*, 219.

41. Manly, "An Address on Agriculture," 337; Robert William Roper, "Anniversary Address, Delivered . . . August 19, 1834," *Southern Agriculturist* 7 (November 1834): 568; Hamilton, "An Address on Agricultural Husbandry," 312.

42. David F. Jamison, *Annual Address Before the State Agricultural Society, of South Carolina* (n.p., n.d.), 353.

43. For a discussion of the way that social ceremonies may be structured around linguistic events see Douglas, *Natural Symbols*, 44; and Basil Bernstein, ed., *Class, Codes and Control*, 2 vols. (London, 1971), 1: *Theoretical Studies towards a Sociology of Language*. On agricultural societies see Mendenhall, "A History of Agriculture," 228. For surviving records see *The Constitution, Acts and Proceedings of the Black Oak Agricultural Society* (Charleston, 1843); *The Constitution and Bye-Laws of the Pendleton Farmers Society* (Columbia, 1820), Charleston County, South Carolina, Agricultural Society of South Carolina Minutes, 1825–1860; Record of the Proceedings of the Beech Island Agricultural Club, 1846–1862; Darlington Agricultural Society Minutes, 1846–1884; Minutes of the Pendleton Farmers' Society, 1824–1919; and State Agricultural Society, Columbia, Proceedings, 1855–1860 (all typescripts in SCL); William J. Ball Books, Elliott and Gonzales Family Papers, and James R. Sparkman Papers, SHC; Black Oak Agricultural Society Minutes, 1842–1844, 1859, 1861, 1862, SHC; Public Improvements: Agriculture, Governors' Papers, South Carolina Department of Archives and History, Columbia, S.C. See also histories: W. A. Clark, ed., *History of the State Agricultural Society of South Carolina* (Columbia, 1916); C. L. Newmann and J. C. Stribling, *Pendleton Farmers' Society* (Atlanta: Foote & Davies, 1908); Cornelius I. Walker, *A History of Agricultural Society of South Carolina* (Charleston: n.p., 1919); David Doar, *A Sketch of the Agricultural Society of St. James, Santee, South Carolina* (Charleston: Calder-Fladger Co., 1908); William M. Frampton, *The Agricultural Society of South Carolina* (Charleston: n.p., 1931); J. M. Napier, *Historical Sketch of the Darlington County Agricultural Society, 1816–1946* (n.p., 1946); *History of the State Agricultural Society of South Carolina from 1839 to 1845, Inclusive, of the State Agricultural Society of South Carolina from 1855 to 1861, Inclusive, of the State Agricultural and Mechanical Society of South Carolina from 1869 to 1916, Inclusive* (Columbia: R. L. Bryan, 1916).

44. Agricola, "Planters' Clubs," *Southern Agriculturist* 4 (November 1844): 402; "Extracts from an Address Delivered Before the Greenville Agricultural Society in August 1841," *Southern Agriculturist* 2 (January 1842): 27–28.

45. Diary entry, July 5, 1843, Edmund Ruffin Papers, VHS; Hall, *The Story of Soil Conservation*, 28.

46. John S. Brisbane, "An Address Delivered Before the St. Andrews Ashley and Stono Agricultural Association, July 1842," *Southern Agriculturist* 3 (February 1843): 41.

47. Ibid., 42; "Report of the Fishing Creek Agricultural Society," *Southern Agriculturist* 3 (November 1843): 420.

48. See Willie Lee Rose, *Rehearsal for Reconstruction: The Port Royal Experiment* (New York: Oxford University Press, 1964), 117, for a discussion of St. Helena Society; "Second Anniversary of the St. Andrew's, Ashley and Stono Agricultural Association, April 3d, 1844," *Southern Agriculturist* 4 (June 1844): 211.

49. J. P. Barrott, "Address Before the Greenwood Agricultural Society, October 30, 1852," *Farmer and Planter* 4 (January 1853): 8–9.

50. William Elliott, *Address Delivered Before the St. Paul's Agricultural Society, May, 1850* (Charleston, 1850), 4; J. E. Byrd, "Agricultural Prospects," *Farmer and Planter* 2 (May 1851): 54.

51. Calhoun, "Address Delivered Before the State Agricultural Society, November 11th, 1856," *Farmer and Planter* 8 (January 1857): 3–10; Carolina, "Mr. Junius Smith's Letter," *Farmer and Planter* 2 (March 1851): 20.

52. Arthur Simkins, *An Address Before the State Agricultural Society of South Carolina . . . November 1855 at Columbia, S. C.* (Edgefield Court House, S.C., 1855), 7–8; Hammond, *Selections from the Letters and Speeches of the Hon. James H. Hammond* (New York, 1866), 317.

53. Channing, *Crisis of Fear*, summarizes the events of secession in South Carolina. For a specific study of the way the planters of the state dominated the secession convention and won their way see Ralph A. Wooster, *The Secession Conventions of the South* (Princeton: Princeton University Press, 1962), 11–25.

54. William Garrott Brown, quoted in Waldo W. Braden, ed., *Oratory in the Old South* (Baton Rouge: Louisiana State University Press, 1970), 3.

55. Geertz, *The Interpretation of Cultures*, 448. See also Paul Ricoeur, "The Model of the Text: Meaningful Action Considered as a Text," *Social Research* 38 (Autumn 1971): 529–62. Treating texts like behavior has, of course, been the foundation of the work of Kenneth Burke and Quentin Skinner. Rhett, "Agricultural Address," 714.

Culture, Conflict, and Community: The Meaning of Power on an Antebellum Plantation

1. These are land miles. Because of bends in the river the distance from Augusta by water is almost thirty miles. See John Shaw Billings, Land Plat Scrapbook, Hammond-Bryan-Cummings Collection, SCL. I am grateful to Richard Beeman, Vernon Burton, Patricia Guthrie, John Reesman, Charles Rosenberg, Allen Stokes, Tom Terrill, and Janet Tighe for comments and criticisms. I especially appreciate the thoughtful suggestions of Peter Wood.

2. Although Hammond later refers to finding 146 slaves at Silver Bluff, he lists 147 in his initial inventory. James Henry Hammond, December 8, 1831, October 16, 1836, February 23, 1838, Hammond Plantation Diary, 1831–1855, Hammond Family Papers, SCL. The Silver Bluff slaves of 1831 had a sex ratio so even as to suggest vigorous family life on the plantation and were indeed listed by Hammond in family groups. By 1846, as a result of extensive purchasing, Hammond had 213 slaves and by 1860, 333. This made him by far the largest slaveholder in his area and one of the largest in the South, for the 1860 census revealed that only eighty-eight planters in the entire region owned more than 300 slaves. In 1860, 48.7 percent of free families in South Carolina held slaves, the highest percentage of slave owners of any southern state. Approximately 440 South Carolinians owned more than 100 slaves in 1860. See Hammond, "List of Negroes," James Henry Hammond Papers, LC; Lewis C. Gray, *History of Agriculture in the Southern United States to 1860*, 2 vols. (1933; repr. Gloucester, Mass.: Peter Smith, 1958), 1:482–83, and Chalmers Gaston Davidson, *The Last Foray: The South Carolina Planters of 1860: A Sociological Study* (Columbia: University of South Carolina Press, 1971). Hammond left a variety of papers dealing specifically with plantation affairs. See in the Hammond Papers, SCL: Plantation Diary, 1831–1855; Silver Bluff, Cathwood, Cowden & Redcliffe, Plantation Records, 1 January 1856; Redcliffe Journal; Plantation Manual. See in the James Henry Hammond Papers, LC: Plantation Book, Silver Bluff, 1832; Plantation Books 1840–1848, 1849–1858, 1857–1858; and "List of Negroes."

3. See Eugene Genovese, *Roll, Jordan, Roll: The World the Slaves Made* (New York: Pantheon, 1974). Because of the nature of available evidence, existing studies of individual plantations have tended recently to stress the demographic and quantitative rather than the qualitative aspects of slavery. See Richard Dunn, "A Tale of Two Plantations: Slave Life at Mesopotamia in Jamaica and Mount Airy in Virginia, 1799–1828," *William and Mary Quarterly*, 3d ser., 34 (1977): 32–65; Michael Craton, *Searching for the Invisible Man: Slaves and Plantation Life in Jamaica* (Cambridge: Cambridge University

Press, 1978); Michael Craton and James Walvern, A *Jamaica Plantation: The History of Worthy Park, 1670–1970* (Toronto: University of Toronto Press, 1970).

4. James Clark to James Henry Hammond, December 19, 1831, LC; Hammond, December 15 and 16, 1831, Plantation Diary, SCL. Black religious autonomy claimed a significant tradition at Silver Bluff even before this time. Silver Bluff has the distinction of being the site of the first separate black church in America, a Baptist congregation founded in 1773 that moved to Augusta, Georgia, after the Revolution. See Albert J. Raboteau, *Slave Religion: The 'Invisible Institution' in the Antebellum South* (New York: Oxford University Press, 1978), 139–40.

5. Hammond, May 11, 1832, May 3, 1835, April 6, 1845, and October 16, 1845, Plantation Diary, SCL. Hammond refers as well to the existence of a Baptist church on his plantation. See Hammond to A. B. Allen, February 2, 1861, LC.

6. Virginia Clay-Clopton, *A Belle of the Fifties* (New York: Doubleday, Page & Co., 1905), 219–20.

7. Hammond, January 14, 1851, Plantation Diary, SCL.

8. Ibid. See also Hammond to Lewis Tappan, September 6, 1850, LC.

9. Hammond to Mr. Walker, December 27, 1836, LC; Hammond, December 13, 14, and 28, 1831, Plantation Diary, SCL.

10. Hammond, May 16, 1836, May 16, 1838, May 26, 1839, September 14, 1854, Plantation Diary, SCL. See also Hammond to Lewis Tappan, September 6, 1850, LC.

11. Hammond, October 12, 1843, December 26, 1847, Plantation Diary, SCL. See also list of Christmas cash rewards for driver, plough driver, midwife, etc., Plantation Book, 1849–1858, LC.

12. Hammond to Mr. Walker, December 27, 1836, LC; Hammond, May 16, 1854, Plantation Diary, SCL.

13. Hammond to M. C. M. Hammond, October 27, 1854, SCL.

14. Hammond, Plantation Manual, SCL. See another version reprinted from the Hammond Papers, LC, in Willie Lee Rose, ed., *A Documentary History of Slavery in North America* (New York: Oxford University Press, 1976), 345–54. On the role of mercy in transforming power into authority see E. P. Thompson, *Whigs and Hunters: The Origins of the Black Act* (New York: Pantheon, 1975), and Douglas Hay, "Property, Authority and the Criminal Law," in Hay et al., *Albion's Fatal Tree: Crime and Society in Eighteenth-Century England* (New York: Pantheon, 1975).

15. See "Governor Hammond's Instructions to His Overseer," in Rose, *A Documentary History*, 348.

16. Hammond, December 18, 1833, January 9, 1945, March 14, 1846, Plan-

tation Diary, SCL. On hog stealing, see also Hammond's remarks in Record of the Proceedings of the Beech Island Agricultural Club, typescript SCL, April 3, 1847. Despite constant complaints during the 1830s and 1840s about theft of hogs by slaves, Hammond was humiliated when Solon Robinson reported on slave thefts at Silver Bluff in an article for the *American Agriculturist*. Hammond felt Robinson had "scandalized my negroes" as well as his own performance as a master. Embarrassed, Hammond was quick to proclaim to the South's eminent agriculturist Edmund Ruffin, "My negroes rarely steal a hog." In the context of his repeated remarks to the contrary, one can only speculate at Hammond's motivations for this statement. See Hammond to Ruffin, February 8, 1850, Edmund Ruffin Papers, VHS.

17. Hammond, October 15, 1862, Redcliffe Journal, SCL; Hammond, October 16, 1835, Plantation Diary, SCL.

18. Hammond, October 27, 1851, Plantation Diary, SCL; Hammond to William Gilmore Simms, November 2, 1862, LC. Hammond recorded a natural decrease of twelve between 1831 and 1854. On medical treatment of slaves generally, see Todd L. Savitt, *Medicine and Slavery: The Diseases and Health Care of Blacks in Antebellum Virginia* (Urbana: University of Illinois Press, 1978), and Peter Wood, "People's Medicine in the Early South," *Southern Exposure* 6 (1978): 50–53.

19. Hammond, December 6, 1856, Redcliffe Journal, SCL; December 7, 1854, Plantation Diary, SCL; Hammond to M. C. M. Hammond, February 12, 1847, March 3, 1864, LC. Most existing studies of runaways have been based on advertisements for escapees. It is not clear that these individuals represent a random sample of runaways, for return of the more valuable slave would be more eagerly sought. More importantly, however, such sources cannot reveal relationships between escapees and the plantation context from which they fled. For examples of the use of advertisements in the study of runaways, see Gerald W. Mullin, *Flight and Rebellion: Slave Resistance in Eighteenth-Century Virginia* (New York: Oxford University Press, 1972), and Philip Morgan, "Black-White Interaction and Culture Change in Colonial South Carolina," unpublished paper delivered at a Symposium on Language and Culture in South Carolina, Department of Anthropology, University of South Carolina, Columbia, March 1979. See also Morgan, "The Development of Slave Culture in Eighteenth Century Plantation America" (Ph.D. diss., University College, London, 1978), and Lathan A. Windley, "A Profile of Runaway Slaves in Virginia and South Carolina from 1730 through 1787" (Ph.D. diss., University of Iowa, 1974).

20. The size of the population that produced these runaways varied considerably during these years, but increased steadily. In 1846, there were 213 slaves, by 1850, 228, and by 1855, 294. Hammond was fearful lest a habitual

runaway spread a propensity for flight amongst his slaves. "Such notions" as escape, he noted to William Gilmore Simms, "do not soon subside & situated as my people are near the abolition town of Augusta, I remit no precaution to guard their morals in this respect." Hammond to Simms, April 17, 1851, LC.

21. Hammond, July 18, 1832, Plantation Diary, SCL.

22. Hammond, March 14, 1834 and April 27, May 11, June 13 and 17, 1833, Plantation Diary, SCL.

23. Hammond, April 29, 1844, Plantation Diary, SCL; July 7, 1864, Redcliffe Journal, SCL.

24. Hammond, October 17, 1839, February 13, 1834, Plantation Diary, SCL.

25. Hammond, February 19, September 19, and November 5, 1844, Plantation Diary, SCL.

26. Hammond, March 18, 1839 and February 28, 1844, Plantation Diary, SCL. Hammond to John C. Calhoun, May 10, 1844, John C. Calhoun Papers, Clemson University. To a northerner criticizing the ignorance slavery had imposed on southern blacks, Hammond claimed he had a dozen slaves who read as well as he. "They teach each other and I never interfere with it, though it is against the law." Hammond to A. B. Allen, February 2, 1861, LC.

27. Hammond, July 7, 1862, Redcliffe Journal, SCL.

28. Hammond, November 10, 1861, January 30, 1862, August 30 and June 28, 1863, Redcliffe Journal, SCL. Eugene Genovese has explored the response of slaves to the war and justified the apparent "docility" of so many (he estimates 80 percent did not flee) in "The Moment of Truth," *Roll, Jordan, Roll*, 97–112. Because he draws on material from plantation settings all over the South, he is unable to portray wartime behavior in the context of a specific individual pattern of master-slave interaction preceding the outbreak of military conflict. On war and slavery see also Leon Litwack, *Been in the Storm So Long: The Aftermath of Slavery* (New York: Alfred A. Knopf, 1979), and James L. Roark, *Masters without Slaves: Southern Planters in the Civil War and Reconstruction* (New York: Norton, 1977).

29. Catherine Hammond to M. C. M. Hammond, September 3, 1865, SCL. Postbellum tenant records kept by Hammond's sons reveal the continuing presence of many former Hammond slaves. See Tenant Records, 1886–1887, SCL.

30. See John W. Blassingame, *The Slave Community: Plantation Life in the Antebellum South* (New York: Oxford University Press, 1972). Patricia Guthrie suggested to me that the presence of ancestral burial grounds might have been an important force keeping the ex-slaves at Silver Bluff. I have found no evidence of such a cemetery, but it is an interesting and plausible suggestion.

31. On the Sea Island situation in the nineteenth century, see Willie Lee

Rose, *Rehearsal for Reconstruction: The Port Royal Experiment* (Indianapolis: Bobbs-Merrill, 1964). On the twentieth-century Sea Island plantation communities, see Patricia Guthrie, "Fosterage, Adoption and Grandkin Parentage: Options for Securing Household Membership on a South Carolina Sea Island," unpublished paper delivered at a Symposium on Language and Culture in South Carolina, Department of Anthropology, University of South Carolina, Columbia, March 1979, and Guthrie, "Catching Sense: The Meaning of Plantation Membership among Blacks on St. Helena Island, South Carolina" (Ph.D. diss., University of Rochester, 1977).

The Proslavery Argument in History

1. David Donald, "The Proslavery Argument Reconsidered," *Journal of Southern History* 37 (1971): 3. For a useful summary of the extensive literature on abolition, see James Brewer Stewart, *Holy Warriors: The Abolitionists and American Slavery* (New York: Hill and Wang, 1976), and Ronald G. Walters, *The Antislavery Appeal: American Abolitionism after 1830* (Baltimore: Johns Hopkins University Press, 1976).

2. The reference to slavery as the "cornerstone" of the southern social order has most frequently been attributed to an 1861 speech of Alexander Stephens, but contemporary southerners recognized the origin of the phrase in a speech by George McDuffie of 1836. See James Henry Hammond to M. C. M. Hammond, July 23, 1859, James Henry Hammond Papers, LC. For other examples of the use of this concept, see Hammond, "Hammond's Letters on Slavery," in *The Pro-Slavery Argument as Maintained by the Most Distinguished Writers of the Southern States* (Charleston: Walker, Richards & Co., 1852), 111; George Frederick Holmes, "Slavery and Freedom," *Southern Quarterly Review* 1 (1856): 87, 92; Edmund Ruffin, *The Political Economy of Slavery* (Washington: L. Towers, 1857), 5, 23.

3. Holmes, "Slavery and Freedom," 95.

4. Larry Edward Tise, "Proslavery Ideology: A Social and Intellectual History of the Defense of Slavery in America, 1790–1840" (Ph.D. diss., University of North Carolina, 1975), 57.

5. See especially William Sumner Jenkins, *Pro-Slavery Thought in the Old South* (1935; repr. Gloucester, Mass.: Peter Smith, 1960); William B. Hesseltine, "Some New Aspects of the Pro-Slavery Argument," *Journal of Negro History* 21 (1936): 1–15; Kenneth M. Stampp, "An Analysis of T. R. Dew's *Review of the Debate in the Virginia Legislature*," *Journal of Negro History* 27 (1942): 380–87.

6. See Charles A. Beard and Mary R. Beard, *The Rise of American Civiliza-*

tion (New York: Macmillan, 1927); Albert Bushnell Hart, *Slavery and Aboli-tion, 1831–1841* (New York: Harper and Bros., 1906); Clement Eaton, *The Growth of Southern Civilization, 1790–1860* (New York: Harper and Row, 1961).

7. See Tise, "Proslavery Ideology"; Larry Morrison, "The Proslavery Argument in the Early Republic, 1790–1830" (Ph.D. diss., University of Virginia, 1975); Robert McColley, *Slavery in Jeffersonian Virginia* (Urbana: University of Illinois Press, 1964); Frederika Teute Schmidt and Barbara Ripel Wilhelm, "Early Proslavery Petitions in Virginia," *William and Mary Quarterly,* 3d ser., 30 (1973): 133–46; Rena Vassar, "William Knox's Defense of Slavery [1768]," *Proceedings of the American Philosophical Society* 114 (1970): 310–26; Anne C. Loveland, "Richard Furman's 'Questions on Slavery,'" *Baptist History and Heritage* 10 (1975): 177–81; Stephen J. Stein, "George Whitfield on Slavery: Some New Evidence," *Church History* 42 (1973): 243–56; Joseph C. Burke, "The Proslavery Argument and the First Congress," *Duquesne Review* 14 (1969): 3–15; Peter Joseph Albert, "The Protean Institution: The Geography, Economy, and Ideology of Slavery in Post-Revolutionary Virginia" (Ph.D. diss., University of Maryland, 1976). Winthrop Jordan also treats the early appearance of racist ideas in particular in *White over Black: American Attitudes toward the Negro, 1550–1812* (Chapel Hill: University of North Carolina Press, 1968).

8. John Saffin, *A Brief and Candid Answer to a late printed sheet, entitled The Selling of Joseph* (Boston: n.p., 1701).

9. Many scholars have noted northern manifestations of proslavery thought, but this aspect of the argument has not been given much consideration in general treatments until recently. See Adelaide Avery Lyons, "The Religious Defense of Slavery in the North," *Trinity College Historical Society Papers* 13 (1919): 5–34; Henry Clyde Hubbart, "Pro-Southern Influence in the Free West, 1840–1865," *Mississippi Valley Historical Review* 20 (1933): 45–62; Howard C. Perkins, "The Defense of Slavery in the Northern Press on the Eve of the Civil War," *Journal of Southern History* 9 (1943): 501–31; Joel H. Silbey, "Pro-Slavery Sentiment in Iowa, 1836–1861," *Iowa Journal of History* 55 (1957): 289–318; Larry Edward Tise, "The Interregional Appeal of Proslavery Thought: An Ideological Profile of the Antebellum American Clergy," *Plantation Society* 1 (1979): 58–72. See Tise, "Proslavery Ideology," for discussion of the proslavery argument in Britain and the West Indies. For an interesting new comparative perspective, see Peter Kolchin, "In Defense of Servitude: American Proslavery and Russian Proserfdom Arguments, 1760–1860," *American Historical Review* 85, No. 4 (October 1980): 809–27.

10. Wilbur J. Cash, *The Mind of the South* (New York: Alfred Knopf, 1941); Charles G. Sellers, Jr., "The Travail of Slavery," in Charles G. Sellers, ed., *The*

Southerner as American (Chapel Hill: University of North Carolina Press, 1960), 40–71. See also William W. Freehling, *Prelude to Civil War: The Nullification Controversy in South Carolina, 1816–1836* (New York: Harper and Row, 1966), and Ralph E. Morrow, "The Proslavery Argument Revisited," *Mississippi Valley Historical Review* 47 (1961): 79–94.

11. E. N. Elliott to James Henry Hammond, September 15, 1859, in Hammond Papers, LC. Elliott was the editor of *Cotton Is King and Pro-Slavery Arguments* (Augusta: Pritchard, Abbott and Loomis, 1860), a collection of proslavery classics.

12. Joseph Walker to James Henry Hammond, May 20, 1848, in Hammond Papers, LC. Walker published *The Pro-Slavery Argument*, which the Charleston *Courier* (May 26, 1853) greeted as a "thesaurus of facts and arguments" on the slavery question.

13. George Frederick Holmes, "Bledsoe on Liberty and Slavery," *De Bow's Review* 21 (1856): 133.

14. Francis Lieber, quoted in Daniel Walker Hollis, *University of South Carolina: South Carolina College* (Columbia: University of South Carolina Press, 1951), 183.

15. Diary entry, January 29, 1859, in Edmund Ruffin Papers, LC.

16. William Harper, *Memoir on Slavery, read before the Society for the Advancement of Learning at its annual meeting in Columbia, 1837* (Charleston: James S. Burges, 1838), 8; George Fitzhugh to George Frederick Holmes, 1855, in George Frederick Holmes Papers, Manuscript Division, Duke.

17. Holmes, "Slavery and Freedom," 132; Henry Hughes, "New Duties of the South," *Southern Reveille*, November 18, 1854, clipping in Henry Hughes Scrapbook, Mississippi Department of Archives and History, Jackson, Mississippi. This quotation was kindly provided me by Bertram Wyatt-Brown. William J. Grayson to James Henry Hammond, November 3, 1849, in Hammond Papers, LC; George Frederick Holmes, "On Slavery and Christianity," *Southern Quarterly Review* 3 (1843): 252.

18. Donald, "The Proslavery Argument Reconsidered," 12, 11, 12.

19. Tise, "Proslavery Ideology," and "The Interregional Appeal of Proslavery Thought." On proslavery clergy, see also Jack P. Maddex, Jr., "Proslavery Millennialism: Social Eschatology in Antebellum Southern Calvinism," *American Quarterly* 31 (1979): 46–62, and Jack P. Maddex, Jr., " 'The Southern Apostasy' Revisited: The Significance of Proslavery Christianity," *Marxist Perspectives* 2 (Fall 1979): 132–41. See also Drew Gilpin Faust, "A Southern Stewardship: The Intellectual and the Proslavery Argument," *American Quarterly* 31 (1979): 63–80, and Faust, *A Sacred Circle: The Dilemma of the Intellectual in the Old South, 1840–1860* (Baltimore: Johns Hopkins University Press, 1977).

20. Jenkins, *The Proslavery Argument in the Old South;* Donald, "The Proslavery Argument Reconsidered," 4; Eugene Genovese, *The World the Slaveholders Made: Two Essays in Interpretation* (New York: Pantheon, 1969). Genovese's concern with planter "hegemony" has focused fresh interest on ideology in the Old South. Other historians have been influenced by anthropological studies of belief systems to regard ideology in new ways. Anthropologist Clifford Geertz has been especially influential. In the realm of proslavery historiography specifically, see Tise, "Proslavery Ideology"; Faust, *A Sacred Circle;* Kenneth Greenberg, "Revolutionary Ideology and the Proslavery Argument: The Abolition of Slavery in Antebellum South Carolina," *Journal of Southern History* 42 (1976): 365–84.

21. Thomas R. Dew, *Review of the Debate in the Virginia Legislature of 1831 and 1832* (Richmond: T. W. White, 1832). This essay was an expansion of "Abolition of Negro Slavery," *American Quarterly Review* 12 (1832): 189–265, and was later reprinted in *The Pro-Slavery Argument,* 287–490.

22. Genovese, *The World the Slaveholders Made,* 133.

23. E. N. Elliott, "Introduction," in *Cotton Is King,* xii.

24. George Frederick Holmes, "The Failure of Free Societies," *Southern Literary Messenger* 21 (1855): 129.

25. Ibid.; Albert Taylor Bledsoe, "Liberty and Slavery; or, Slavery in the Light of Political Philosophy," in *Cotton Is King,* 274; Charleston *Courier,* May 26, 1853. See chart of personal interactions among slavery's defenders in Faust, "A Southern Stewardship," 68.

26. A. B. Longstreet, *Letters on the Epistle of Paul to Philemon* (Charleston: B. Jenkins, 1845); Howell Cobb, *A Scriptural Examination of the Institution of Slavery in the United States* (Perry, Ga.: Printed for the author, 1856); Thornton Stringfellow, "The Bible Argument, or Slavery in the Light of Divine Revelation," in *Cotton Is King,* 461–546.

27. For the impact of the emergence of "social science" upon the career of one of slavery's defenders, see Neal C. Gillespie, *The Collapse of Orthodoxy: The Intellectual Ordeal of George Frederick Holmes* (Charlottesville: University of Virginia Press, 1972). See also H. G. Duncan and Winnie Leach Duncan, "The Development of Sociology in the Old South," *American Journal of Sociology* 39 (1934): 649–56. Thornton Stringfellow, *Scriptural and Statistical Views in Favor of Slavery* (Richmond: J. W. Randolph, 1856); George Fitzhugh, *Sociology for the South or the Failure of Free Society* (Richmond: A. Morris, 1854); Henry Hughes, *Treatise on Sociology: Theoretical and Practical* (Philadelphia: Lippincott, Grambo and Co., 1854).

28. On the emergence of social science from moral philosophy, see Gladys Bryson, "The Emergence of Social Sciences from Moral Philosophy," *International Journal of Ethics* 42 (1932): 304–23; on moral science, see Donald H.

Meyer, *The Instructed Conscience: The Shaping of the American National Ethic* (Philadelphia: University of Pennsylvania Press, 1972).

29. See Thomas Cooper, "Slavery," *Southern Literary Journal* 1 (1835): 188; James Henry Hammond, "Law of Nature—Natural Rights—Slavery," Tucker-Coleman Papers, Manuscript Department, Earl Gregg Swem Memorial Library, College of William and Mary, Williamsburg, Virginia; J. P. Holcombe, "Is Slavery Consistent with Natural Law?" *Southern Literary Messenger* 27 (1858): 408.

30. William J. Grayson, "The Hireling and the Slave," in Eric L. McKitrick, ed., *Slavery Defended: The Views of the Old South* (Englewood Cliffs, N.J.: Prentice Hall, 1963), 66, 68. On the notion of rights and duties, see W. T. Hamilton, D.D., *The Duties of Masters and Slaves Respectively: Or Domestic Servitude as Sanctioned by the Bible* (Mobile: F. A. Brooks, 1845), and James Henley Thornwell, *The Rights and Duties of Masters: A Sermon Preached at the Dedication of a Church Erected in Charleston for the Benefit and Instruction of the Coloured Population* (Charleston: Walker and James, 1850). On social organicism, see Theodore Dwight Bozeman, "Joseph LeConte: Organic Science and a 'Sociology for the South,'" *Journal of Southern History* 39 (1973): 565–82.

31. Abel P. Upshur, "Domestic Slavery," *Southern Literary Messenger* 5 (1839): 685; James Henry Hammond, Speech in the Senate, March 4, 1858, *Congressional Globe*, 35th Cong., 1st Sess., App., 71.

32. William Harper, "Slavery in the Light of Social Ethics," 569; Hammond, "Hammond's Letters," 122; Nathaniel Beverley Tucker, *A Series of Lectures on the Science of Government Intended to Prepare the Student for the Study of the Constitution of the United States* (Philadelphia: Carey and Hart, 1845), 349.

33. On these changes, see Charles C. Gillespie, *Genesis and Geology* (Cambridge: Harvard University Press, 1951); Theodore Dwight Bozeman, *Protestants in an Age of Science: The Baconian Ideal and Antebellum American Religious Thought* (Chapel Hill: University of North Carolina Press, 1977); Charles E. Rosenberg, *No Other Gods: On Science and Social Thought in America* (Baltimore: Johns Hopkins University Press, 1976).

34. Samuel Cartwright to William S. Forwood, March 24, 1858, in William S. Forwood Papers, Trent Collection, Duke Medical Library, Duke University, Durham, North Carolina.

35. Samuel Cartwright to William S. Forwood, February 13, 1861, in William S. Forwood Papers.

36. Josiah C. Nott, *Two Lectures on the Connection Between the Biblical and Physical History of Man* (1849; repr. New York: Negro Universities Press, 1969), 7, 14.

37. S. W. Butler to W. S. Forwood, June 26, 1857, in Forwood Papers. Like

many of Nott's nineteenth-century readers, William Stanton also failed to distinguish between Nott's anticlericalism and antireligionism and greatly overstated the level of conflict between religion and science in the 1850s. Nevertheless, Stanton's study of the rise of ethnology is the most complete to date. See *The Leopard's Spots: Scientific Attitudes toward Race in America, 1815–1859* (Chicago: University of Chicago Press, 1960). For the attack upon Nott, see Moses Ashley Curtis, "The Unity of the Races," *Southern Quarterly Review* 7 (1845): 372–448, and John Bachman, *The Doctrine of the Unity of the Human Race Examined on the Principles of Science* (Charleston: C. Canning, 1850). Note that Bachman, a Lutheran clergyman, invoked the "principles of science."

38. George Frederick Holmes to Daniel Whitaker, September 25, 1844, in George Frederick Holmes Letterbook, Holmes Papers; Diary entry, January 10, 1864, Edmund Ruffin Papers, LC; George Fitzhugh, "Southern Thought," *De Bow's Review* 13 (1857): 347.

39. In a recent reassessment of proslavery thought, historian George Fredrickson has portrayed the role of racial defenses quite differently, proclaiming the existence of significant opposition between racial and moral-philosophical rationalizations for the South's system of human bondage. Instead of proslavery unity, he found two distinct proslavery arguments, one in the aristocratic seaboard South and one in the more democratic Southwest. These latter egalitarian areas, he asserted, were unsympathetic to the hierarchical views of slavery's moral-philosophical defenders; racial arguments could provide the only convincing foundation for human bondage within the Old Southwest's "herrenvolk democracy." There is little evidence for these geographical differences in proslavery sentiment. A best-selling collection of defenses of slavery edited by E. N. Elliott of Mississippi included the most famous hierarchical arguments and emphasized the consistency of all proslavery thought; eastern apologists devoted considerable attention to racial justifications in their own tracts; seaboard and southwestern defenders exchanged pamphlets and essays and eagerly sought each other's advice. Fredrickson may err in regarding the mainstream proslavery position as uncongenial to the more democratic Southwest. As early as 1936, William B. Hesseltine made a convincing case that proslavery was motivated in large part by a desire to promote the loyalty of nonslaveholding whites, and he contended that all proslavery theories were designed to be attractive to these common folk. Even though the arguments "carried but little promise to the lower classes," he remarked, "[they] sufficed to draw a line of demarkation between the exploited groups of the South." The complex factors that kept the southern yeoman loyal to the region's master class may also have attracted them to the proslavery argument. Slavery, its defenders insisted, made republicanism and white freedom possible. Because blacks served as the necessary "mud-sill"

class, whites all enjoyed enhanced liberty. George M. Fredrickson, *The Black Image in the White Mind: The Debate on Afro-American Character and Destiny, 1817–1914* (New York: Harper and Row, 1971); William B. Hesseltine, "Some New Aspects of the Pro-Slavery Argument," 11. On the position of the yeoman, see Eugene Genovese, "Yeoman Farmers in a Slaveholders Democracy," *Agricultural History* 49 (1975): 331–42.

40. E. N. Elliott, "Concluding Remarks," in *Cotton Is King*, 897; "Critical Notices," *Southern Quarterly Review* 16 (1849): 265; Holmes, "Slavery and Freedom," 65.

41. George Fitzhugh to George Frederick Holmes, March 27, 1855, in Holmes Papers; Robert Walsh, *An Appeal from the Judgments of Great Britain Respecting the United States of America* (Philadelphia: Mitchell, Ames and White, 1819).

42. George Fitzhugh to George Frederick Holmes, 1855, in Holmes Papers.

43. Diary entry, February 21, 1857, George Frederick Holmes Papers; Diary entry, October 26, 1858, Edmund Ruffin Papers, LC.

44. Donald, "The Proslavery Argument Reconsidered," 3.

45. Arthur C. Cole presents evidence for the direct influence of Fitzhugh on Lincoln's "house divided" speech. See Cole, *Lincoln's House Divided Speech* (Chicago: University of Chicago Press, 1923).

46. Genovese, *The World the Slaveholders Made*, 129. Part of Genovese's attraction to Fitzhugh arises, of course, from the hostility to capitalism that this Marxist historian shares with the nineteenth-century southerner.

47. Diary entry, October 21, 1858, Edmund Ruffin Papers, LC.

48. The nature of this conflict between tradition and modernity has been a central concern in the extensive historical literature on the nineteenth-century North, especially on evangelicalism and reform. For two examples, see Marvin Meyers, *The Jacksonian Persuasion* (Stanford: Stanford University Press, 1960), and Clifford S. Griffin, *Their Brothers Keepers: Moral Stewardship in the United States, 1800–1865* (New Brunswick: Rutgers University Press, 1960).

Christian Soldiers: The Meaning of Revivalism in the Confederate Army

1. "Rev. A. E. Dickinson's Annual Report to the General Association of Va.," *Confederate Baptist*, June 24, 1863. I would like to thank the Stanford Humanities Center, the several audiences who made helpful comments on preliminary versions of this paper, and especially Lizabeth Cohen, Steven

Hahn, Randall Miller, Reid Mitchell, Charles Rosenberg, and Morton Sosna for their suggestions and criticism.

2. For example, James M. McPherson's excellent recent overview of the war does not mention the revivals. See *Ordeal by Fire: The Civil War and Reconstruction* (New York: Alfred A. Knopf, 1982). The best discussion of the revivals is still Bell Irvin Wiley, "Consolations of the Spirit," in *The Life of Johnny Reb: The Common Soldier of the Confederacy* (1943; repr. Baton Rouge: Louisiana State University Press, 1978), but in my view Wiley underestimates their significance. See also Gorrell Clinton Prim, Jr., "Born Again in the Trenches: Revivalism in the Confederate Army" (Ph.D. diss., Florida State University, 1982), for a recent but largely unanalytical account. Equally unanalytical are G. Clinton Prim, Jr., "Revivals in the Armies of Mississippi during the Civil War," *Journal of Mississippi History* 44 (August 1982): 227–34; Herman Norton, "Revivalism in the Confederate Armies," *Civil War History* 6 (December 1960): 410–24; John Shepard, Jr., "Religion in the Army of Northern Virginia," *North Carolina Historical Review* 25 (July 1948): 341–76; Sidney J. Romero, *Religion in the Rebel Ranks* (Lanham, Md.: University Press of America, 1983); and Benjamin Rice Lacy, Jr., *Revivals in the Midst of the Years* (Richmond: John Knox Press, 1943). Two accounts published shortly after the war by participants are useful. See J. Wm. Jones, *Christ in the Camp: or Religion in Lee's Army* (Richmond, 1887); and William W. Bennett, *A Narrative of the Great Revival in the Southern Armies . . .* (Philadelphia, 1877). A work that appeared after the completion of this essay deals in some detail with the role of religion during the war, although it does not devote particular attention to its significance in the Confederate army. See Richard E. Beringer, Herman Hattaway, Archer Jones, and William N. Still, Jr., *Why the South Lost the Civil War* (Athens: University of Georgia Press, 1986). For my reservations about their viewpoint see Drew Gilpin Faust, "Reassessing the Lost Cause of the South," *Books/Leisure* section, *Philadelphia Inquirer,* June 29, 1986, pp. 1, 8–9.

3. For a useful overview of this literature see Leonard I. Sweet, "The Evangelical Tradition in America," in Leonard I. Sweet, ed., *The Evangelical Tradition in America* (Macon, Ga.: Mercer University Press, 1984), 1–86.

4. See Donald G. Mathews, *Religion in the Old South* (Chicago: University of Chicago Press, 1977); Samuel S. Hill, Jr., *The South and the North in American Religion* (Athens: University of Georgia Press, 1980); John B. Boles, *The Great Revival, 1787–1805: The Origins of the Southern Evangelical Mind* (Lexington: University of Kentucky Press, 1972); Anne C. Loveland, *Southern Evangelicals and the Social Order, 1800–1860* (Baton Rouge: Louisiana State University Press, 1980); Dickson D. Bruce, Jr., *And They All Sang Hallelujah: Plain-Folk Camp-Meeting Religion, 1800–1845* (Knoxville: University of Tennessee Press, 1974); Drew Gilpin Faust, ed., *The Ideology of Slavery: Proslavery Thought in the Ante-*

bellum South, 1830–1860 (Baton Rouge: Louisiana State University Press, 1981); James W. Silver, *Confederate Morale and Church Propaganda* (Tuscaloosa: University of Alabama Press, 1957); and William A. Clebsch, "Christian Interpretations of the Civil War," *Church History* 30 (June 1961): 212–22. On the Civil War as total war see T. Harry Williams, *The History of American Wars from 1745–1918* (New York: Alfred A. Knopf, 1981); Russell F. Weigley, *The American Way of War: A History of United States Military Strategy and Policy* (New York: Macmillan, 1973); and Jay Luvaas, *The Military Legacy of the Civil War: The European Inheritance* (Chicago: University of Chicago Press, 1959). On evangelicalism as a vehicle of national organization and integration see Donald G. Mathews, "The Second Great Awakening as an Organizing Process, 1780–1830: An Hypothesis," *American Quarterly* 21 (Spring 1969): 23–43.

5. Jones, *Christ in the Camp*, 336. For examples of early reports of conversions see *Religious Herald*, August 29, September 12, and October 17, 1861; April 17, June 5, and August 21, 1862. See Jones, *Christ in the Camp*, 535–624; Lacy, *Revivals*, 119; James Cooper Nisbet, *Four Years on the Firing Line*, ed. Bell Irvin Wiley (1914; repr. Jackson, Tenn.: McCowat-Mercer Press, 1963), 175; "Great Trans-Mississippi Revival," *Southern Christian Advocate*, August 25, 1864; and *Confederate Baptist*, June 1, 1864. Jones, *Christ in the Camp*, 390. For an assessment of different estimates of numbers of converts see Herman Norton, *Rebel Religion: The Story of Confederate Chaplains* (St. Louis: BeMany Press, 1961), 64.

6. Jones, *Christ in the Camp*, 33–34; John Kent Folmar, ed., *From That Terrible Field: Civil War Letters of James M. Williams, Twenty-first Alabama Infantry Volunteers* (University, Ala.: Alabama University Press, 1981), 13; Anne King Gregorie, ed., "Diary of Captain Joseph Julius Westcoat, 1863–1865," *South Carolina Historical Magazine* 49 (January 1958): 13. See also J. Charles Mundy to Beverly Preston Morriss, September 28, 1863, Beverly Preston Morriss Papers, Duke; and George W. Cherry to Dear Sister, October 7, 1863, Lunceford R. Cherry Papers, Duke.

7. Jones, *Christ in the Camp*, 504. See also the preaching schedule of John DeWitt McCollough, March-May, 1862, Journal, John DeWitt McCollough Papers, SCL.

8. *Christian Observer*, January 26, 1865; John H. Worsham, *One of Jackson's Foot Cavalry* . . . , ed. James I. Robertson, Jr. (1912; repr. Jackson, Tenn.: McCowat-Mercer Press, 1964), 113–14; *Religious Herald*, February 11, 1864, October 10, 1861; R. S. Webb to his mother, April 16, 1864, Webb Family Papers, SHC; *Central Presbyterian*, April 2, 1863. See also Samuel P. Lockhart to Ellen Lockhart, March 14, 1864, Hugh Conway Browning Papers, Duke.

9. *Confederate Baptist*, May 16, 1863; *Religious Herald*, May 8, 1862, October

10, 1861; James W. Silver, ed., *A Life for the Confederacy, as Recorded in the Pocket Diaries of Pvt. Robert A. Moore* . . . (Jackson, Tenn.: McCowat-Mercer Press, 1959), 95. On tracts see Romero, *Religion in the Rebel Ranks*, 163; Silver, *Confederate Morale and Church Propaganda*; and Wiley, *The Life of Johnny Reb*, 177. Much of the research for this paper was made possible by the availability on microfilm of almost all surviving Confederate tracts and sermons as well as most other extant printed Confederate material. See *Confederate Imprints* (New Haven: Research Publications, 1974).

10. *Religious Herald*, April 8, 1864. On the lack of religious fervor on the home front see "Revivals at Home," *Southern Christian Advocate*, September 8, 1864; *Biblical Recorder*, June 17, 1863; *Army and Navy Messenger*, March 1, 1864; William Flinn to William Letcher Mitchell, April 24, 1863, William Letcher Mitchell Papers, SHC.

11. John G. Nicolay and John Hay, eds., *Complete Works of Abraham Lincoln*, 12 vols. (New York: Francis D. Tandy, 1905), 8:29–30. On comparison with religion in the northern armies see Bell Irvin Wiley, *The Life of Billy Yank: The Common Soldier of the Union* (New York: Bobbs-Merrill, 1952); William Warren Sweet, *Methodism in American History* (New York: Methodist Book Concern, 1933), 287.

12. [Mrs. Frances Blake Brockenbrough], *A Mother's Parting Words to her Soldier Boy* (Petersburg, Va., [186-]), 3, 5; *Are You a Soldier?* (n.p., n.d.), 1; Charles Colcock Jones to Charles Colcock Jones, Jr., March 24, 1862, in Robert Manson Myers, ed., *The Children of Pride: A True Story of Georgia and the Civil War* (New Haven: Yale University Press, 1972), 866; *Confederate Baptist*, July 6, 1864, December 17, 1862; *The Open Sepulchre* (Charlotte, N.C., 1864), 2. See also Drury Lacy, *Address Delivered at the General Military Hospital, Wilson, N.C.* (Fayetteville, N.C., 1863), 7.

13. Silver, ed., *A Life for the Confederacy*, 83; William C. Childers, ed., "A Virginian's Dilemma: The Civil War Diary of Isaac Noyes Smith . . . Sept. to Nov., 1861," *West Virginia History* 27 (April 1966): 184, 199; *Religious Herald*, June 20, 1861; *Biblical Recorder*, June 19, 1861; Jones, *Christ in the Camp*, 271.

14. *Proceedings of the Ninth Biennial Session, of the Southern Baptist Convention . . . Augusta, Ga., 1863* (Macon, Ga., 1863), 54; Jones, *Christ in the Camp*, 555; *Religious Herald*, May 16, 1861; Ja[me]s. McGready, *An Appeal to the Young* (Raleigh, [186-]), 2; Donald M. Scott, *From Office to Profession: The New England Ministry, 1750–1850* (Philadelphia: University of Pennsylvania Press, 1978), 37; T. C. Teasdale, *The Season of Divine Mercy* (Raleigh, [186-]), 6; *Religious Herald*, March 14, 1861; B. W. McDonnald, *Address to Chaplains and Missionaries* (Petersburg, Va., 1863), 2, 3. Almost two out of three church members in the Old South were women; see Mathews, *Religion in the Old South*, 47; John E[llis]. Edwards, *The Wounded Soldier* (Raleigh, [186-]), 5. On adolescence

and conversion see Carl W. Christensen, "Religious Conversion," *Archives of General Psychiatry* 9 (September 1963): 210.

15. McDonnald, *Address to Chaplains and Missionaries*, 8, 13.

16. Jones, *Christ in the Camp*, 360, 365; *Southern Presbyterian*, June 25, 1863; *Southern Churchman*, December 18, 1863; *Biblical Recorder*, December 9, 1863 and February 5, 1862; T. Conn Bryan, ed., "Letters of Two Confederate Officers: William Thomas Conn and Charles Augustus Conn," *Georgia Historical Quarterly* 46 (June 1962): 177; Stephen Cocke to Charles T. Quintard, April 25, 1863, and William Bennett to Charles T. Quintard, March 25, 1863, Charles Todd Quintard Papers, Duke; "The Office of Evangelist," *Central Presbyterian*, April 3, 1862; Joseph T. Durkin, ed., *Confederate Chaplain: A War Journal of Rev. James B. Sheeran, . . . 14th Louisiana, C.S.A.* (Milwaukee: Bruce Publishing Co., 1960), 57; *Confederate Baptist*, May 20, 1863. Episcopalians and Presbyterians expressed some doubts about evangelical fervor but were for the most part won over by the revivals' power and effectiveness. See William S. Lacy to Bessie L. Dewey, September 23, 1863, Drury Lacy Papers, SHC; and Diary entry, March 16, 1863, Abner Crump Hopkins Papers, VHS. As one Episcopal paper rationalized, "Anything is better than the quietness of moral death" (*Southern Churchman*, June 5, 1863). Some members of the more literalistic denominations indicated concern about the doctrinal compromises implicit in cooperation. See for example *Biblical Recorder*, July 30, 1862, December 9, 1863, January 16 and October 19, 1864. On hostility to chaplains see *Confederate Baptist*, November 4, 1863; and R. S. Webb to his mother, February 13, 1864, Webb Family Papers. On lobbying for improved status see for example *Southern Christian Advocate*, February 19, 1863; and *Central Presbyterian*, January 11, 1862. On chaplains generally see W. Harrison Daniel, "An Aspect of Church and State Relations in the Confederacy: Southern Protestantism and the Office of Army Chaplain," *North Carolina Historical Review* 36 (January 1959): 47–71; Frank L. Hieronymus, "For Now and Forever: The Chaplains of the Confederate States Army" (Ph.D. diss., University of California-Los Angeles, 1964); Bell Irvin Wiley, " 'Holey Joes' of the Sixties: A Study of Civil War Chaplains," *Huntington Library Quarterly* 16 (May 1953): 287–304; Sidney J. Romero, "The Confederate Chaplain," *Civil War History* 1 (June 1955): 127–40; Romero, *Religion in the Rebel Ranks*; James W. Silver, "The Confederate Preacher Goes to War," *North Carolina Historical Review* 33 (October 1956): 499–509; Norton, *Rebel Religion*; Charles Frank Pitts, *Chaplains in Gray: The Confederate Chaplains' Story* (Nashville: Broadman Press, 1957); Arthur Howard Noll, *Doctor Quintard: Chaplain C.S.A. and Second Bishop of Tennessee* (Sewanee, Tenn.: University of the South, 1905); Joseph Cross, *Camp and Field: Papers from the Portfolio of an Army Chaplain* (Macon, Ga., 1864); Donald E. Everett, ed., *Chaplain Davis and Hood's Texas*

Brigade . . . (1863; repr. San Antonio, Principia Press, 1962); Randolph H. McKim, *A Soldier's Recollections: Leaves from the Diary of a Young Confederate* (New York: Longmans, Green, 1921); A. D. Betts, *Experiences of a Confederate Chaplain, 1861–1864*, ed. W. A. Betts (n.p., n.d.); Durkin, ed., *Confederate Chaplain*; Jones, *Christ in the Camp*; and Bennett, *A Narrative of the Great Revival*.

17. Bennett, *A Narrative of the Great Revival*, 246; Jones, *Christ in the Camp*, 272; *Religious Herald*, August 21, 1862; Addams to Dear Brother, January 5, 1863, William Miller McAllister Papers, Duke; *Central Presbyterian*, November 6, 1862; *Religious Herald*, October 23 and November 27, 1862; *Biblical Recorder*, September 2, 1863; *Camp Nineveh* (Petersburg, Va., [186-]); Everett, ed., *Chaplain Davis*, 107. On conversions after the Wilderness see *Southern Christian Advocate*, July 28, 1864. On Antietam see Stephen W. Sears, *Landscape Turned Red: The Battle of Antietam* (New York: Ticknor & Fields, 1983). Wiley overlooks these 1862 outbursts but emphasizes the significance of Gettysburg in the 1863 revivals. Wiley, *The Life of Johnny Reb*, 174–91.

18. *Confederate Baptist*, April 6, 1864; Mat[hew]. A[ndrew]. Dunn to Nora, August 22, 1864, in Weymouth T. Jordan, ed., "Mathew Andrew Dunn Letters," *Journal of Mississippi History* 1 (April 1939): 110–26 (second quotation on p. 125); Jones, *Christ in the Camp*, 245; *Religious Herald*, September 3, 1863.

19. *Confederate Baptist*, November 4, 1863 (first quotation). David Lang to Cousin Annie, September 13, 1863, in Bertram H. Groene, ed., "Civil War Letters of Colonel David Lang," *Florida Historical Quarterly* 54 (January 1976): 359. See also *Religious Herald*, November 5, 1863 and August 21, 1862. Cromwell's army was frequently cited as evidence of the military effectiveness of religion; see *Religious Herald*, July 31, 1862. Note the observation of one officer who felt that a town regiment was always twice as efficient as one from the country (cited in Horace H. Cunningham, *Field Medical Services at the Battle of Manassas [Bull Run]* [Athens: University of Georgia Press, 1968], 25).

20. Jones, *Christ in the Camp*, 501, 465–66: Durkin, ed., *Confederate Chaplain*, 50–51; *Confederate Baptist*, May 16, 1863; *Religious Herald*, August 21, 1862 (quotation). On religion and officers see also Thomas Hart Law, July 20, 1863, Journal, Thomas Hart Law Papers, SCL; and William S. Lacy to Bessie L. Dewey, September 23, 1863, Lacy Papers. Other religious generals included Leonidas L. Polk, John B. Gordon, Daniel H. Hill, Ambrose P. Hill, John B. Hood, and Joseph E. Johnston.

21. James S. Beavers to Isham Sims Upchurch, July 2, 1861, Isham Sims Upchurch Papers, Duke. On discipline see David Donald, "Died of Democracy," in David Donald, ed., *Why the North Won the Civil War* (Baton Rouge: Louisiana State University Press, 1960), 77–90; Everett, ed., *Chaplain Davis*, 150–51; also Jefferson Davis's call for greater discipline, quoted in the *Confed-*

erate Baptist, November 12, 1862; and "Address of General D[aniel]. H[arvey]. Hill, Reunion of the Virginia Division Army of Northern Virginia Association," *Southern Historical Society Papers* 13 (January-December 1885), 261. The Confederate army contained a significantly greater proportion of previously masterless men than did the northern army. By 1870, when the first complete occupational census was taken, 60 to 70 percent of the northern labor force worked under masters. Agricultural areas of the North, and the white South generally, averaged well below this. Daniel T. Rodgers, *The Work Ethic in Industrial America, 1850–1920* (Chicago: University of Chicago Press, 1978), 37. See also David Montgomery, *Beyond Equality: Labor and the Radical Republicans, 1862–1872* (New York: Alfred A. Knopf, 1967), 30; and Eric Foner, *Free Soil, Free Labor, Free Men: The Ideology of the Republican Party before the Civil War* (New York: Oxford University Press, 1970), 32. Both the less detailed 1860 census (which lacks complete occupational data) and data collected by Bell Wiley indicate marked prewar differentials as well. Also note that 20 percent of the Confederate army was made up of draftees and substitutes as compared with 8 percent of the Union forces; see McPherson, *Ordeal by Fire*, 359, 182. On the devotion of the southern common people to their personal independence see J. Mills Thornton III, *Politics and Power in a Slave Society: Alabama, 1800–1860* (Baton Rouge: Louisiana State University Press, 1978); and Steven Hahn, *The Roots of Southern Populism: Yeoman Farmers and the Transformation of the Georgia Upcountry, 1850–1890* (New York: Oxford University Press, 1983).

22. E. P. Thompson, *The Making of the English Working Class* (New York: Pantheon, 1963); "Time, Work-Discipline, and Industrial Capitalism," *Past and Present* 38 (December 1967): 56–97; Anthony F. C. Wallace, *Rockdale: The Growth of an American Village in the Early Industrial Revolution* (New York: Alfred A. Knopf, 1978); Élie Halévy, *Histoire du peuple anglais au XIXe siecle* (Paris: Librairie Hachette, 1913). Daniel T. Rodgers, "Tradition, Modernity, and the American Industrial Worker: Reflections and Critique," *Journal of Interdisciplinary History* 7 (Spring 1977): 656; Herbert G. Gutman, *Work, Culture, and Society in Industrializing America: Essays in American Working-Class and Social History* (New York: Alfred A. Knopf, 1976); Bruce Tucker, "Class and Culture in Recent Anglo-American Religious Historiography: A Review Essay," *Labour/Le Travailleur* 6 (Autumn 1980): 159–69; *Religious Herald*, July 31, 1862; *Biblical Recorder*, July 10, 1861. See also *Central Presbyterian*, February 6, 1862; *Christian Observer*, June 30, 1864; *Army and Navy Messenger*, May 1, 1863. On the weakness of the work ethic in the South see C. Vann Woodward, "The Southern Ethic in a Puritan World," in *American Counterpoint: Slavery and Racism in the North-South Dialogue* (Boston: Little, Brown, 1971), especially 29 and 42. As E. P. Thompson has noted the relevance of

timepieces to industrial work, David Landes has similarly related their development and dissemination to industrialized warfare. David S. Landes, *Revolution in Time: Clocks and the Making of the Modern World* (Cambridge: Harvard University Press, 1983).

23. W. H. Christian, *The Importance of a Soldier Becoming a Christian* (Richmond, [186-]), 3; Jones, *Christ in the Camp*, 380–81; *North Carolina Presbyterian*, August 4, 1862; *Confederate Baptist*, July 6, 1864 and May 16, 1863. On the religious cure for desertion see John Paris, *A Sermon: Preached Before Brig.-Gen. Hoke's Brigade, . . . Upon the Death of Twenty-Two Men . . . Executed in the Presence of the Brigade for the Crime of Desertion* (Greensborough, N.C., 1864), 12. On the severe military problem presented by persistent straggling see *The War of the Rebellion: A Compilation of the Official Records of the Union and Confederate Armies* 70 vols. (Washington: GPO, 1880–1901), ser. 1, vol. 19, pt. 1, 1026; and Worsham, *One of Jackson's Foot Cavalry*, 151.

24. R. N. Sledd, *A Sermon; Delivered in the Market Street M. E. Church, Petersburg, Va., Before the Confederate Cadets, on the Occasion of Their Departure for the Seat of War, Sunday, Sept. 22d, 1861* (Petersburg, 1861), 14; *Religious Herald*, April 23 and June 11, 1863.

25. T. J. Koger, June 22, 1862, quoted in John K. Bettersworth, ed., *Mississippi in the Confederacy: As They Saw It* (Baton Rouge: Louisiana State University Press, 1961), 346. See also the volunteer cavalry colonel who early in the war resigned because of "the uncontrollable wickedness of soldiers in camp." John N. Waddel, *Memorials of Academic Life: Being an Historical Sketch of the Waddel Family* (Richmond, 1891), 398; A. Curtis to Matthias Murray Marshall, December 20, 1862, Matthias Murray Marshall Papers, Duke; Samuel P. Lockhart to Emeline Lockhart, May 11 and July 27, 1862, Browning Papers; Unidentified to Dear Willie on back of Dr. G. McAllister to Dear Clara, October 26, 1861, McAllister Papers.

26. *Religious Herald*, February 23, 1865; Rhys Isaac, *The Transformation of Virginia, 1740–1790* (Chapel Hill: University of North Carolina Press, 1982); Bertram Wyatt-Brown, "The Antimission Movement in the Jacksonian South: A Study in Regional Folk Culture," *Journal of Southern History* 36 (November 1970), 522. In this article Wyatt-Brown details the prewar resistance among many of the southern lower orders to attempts to impose evangelical order from above. On class divisions in antebellum southern religion see also Wayne Flynt, "One in the Spirit, Many in the Flesh: Southern Evangelicals," in David Edwin Harrell, Jr., ed., *Varieties of Southern Evangelicalism* (Macon, Ga.: Mercer University Press, 1981), 25. See *Confederate Baptist* diatribes against dueling, December 3, 1862, and April 29, 1863; on reading see for example Jordan, ed., "Mathew Andrew Dunn Letters," 116; and Jones, *Christ in the Camp*, 363, 500. On hostility to evangelicalism see Folmar, ed., *From That*

Terrible Field, 13; Wiley, "'Holey Joes,'" 291, 294; *The Christian Sergeant* (Richmond, [186-]). On similar complexity in the relationship between evangelicalism and class in the North see Paul E. Johnson, *A Shopkeeper's Millennium: Society and Revivals in Rochester, New York, 1815–1837* (New York: Hill & Wang, 1978).

27. *Religious Herald*, quoted in E. M. Boswell, "Rebel Religion," *Civil War Times Illustrated* 11 (October 1972): 28; *A Kind Word to the Officers of our Army* (Charleston, [186-]), 2; *Soldier's Paper*, February 15, 1864; *Confederate Baptist*, October 21, 1863; Addams to Dear Brother, June 12, 1862, McAllister Papers; *Confederate Baptist*, April 8, 1863. For an outstanding treatment of the role of class in the Confederacy see Armstead Louis Robinson, "Day of Jubilo: Civil War and the Demise of Slavery in the Mississippi Valley, 1861–1865" (Ph.D. diss., University of Rochester, 1977).

28. *Swearing* (Raleigh, [186-]), 2; the same phrase appears also in [Jabez Lamar Monroe Curry], *Swearing* (Raleigh, [186-]), 2; [Brockenbrough], *A Mother's Parting Words*, 5; D[aniel]. R. Hundley, *Social Relations in Our Southern States* (1860; repr. Baton Rouge: Louisiana State University Press, 1979), 226, 239–40. Also see literary treatments of antebellum southern language in which swearing is restricted to a particular, often morally depraved segment of the lower class, or, as in William Gilmore Simms's *Woodcraft*, soldiers (*Woodcraft, or Hawks about the Dovecote: A Story of the South at the Close of the Revolution* [New York, 1854]). See also A. B. Longstreet, "Georgia Theatrics," and "The Flight," in *Georgia Scenes: Characters, Incidents . . . in the First Half Century of the Republic* (1835; repr. Gloucester, Mass.: Peter Smith, 1970); Merrill Maguire Skaggs, *The Folk of Southern Fiction* (Athens: University of Georgia Press, 1972), 23; and Shields McIlwaine, *The Southern Poor-White from Lubberland to Tobacco Road* (Norman: University of Oklahoma Press, 1939), 50.

29. Sylvanus Landrum, *The Battle is God's* (Savannah, 1863), 12; R[obert]. L[ewis]. Dabney, *Swear Not* (Petersburg, Va., 1863), 1; *Southern Christian Advocate*, February 5, 1863; *Profane Swearing* (Charlotte, N.C., 1864), 3; J[eremiah]. B[ell]. Jeter, *Don't Swear!* (Raleigh, [186-]), 1; *Why Do You Do It?* (Richmond, [186-]), 1; J. N. Andrews, *Why Do You Swear?* (Raleigh, [186-]), 6; J. C. Mitchell, *A Sermon Delivered in the Government Street Church* (Mobile, 1861), 20. See also *The Bold Blasphemer. A Narrative of Facts* (Richmond, [186-]); B[enjamin]. M[organ]. Palmer, *National Responsibility Before God* (New Orleans, 1861); Sam'l Barnett, *The Tongue* (Richmond, [186-]); *The Silly Fish* (Columbia, S.C., [186-]); and "Profane Swearing," *Biblical Recorder*, August 20, 1862. On the social role of swearing see K. C. Phillipps, *Language and Class in Victorian England* (New York: Blackwell, 1984), 54; Robert Graves, *Lars Porsena: Or the Future of Swearing and Improper Language* (New York: E. P. Dutton, 1927), 37 n.; Ashley Montagu, *The Anatomy of Swearing* (New York:

Macmillan, 1967), 224, 226, 237; Henry Cecil Wyld, *A History of Modern Colloquial English* (1920; repr. Oxford: Basil Blackwell, 1936), 386; Eric Partridge, *Words at War, Words at Peace: Essays on Language in General and Particular Words* (1948; repr. Freeport, N.Y.: Books for Libraries Press, 1970).

30. Eric J. Leed, *No Man's Land: Combat & Identity in World War I* (Cambridge: Cambridge University Press, 1979), 94; John O. Casler, *Four Years in the Stonewall Brigade*, ed. James I. Robertson, Jr. (1893; repr. Dayton, Ohio: Morningside Book Publishers, 1971), 291; Rodgers, *The Work Ethic in Industrial America*, 32; *The Sentinel* (Petersburg, Va., 1861), 1.

31. See Adam to Harriet C. Lewis, November 1, 1864, Harriet C. Lewis Papers, Duke; James N. Riddle to Dear Sisters, August 11, 1863, James N. Riddle Papers, Duke. On social control and religion see Lois W. Banner, "Religious Benevolence as Social Control: A Critique of an Interpretation," *Journal of American History* 60 (June 1973): 23–41. On opposition to evangelicalism see Wyatt-Brown, "Antimission Movement," and Flynt, "One in the Spirit, Many in the Flesh," 23–44.

32. *The Sentinel*, 1; Thompson, *The Making of the English Working Class*, 354–55; Eugene D. Genovese, *Roll, Jordan, Roll: The World the Slaves Made* (New York: Pantheon, 1974).

33. For an excellent portrait of the quality of the evangelical community see Isaac, *The Transformation of Virginia*, 161–72; *Religious Herald*, September 3, 1863.

34. On the importance of the primary group in battle see S. L. A. Marshall, *Men against Fire: The Problem of Battle Command in Future War* (New York: William Morrow, 1947); Richard A. Gabriel and Paul L. Savage, *Crisis in Command: Mismanagement in the Army* (New York: Hill & Wang, 1978); and Anthony Kellett, *Combat Motivation: The Behavior of Soldiers in Battle* (Boston: Kluwer-Nishoff, 1982). For a sensitive consideration of the place of religion in another army see Charles Royster, *A Revolutionary People at War: The Continental Army and American Character, 1775–1783* (Chapel Hill: University of North Carolina Press, 1979), 13–23. *Constitution, By-Laws, and Catalogue of Members of the Christian Association of the Stonewall Brigade* (Richmond, 1864), 2; *Religious Herald*, June 4, 1863. See also Edmund Cody Burnett, ed., "Letters of a Confederate Surgeon: Dr. Abner Embry McGarity, 1862–1865," *Georgia Historical Quarterly* 29 (September 1945): 182–83; W. Harrison Daniel, "The Christian Association: A Religious Society in the Army of Northern Virginia," *Virginia Magazine of History and Biography* 69 (January 1961): 95–96; Daniel, "The Southern Baptists in the Confederacy," *Civil War History* 6 (December 1960): 397; Robert Emory Park, "War Diary of Capt. Robert Emory Park, Twelfth Alabama Regiment, January 28th, 1863–January 27th, 1864," *Southern Historical Society Papers* 26 (January-December 1898): 22; Jesse

M. Frank to K. M. Frank, April 16, 1864, Alexander Frank Papers, Duke; Prim, "Born Again in the Trenches," 52. Religion also no doubt benefited from soldiers' close personal ties. See Rodney Stark and William Sims Bainbridge, "Networks of Faith: Interpersonal Bonds and Recruitments to Cults and Sects," *American Journal of Sociology* 85 (May 1980): 1376–95; John Lofland and Rodney Stark, "Becoming a World-Saver: A Theory of Conversion to a Deviant Perspective," *American Sociological Review* 30 (December 1965): 862–75.

35. Leo H. Bartemeier, Lawrence S. Kubie, Karl A. Menninger, John Romano, and John C. Whitehorn, "Combat Exhaustion, Part I and Part II," *Journal of Nervous and Mental Disease* 104 (October and November 1946): 358–89, 489–525; Jones, *Christ in the Camp*, 281; *North Carolina Presbyterian*, September 20, 1862; *Central Presbyterian*, September 24, 1863; *Soldier's Visitor*, February 1864; *Biblical Recorder*, December 10, 1862; Prim, "Born Again in the Trenches," 40. See also William Sargant, *Battle for the Mind: A Physiology of Conversion and Brain-Washing* (Garden City, N.Y.: Doubleday, 1957). A study of post-traumatic stress in Vietnam soldiers estimates that half of all veterans suffer from the syndrome and that stress disorders existed unrecognized in combat veterans well before World War I when they first drew sustained attention. Herbert Hendin and Ann Pollinger Haas, *Wounds of War: The Psychological Aftermath of Combat in Vietnam* (New York: Basic Books, 1984), 6, 9.

36. Marcus Cunliffe, *Soldiers and Civilians: The Martial Spirit in America, 1775–1865* (Boston: Little, Brown, 1968), 435; Luvaas, *The Military Legacy of the Civil War*; Daniel Aaron, *The Unwritten War: American Writers and the Civil War* (New York: Oxford University Press, 1973); Thomas C. Leonard, *Above the Battle: War Making in America from Appomattox to Versailles* (New York: Oxford University Press, 1978). See also Paul Fussell, *The Great War and Modern Memory* (New York: Oxford University Press, 1975). Casler, *Four Years in the Stonewall Brigade*, 37; Kate Cumming, *Kate: The Journal of a Confederate Nurse*, ed. Richard Barksdale Harwell (1866; repr. Baton Rouge: Louisiana State University Press, 1959), 13–14. On numbness see also *Obstacles to Conversion* (Petersburg, Va., [186-]), 2–3.

37. On indifference see the first page of *The Soldiers' Almanac* (Richmond, 1863), 9: "WARNING TO SOLDIERS. Guard against unfeeling recklessness. By unfamiliarity with scenes of violence and death, soldiers often become apparently indifferent to suffering and anguish, and appear to be destitute of the ordinary sensibilities of our humanity." See also William L. Nugent to his wife, September 7, 1863, in Bettersworth, ed., *Mississippi in the Confederacy*, 354; Dunn to his wife, October 13, 1863, in Jordan, ed., "Mathew Andrew Dunn Letters," 112; H[ugh]. H[arris]. Robison to his wife, November 11, 1861,

in Weymouth T. Jordan, ed., "Hugh Harris Robison Letters," *Journal of Mississippi History* 1 (January 1939): 54; *Religious Herald*, July 24, 1862. See also N. M. Osborne, Jr., to my dear Aunt, June 28, 1863, Elizabeth Moorman Smithson Papers, Duke.

38. On combat stress see Mardi Jon Horowitz, *Stress Response Syndromes* (New York: Jason Aronson, 1976); Norman Q. Brill, "Gross Stress Reaction, II: Traumatic War Neurosis," in Alfred M. Freedman and Harold I. Kaplan, eds., *Comprehensive Textbook of Psychiatry* (Baltimore: Williams & Wilkins, 1967), 1031–35; Peter G. Bourne, *Men, Stress, and Vietnam* (Boston: Little, Brown, 1970); Roy R. Grinker and John P. Spiegel, *Men under Stress* (Philadelphia: McGraw-Hill, 1945); Abram Kardiner and Herbert Spiegel, *War Stress and Neurotic Illness* (New York: Paul B. Hober, 1947); Nolan D. C. Lewis and Bernice Engle, *Wartime Psychiatry: A Compendium of the International Literature* (New York: Oxford University Press, 1954); E. E. Southard, *Shell-Shock and Other Neuropsychiatric Problems* (Boston: W. M. Leonard, 1919); Albert Deutsch, "Military Psychiatry: The Civil War, 1861–1865," in American Psychiatric Association, *One Hundred Years of American Psychiatry* (New York: Columbia University Press, 1944), 367–84; Peter Watson, *War on the Mind: The Military Uses and Abuses of Psychology* (New York: Basic Books, 1978). Folmar, ed., *From That Terrible Field*, 60; and *Camp Nineveh*, 4. See also Jones, *Christ in the Camp*, 289, and for a description of symptoms of "congestion of the brain" in a fearful soldier, James K. Street to My Dear Ninnie, May 8, 1863, James K. and Melinda East (Pace) Street Papers, SHC. See also Stephen Cocke to Charles T. Quintard, April 25, 1862, Quintard Papers.

39. *Confederate Baptist*, June 17, 1863; *Religious Herald*, March 20, 1862; *Biblical Recorder*, October 8, 1862.

40. *Why Will You Die?* (Petersburg, Va., [186-]); and A. M. Poindexter, *Why Will Ye Die?* (Raleigh, [186-]); E[dwin]. T[heodore]. Winkler, *Duties of the Citizen Soldier. A Sermon . . . Before the Moultrie Guards* (Charleston, 1861), 14; [Brockenbrough], *Mother's Parting Words*, 2. J[ohn]. C[owper]. Granbery, *An Address to the Soldiers of the Southern Armies* (Raleigh, [186-]), 8; *Are You Prepared?* (Raleigh, [186-]), 1. On the role of loss of control in inducing stress see Horowitz, *Stress Response Syndromes*.

41. For the identification of religion as war see other examples: *Can I Be Religious While I Am A Soldier?* (Richmond, [186-]); Charles F[orce]. Deems, *"Christ in You"* (Raleigh, [186-]), 2; *Bread Upon the Waters, or a True Story of Lucknow* (Petersburg, Va., [186-]), 2; [Herbert T. Bacon], *The Countersign* (Richmond, [186-]); *The Muster* (Charleston, [186-]); B[asil]. Manly, Jr., *Halting on this Side of Jordan* (Raleigh, [186-]).

42. Brill, "Gross Stress Reactions," 1032; Albert J. Glass, "Psychotherapy in the Combat Zone," *American Journal of Psychiatry* 110 (April 1954): 727. On

guilt and its role in war neuroses see Bartemeier et al., "Combat Exhaustion"; Southard, *Shell-Shock*, 256; Joseph Lander, "The Psychiatrically Immunizing Effect of Combat Wounds," *American Journal of Orthopsychiatry* 15 (July 16, 1946): 536–41. On suggestibility in early stages of combat stress see Glass, "Psychotherapy in the Combat Zone," 726. For a discussion of guilt as a standard vehicle of conversion see Edmund S. Morgan, *Visible Saints: The History of a Puritan Idea* (New York: New York University Press, 1963); Murray G. Murphey, "The Psychodynamics of Puritan Conversion," *American Quarterly* 31 (Summer 1979): 135–47; and John Lofland and Norman Skonovd, "Conversion Motifs," *Journal for the Scientific Study of Religion* 20 (December 1981): 373–85.

43. J. Milton Yinger, *The Scientific Study of Religion* (New York: Macmillan, 1970), 152; Julian Silverman, "Shamans and Acute Schizophrenia," *American Anthropologist* 59 (February 1967): 21–31. See Bourne, *Men, Stress, and Vietnam*, 79, on cultural influences in differences in reactions to combat of Americans and Vietnamese.

44. *Biblical Recorder*, September 2, 1863.

45. On social conflict see Paul D. Escott, " 'The Cry of the Sufferers': The Problem of Welfare in the Confederacy," *Civil War History* 23 (September 1977): 228–40; Hahn, *The Roots of Southern Populism*, 86–133; Stephen E. Ambrose, "Yeoman Discontent in the Confederacy," *Civil War History* 8 (September 1962): 259–68; Georgia Lee Tatum, *Disloyalty in the Confederacy* (Chapel Hill: University of North Carolina Press, 1934); Ella Lonn, *Desertion during the Civil War* (New York: Century Co., 1928); Bessie Martin, *Desertion of Alabama Troops from the Confederate Army: A Study in Sectionalism* (New York: Columbia University Press, 1932); Maurice Melton, "Disloyal Confederates," *Civil War Times Illustrated* 16 (August 1977): 12–19.

46. On the postwar period see Charles Reagan Wilson, *Baptized in Blood: The Religion of the Lost Cause, 1865–1920* (Athens: University of Georgia Press, 1980); Rufus B. Spain, *At Ease in Zion: A Social History of Southern Baptists, 1865–1900* (Nashville: Vanderbilt University Press, 1967); Hunter Dickinson Farish, *The Circuit Rider Dismounts: A Social History of Southern Methodism, 1865–1900* (Richmond: Dietz Press, 1938); and Ernest Trice Thompson, *Presbyterians in the South, 1861–1890*, 3 vols. (Richmond: John Knox Press, 1973). On Populists and religion see Frederick A. Bode, *Protestantism and the New South: North Carolina Baptists and Methodists in Political Crisis, 1894–1903* (Charlottesville: University of Virginia Press, 1975); Bode, "Religion and Class Hegemony: A Populist Critique in North Carolina," *Journal of Southern History* 37 (August 1971): 417–38; and Robert C. McMath, Jr., *Populist Vanguard: A History of the Southern Farmers' Alliance* (Chapel Hill: University of North Carolina Press), 75.

47. See Hahn, *Roots of Southern Populism*, 137–289; Forrest McDonald and Grady McWhiney, "The South from Self-Sufficiency to Peonage: An Interpretation," *American Historical Review* 85 (December 1980): 1095–118; and Broadus Mitchell, *The Rise of Cotton Mills in the South* (Baltimore: Johns Hopkins University Press, 1921).

48. Hendin and Haas, *Wounds of War*. See also the striking descriptions of postwar southern "lethargy and listlessness" that sound much like other, less violent manifestations of post-Vietnam syndrome, in Dan T. Carter, *When the War Was Over: The Failure of Self-Reconstruction in the South, 1865–1867* (Baton Rouge: Louisiana State University Press, 1985), 271. See also David Herbert Donald, "A Generation of Defeat," in Walter J. Fraser, Jr., and Winifred B. Moore, Jr., eds., *From the Old South to the New: Essays on the Transitional South* (Westport, Conn.: Greenwood Press, 1981), 3–20.

Altars of Sacrifice: Confederate Women and the Narratives of War

1. Richmond Lattimore, trans., *The Iliad of Homer* (Chicago: University of Chicago Press, 1951), 166. Margaret Randolph Higonnet et al., eds., *Behind the Lines: Gender and the Two World Wars* (New Haven: Yale University Press, 1987), 4. See also Jean Bethke Elshtain, *Women and the War* (New York: Basic Books, 1987); and Eric Leed, *No Man's Land: Combat and Identity in World War I* (New York: Cambridge University Press, 1979). I would like to thank John Boles, Anne Boylan, Evelyn Brooks, Elizabeth Fox-Genovese, Eugene Genovese, Steven Hahn, Jacquelyn Hall, Lynn Hunt, Michael Johnson, Anne Goodwyn Jones, Mary Kelley, Linda Kerber, Stephanie McCurry, James McPherson, Reid Mitchell, Sharon O'Brien, Philip Racine, Janice Radway, Armstead Robinson, Charles Rosenberg, Barry Shank, and David Thelen for their acute criticisms and helpful suggestions, many of which I admit to having been foolhardy enough to ignore.

2. Julia Ellen (Le Grand) Waitz, *The Journal of Julia Le Grand, New Orleans, 1862–1863*, ed. Kate Mason Rowland and Mrs. Morris L. Croxall (Richmond: Everett Waddey, 1911), 52. The special experience of Confederate women arose both from the newness of the kind of combat the Civil War produced and from the growing scarcity of southern resources. For comparisons, see Claudia Koonz, *Mothers in the Fatherland: Women, the Family, and Nazi politics* (New York: St. Martin's Press, 1987); Higonnet et al., eds., *Behind the Lines*; Joan Hoff Wilson, "The Illusion of Change: Women and the American Revolution," in *The American Revolution: Explorations in the History of American Radicalism*, ed. Alfred F. Young (DeKalb: Northern Illinois University Press,

1976), 383–446; Linda K. Kerber, *Women of the Republic: Intellect and Ideology in Revolutionary America* (Chapel Hill: University of North Carolina Press, 1980); Mary Beth Norton, *Liberty's Daughters: The Revolutionary Experience of American Women, 1750–1800* (Boston: Little, Brown, 1980); and D'Ann Campbell, *Women at War with America: Private Lives in a Patriotic Era* (Cambridge: Harvard University Press, 1984). On northern women during the Civil War, see Philip Shaw Paludan, *A People's Contest: The Union and the Civil War, 1861–1865* (New York: Harper & Row, 1988), 156–60, 182–83, 327–30.

3. John Keegan, *The Face of Battle* (New York: Viking, 1977). For a similar ideological use of the "hegemony of gender," see Christine Stansell, *City of Women: Sex and Class in New York, 1789–1860* (New York: Alfred A. Knopf, 1986). On yeoman dissent, see Paul D. Escott, *After Secession: Jefferson Davis and the Failure of Confederate Nationalism* (Baton Rouge: Louisiana State University Press, 1978); and Paul D. Escott, " 'The Cry of the Sufferers': The Problem of Welfare in the Confederacy," *Civil War History* 23 (September 1977): 228–40. On the history and historiography of Confederate morale, see Richard E. Beringer et al., *Why the South Lost the Civil War* (Athens: University of Georgia Press, 1986); and Drew Gilpin Faust, *The Creation of Confederate Nationalism: Ideology and Identity in the Civil War South* (Baton Rouge: Louisiana State University Press, 1988). On the greater vulnerability of southern men, see Maris Vinovskis, "Have Social Historians Lost the Civil War? Some Preliminary Demographic Speculations," *Journal of American History* 76 (June 1989): 39.

4. James D. Richardson, comp., "Resolutions of Thanks," in *The Messages and Papers of Jefferson Davis and the Confederacy, 1861–1865*, 2 vols. (New York: Confucian Press, 1981), 1:176; *Laws of the State of Mississippi, passed at a called and regular session of the Mississippi Legislature. Held in Jackson and Columbus, Dec. 1862 and Nov. 1863* (Selma: 1864), 226.

5. An important departure from the celebratory historiographical tradition is George C. Rable, *Civil Wars: Women and the Crisis of Southern Nationalism* (Urbana: University of Illinois Press, 1989). Monuments to Confederate women were planned in Mississippi, North Carolina, South Carolina, Arkansas, Tennessee, and Florida. See also Gaines M. Foster, *Ghosts of the Confederacy: Defeat, the Lost Cause, and the Emergence of the New South, 1865 to 1913* (New York: Oxford University Press, 1987), 175–79; J. L. Underwood, *The Women of the Confederacy* (n.p., 1906); Mary Elizabeth Massey, *Bonnet Brigades* (New York: Alfred A. Knopf, 1966); and H. E. Sterkx, *Partners in Rebellion: Alabama Women in the Civil War* (Rutherford: Farleigh Dickinson University Press, 1970). For the poem by Henry Timrod, see H. M. Wharton, *War Songs and Poems of the Southern Confederacy, 1861–1865* (Philadelphia: John C. Winston, 1904),

215. For the notion of "two armies," see *Charleston Daily Courier*, November 28, 1861.

6. A popular work, dedicated by its author as a "monument" to female contributions to the southern cause, is Rita Mae Brown, *High Hearts* (New York: Bantam, 1986). For a more scholarly consideration, see Janet E. Kaufmann, " 'Under the Petticoat Flag': Women Soldiers in the Confederate Army," *Southern Studies* 23 (Winter 1984): 363–75. For examples of the new women's historiography, see Nancy A. Hewitt, "Beyond the Search for Sisterhood: American Women's History in the 1980s," *Social History* 10 (October 1985): 299–321; Elizabeth Fox-Genovese, *Within the Plantation Household: Black and White Women of the Old South* (Chapel Hill: University of North Carolina Press, 1988); Joan Wallach Scott, *Gender and the Politics of History* (New York: Columbia University Press, 1988); Koonz, *Mothers in the Fatherland;* and Nancy MacLean, "Behind the Mask of Chivalry: Gender, Race, and Class in the Making of the Ku Klux Klan of the 1920s in Georgia" (Ph.D. diss., University of Wisconsin–Madison, 1989).

7. "Educated Woman—In Peace and War," *Southern Field and Fireside*, April 11, 1863; *Augusta Weekly Constitutionalist*, July 17, 1861.

8. Sarah Katherine Stone, *Brokenburn: The Journal of Kate Stone, 1861–1868*, ed. John Q. Anderson (Baton Rouge: Louisiana State University Press, 1955), 17; Julia Le Grand to Mrs. Shepherd Brown, November 17, 1862, in *Journal of Julia Le Grand*, ed. Rowland and Croxall, 52–53; Kate Cumming, *Kate: The Journal of a Confederate Nurse*, ed. Richard Barksdale Harwell (Baton Rouge: Louisiana State University Press, 1959), 38–39. See also C. W. Dabney to "My Dear Brother," May 1, 1861, Charles W. Dabney Papers, SHC.

9. Francis Butler Simkins and James Welch Patton, *The Women of the Confederacy* (Richmond: Garrett & Massie, 1936), 22; Diary entry, August 9, 1861, Clara D. MacLean Papers, Manuscript Division, Duke; Greenville Ladies Association Records and Ladies Relief Association, Spartanburg, SCL.

10. Sarah Lois Wadley Diary, August 20, 1863, SHC; Amanda Chappelear Diary, April 19, 1862, VHS; Clara to "My dear Friend Jesse," May 4, 1863, Warren Ogden, Collector, Miscellaneous Civil War Letters, Manuscripts Section, Special Collections Division, Howard-Tilton Memorial Library, Tulane University, New Orleans, Louisiana; *The Diary of Miss Emma Holmes, 1861–1866*, ed. John F. Marsalek (Baton Rouge: Louisiana State University Press, 1979), 251, 323; Sarah Morgan Dawson, *A Confederate Girl's Diary*, ed. James I. Robertson, Jr. (Bloomington: Indiana University Press, 1960), 119; Caroline Kean Hill Davis Diary, February 13, 1865, VHS. See also Mary Eliza Dulany Diary, June 10, 1862, VHS. Cornelia McDonald, quoted in Douglas Southall Freeman, *The South to Posterity: An Introduction to the Writings of Confederate History* (New York: Charles Scribner's Sons, 1939), 152.

11. Elizabeth Collier Diary, April 11, 1862, SHC; Emma Walton to J. B.

Walton, May 12 and July 15, 1863, Historic New Orleans Collection, New Orleans, Louisiana; Sallie Munford, quoted in Freeman, *South to Posterity*, 109; Dawson, *Confederate Girl's Diary*, ed. Robertson, 318. For an example of a southern woman disguising herself as a man, see J. M Fain to E. Fain, December 10, 1861, Huldah Annie Briant Collection, Duke; and Annie Samuels et al. to James Seddon, December 2, 1864, Letters Received, Confederate Secretary of War, RG 109, M437, reel 122, B692, NA. For an extended fictional treatment, see Brown, *High Hearts*.

12. Alexander St. Clair Abrams, *The Trials of a Soldier's Wife: A Tale of the Second American Revolution* (Atlanta, 1864), 165.

13. Leila W., "Woman a Patriot," *Southern Monthly* 1 (October 1861): 115; *Mobile Evening News*, January 25, 1864; *Natchez Weekly Courier*, March 12, 1862. See also Faust, *Creation of Confederate Nationalism*.

14. Mary B. Clarke to Macfarlane and Fergusson, September 21, 1861, Macfarlane and Fergusson Papers, VHS; *Augusta Weekly Constitutionalist*, October 16, 1861.

15. Theodore von La Hache, *I Would Like to Change My Name: A Favorite Encore Song* (Augusta, Ga., 1863).

16. *Charleston Daily Courier*, August 15, 1861; Davis quoted in unidentified newspaper clipping in George Bagby Scrapbook, 2:128, George Bagby Papers, VHS.

17. "Heart Victories," in *Songs of the South* (Richmond: 1862), 68–69.

18. "Our Mothers Did So Before Us," 70–71, and "The Dead," 47–48, in *Songs of the South*.

19. *Record of News, History and Literature*, September 3, 1863, 105; Diary entry, May 19, 1862, Chappelear Papers.

20. *Charleston Daily Courier*, August 19, 1861.

21. "I've Kissed Him and Let Him Go," in clipping in George Bagby Scrapbook, 5:99, Bagby Papers.

22. J. M. Fain to Huldah Fain Briant, May 19, 1862, Briant Papers; June 29, 1862, Priscilla Munnikhuysen Bond Diary, Hill Memorial Library, Louisiana State University, Baton Rouge.

23. *Huntsville Democrat*, August 21, 1861; *Countryman*, March 18, 1862.

24. *Richmond Daily Enquirer*, August 5, 1863. One in eight Confederate soldiers deserted, as contrasted with one in ten from the North. Vinovskis, "Have Social Historians Lost the Civil War?" 41.

25. Barnwell quoted in *Diary of Miss Emma Holmes*, ed. Marsalek, 101–2.

26. Margaret Beckwith Reminiscences, 2:10, VHS; Diary entry, July 2, 1862, Chappelear Papers.

27. *Record of News, History and Literature*, July 16, 1863, 37; "Slap-By Klubs," in *Songs of the South*, 67; Catherine Cochran Reminiscences, vol. 1, VHS;

U. S. War Department, *The War of the Rebellion: A Compilation of the Official Records of the Union and Confederate Armies*, 128 vols. (Washington, 1880–1901), ser. 1, 52, pt. 2, pp. 667–68. Statistical information on the Confederate army is incomplete, and thus casualty estimates necessarily involve guesswork. These figures are James M. McPherson's revisions, made in a telephone conversation to Drew Gilpin Faust on October 26, 1989, of numbers he offers in *Ordeal by Fire: The Civil War and Reconstruction* (New York: Alfred A. Knopf, 1982), 18; and *Battle Cry of Freedom: The Civil War Era* (New York: Oxford University Press, 1988), 471, 854. For his computations, McPherson considers 18–40 to be effective military age.

28. Addie Harris to G. W. Randolph, October 29, 1862, Letters Received, Confederate Secretary of War, RG 109, M437, reel 53, H1166.

29. Letters Received, Confederate Secretary of War, RG 109, M437: Amanda Walker to the Secretary of War, October 31, 1862, reel 79, W1106, and Lucy Sharp to John Randolph, October 1, 1862, reel 72, S1000. It is important to recognize that many of these letters complaining about slave management were prompted by the passage of the Confederate law exempting slave managers from military service and thus were not simply disinterested cries of pain. Alice Palmer to Hattie Palmer, July 20, 1865, Palmer Family Papers, SCL.

30. Cumming, *Kate*, 191–92. See also Patricia R. Loughridge and Edward D. C. Campbell, Jr., *Women and Mourning* (Richmond: Museum of the Confederacy, 1985); and in this volume, Drew Gilpin Faust, "Race, Gender, and Confederate Nationalism: William D. Washington's *Burial of Latané*," 148–59.

31. *Richmond Daily Enquirer*, March 7, 1862; *Confederate Baptist*, October 15, 1862; Phoebe Yates Pember, *A Southern Woman's Story: Life in Confederate Richmond*, ed. Bell Irvin Wiley (Jackson, Tenn.: McCowat-Mercer, 1959), 25; C. Vann Woodward, ed., *Mary Chesnut's Civil War* (New Haven: Yale University Press, 1981), 641. For expression of similar concerns in the North, see Susan M. Reverby, *Ordered to Care: The Dilemma of American Nursing, 1850–1945* (New York: Cambridge University Press, 1987), 43–47.

32. Pember, *Southern Woman's Story*, 25; Simkins and Patton, *Women of the Confederacy*, 86; Cordelia Scales, "Civil War Letters of Cordelia Scales," ed. Percy L. Rainwater, *Journal of Mississippi History* 1 (July 1939): 173.

33. Cumming, *Kate*, 65.

34. Phebe Levy to Eugenia Phillips, September 13, 1863, Philip Phillips Family Papers, LC; Diary entry, March 3, 1862, Clara D. MacLean Collection, Duke; Woodward, ed., *Mary Chesnut's Civil War*, 677.

35. *Augusta Daily Constitutionalist*, May 14, 1863.

36. W. Buck Yearns and John G. Barrett, eds., *North Carolina Civil War Documentary* (Chapel Hill: University of North Carolina Press, 1980), 237; "Pro-

ceedings of the 6th Annual Meeting of the State Education Association," *North Carolina Journal of Education* 4 (November 1861): 326. By the end of the war, the percentage of female teachers in North Carolina had risen from 7 percent to 50 percent. Yearns and Barrett, eds., *North Carolina Civil War Documentary*, 231.

37. Yearns and Barrett, eds., *North Carolina Civil War Documentary*, 244; *Sixth Annual Circular of Wytheville Female College* (Wytheville, 1861); *Minutes of the Bethel Baptist Association* (Macon, 1863). See also *Catalogue of the Trustees, Faculty, and Students of the Wesleyan Female College, Macon, Georgia* (Macon, 1862); and Farmville Female College, *The Next Term of this Institution*, broadside [n.p., 1863].

38. *Diary of Miss Emma Holmes*, ed. Marsalek, 172; Grimball quoted in Fox-Genovese, *Within the Plantation Household*, 46; *Proceedings of the Convention of Teachers of the Confederate States* (Macon, 1863), 4; *North Carolina Journal of Education* 7 (July 1864): 88. On teaching, see also Rable, *Civil Wars*, 129–31.

39. For a consideration of painting, see Faust, "Race, Gender, and Confederate Nationalism," 148–59 in this volume.

40. [Augusta Jane Evans], *Macaria; or, Altars of Sacrifice* (Richmond: West and Johnston, 1864). On Evans and women's fiction generally, see Anne Goodwyn Jones, *Tomorrow Is Another Day: The Woman Writer in the South, 1859–1936* (Baton Rouge: Louisiana State University Press, 1981); Nina Baym, *Woman's Fiction: A Guide to Novels by and about Women in America, 1820–1870* (Ithaca: Cornell University Press, 1978); and Mary Kelley, *Private Woman, Public Stage: Literary Domesticity in Nineteenth Century America* (New York: Oxford University Press, 1984).

41. Because *Macaria* is extensively discussed in this volume (160–73), the material on it included in the original version of this article has been largely omitted.

42. *Montgomery Daily Advertiser*, June 15, 1864.

43. A. Grima to Alfred Grima, November 27, 1863, Grima Family Papers, Historic New Orleans Collection; Mary L. Scales to the secretary of war, September 8, 1862, Letters Received, Confederate Secretary of War, RG 109, M437, reel 72, S890.

44. G. Glenn Clift, ed., *The Private War of Lizzie Hardin* (Frankfurt, Ky.: Kentucky Historical Association, 1963), 17; Constance Cary Harrison, *Recollections Grave and Gay* (New York: Charles Scribner's Sons, 1911), 83; Elizabeth Preston Allan, *The Life and Letters of Margaret Junkin Preston* (New York: Houghton Mifflin, 1903), 148; Sarah Jane Sams to Randolph Sams, March 14, 1865, Sarah Jane Sams Collection, SCL; Waitz, *Journal of Julia Le Grand*, ed. Rowland and Croxall, 44–45; Margaret Crawford, "Tales of a Grandmother," in *South Carolina Women in the Confederacy*, ed. Mrs. A. T. Smythe, Miss M. B.

Poppenheim, and Mrs. Thomas Taylor, 2 vols. (Columbia, S.C.: The State Co., 1903), 1:210; Diary entry, November 18, 1864, David Harris Papers, College Library, Winthrop College, Rock Hill, S.C.

45. Lila Chunn to Willie Chunn, May 19, 1863, Willie Chunn Papers, Duke; Myrna Lockett Avary, ed., *A Virginia Girl in the Civil War, 1861–1865* (New York: D. Appleton, 1903), 41; Annie Upshur to Jefferson Davis, January 24, 1863, Letters Received, Confederate Secretary of War, RG 109, M437, reel 114, U2. Cornelia McDonald, *A Diary with Reminiscences of the War and Refugee Life in the Shenandoah Valley* (Nashville: Cullom & Ghertner, 1935), 165, 167, 114–15; Mary A. Blackburn to David B. Blackburn, December 19, 1864, Point Lookout Letters, Miscellaneous Files, Adjutant General's Office, RG 109, NA. On stress reaction among soldiers, see "Christian Soldiers: The Meaning of Revivalism in the Confederate Army," 88–109 in this volume.

46. Letters Received, Confederate Secretary of War, RG 109, M437: Ella Stuart to secretary of war, April 28, 1863, reel 111, S312; Miranda Sutton to secretary of war, January 28, 1864, reel 140, S79; Harriet Stephenson to secretary of war, January 18, 1864, reel 140, S47; Nancy Williams to Jefferson Davis, April 1, 1863, October 29, 1863, reel 116, W246; Frances Brightwell to Davis, March 17, 1862, reel 31, B167.

47. Letters Received, Confederate Secretary of War, RG 109, M437: Anonymous to Davis, May 14, 1864, reel 118, A134; Mrs. M. L. Nelson to Davis, n.d., reel 137, N77; Nelson to Seddon, October 12, 1864, reel 137, N80; Almira Acors to Davis, March 23, 1862, reel 29, A62. The appearance of the instruction "file" on letters describing such desperate circumstances is striking and is also noted by Rable, *Civil Wars*, 75.

48. In their growing discontent with their situation, some women even came to question the paternalistic justice of God. See Grace Brown Elmore Reminiscences, June 20, 1865, SCL.

49. Yearns and Barrett, eds., *North Carolina Civil War Documentary*, 22, 97; M. Chichester to Captain Arthur Chichester, May 2, 1864, Point Lookout Letters; Charles Fenton James to "Dear Sister," February 13, 1864, Charles Fenton James Papers, SHC.

50. See, for example, the report of applicants requesting permission to leave the Confederacy, July 25, 1864, Letters Received, Confederate Secretary of War, RG 109, M437, reel 124, C429.

51. *Children's Friend*, December 1862.

52. Diary entry, August 10, 1862, Dulany Papers; Stone, *Brokenburn*, ed. Anderson, 277; Harrison, *Recollections*, 188.

53. *Countryman*, May 3, 1864. On bread riots and female violence, see Michael Chesson, "Harlots or Heroines? A New Look at the Richmond Bread

Riot," *Virginia Magazine of History and Biography* 92 (April 1984): 131–75; Paul
D. Escott, *Many Excellent People: Power and Privilege in North Carolina, 1850–
1900* (Chapel Hill: University of North Carolina Press, 1986), 67; Victoria
Bynum, "'War within a War': Women's Participation in the Revolt of the
North Carolina Piedmont," *Frontiers* 9 (1987): 43–49.

54. Woodward, ed., *Mary Chesnut's Civil War*, 430; *Richmond Daily Enquirer*,
February 11, 1864; Minutes of the Tombeckbee Presbytery, April 8, 1865, Historical Foundation of the Presbyterian Church, Montreat, N.C.; unidentified
clipping in George Bagby Scrapbook, 5:131, Bagby Papers; James to "Dear
Sister," February 13, 1865, Charles Fenton James Collection.

55. Cumming, *Kate*, 4; Robert E. Lee quoted in Douglas Southall Freeman,
Lee's Lieutenants: A Study in Command, 3 vols. (New York: Charles Scribner's
Sons, 1972), 2:752. See also Rable, *Civil Wars*, 207; Waitz, *Journal of Julia Le
Grand*, ed. Rowland and Croxall, 16.

In Search of the Real Mary Chesnut

1. C. Vann Woodward, *Mary Chesnut's Civil War* (New Haven: Yale Univer-
sity Press, 1981); Kenneth S. Lynn, "The Masterpiece That Became a Hoax,"
New York Times Book Review, April 26, 1981; William R. Taylor and Steven M.
Stowe, "Mary Chesnut's Diary," *New York Times Book Review*, May 17, 1981;
William Styron, "In the Southern Camp," *New York Review of Books*, August
13, 1981; Elisabeth Muhlenfeld, *Mary Boykin Chesnut: A Biography* (Baton
Rouge: Louisiana State University Press, 1981), 11. This chapter is the only
review represented in this collection, which explains its focus on the Wood-
ward and Muhlenfeld volumes.

Race, Gender, and Confederate Nationalism: William D. Washington's *Burial of Latané*

1. Two recent works have greatly facilitated access to southern arts. See
Painting in the South: 1564–1980 (Richmond: Virginia Museum, 1983), and
Jessie Poesch, *The Art of the Old South: Painting, Sculpture, Architecture & the
Products of Craftsmen, 1560–1860* (New York: Alfred Knopf, 1983). I am very
grateful to Malcolm Campbell for his comments and suggestions.

2. Emily Salmon, "The Burial of Latané: Symbol of the Lost Cause," *Vir-
ginia Cavalcade* 28 (Winter 1979): 126; Vandiver quoted in Mark E. Neely, Jr.,
Harold Holzer, and Gabor S. Boritt, *The Confederate Image: Prints of the Lost
Cause* (Chapel Hill: University of North Carolina Press, 1987), ix. See also

Ethelbert Nelson Ott, "William D. Washington: Artist of the Old South" (M.A. thesis, University of Delaware, 1968).

3. "Lucy Ashton" to John R. Thompson, July 25, 1862 and August 5, 1862, John R. Thompson Papers, VHS. John R. Thompson, "The Burial of Latane" (Richmond, 1862), *broadside*.

4. On history painting see Ann Uhry Abrams, *The Valiant Hero: Benjamin West and Grand-Style History Painting* (Washington, D.C.: Smithsonian Institution Press, 1985); Dennis Montagna, "Benjamin West's 'The Death of Wolfe': A Nationalist Narrative," *American Art Journal* 8 (Spring 1981): 72–88; Edgar Wind, "The Revolution of History Painting," *Journal of the Warburg and Courtauld Institutes* 2 (October 1938): 117–21; Charles Mitchell, "Benjamin West's 'Death of General Wolfe' and the Popular History Piece," *Journal of the Warburg and Courtauld Institutes* 2 (1944): 20–33.

5. Ferdinand Jacobs, *A Sermon, for the times . . .* (Marion, Ala., 1861), 3. For a more extensive discussion of the ideology of Confederate nationalism see Drew Gilpin Faust, *The Creation of Confederate Nationalism: Ideology and Identity in the Civil War South* (Baton Rouge: Louisiana State University Press, 1988).

6. Margaret Mead, "Warfare Is Only an Invention," *Asia* 40 (1940): 402–5; Nancy Huston, "Tales of War and Tears of Women," *Women's Studies International Forum* 5 (1982): 271–82.

7. Stephen Elliott, *Our Cause in Harmony with the Purposes of God in Christ Jesus. A Sermon . . . in Christ Church, Savannah* (Savannah: John M. Cooper, 1862), 14.

8. For more detailed discussion see Faust, *The Creation of Confederate Nationalism*, 4.

9. For more detailed discussion of women's wartime roles, see "Altars of Sacrifice," 113–40 in this volume.

10. John Andrew Rice, quoted in Anne Firor Scott, *The Southern Lady: From Pedestal to Politics, 1830–1930* (Chicago: University of Chicago Press, 1970), 100.

A War Story for Confederate Women:
Augusta Jane Evans's *Macaria*

1. For assistance, comments and criticism, I want to thank Todd Barnett, Nancy Bercaw, Brian Crane, Elizabeth Fox-Genovese, John Gamba, Larry Goldsmith, Mary Kelley, Frances Kohler, Elizabeth Moss, Michael O'Brien, Janice Radway, Charles Rosenberg, Jane Schultz, Kathryn Wilson. Margaret Mead, "Warfare Is Only an Invention," *Asia* 40 (1940): 402–5; see also Nancy

Huston, "Tales of War and Tears of Women," *Women's Studies International Forum* 5 (1982): 271–82. I have written in similar terms about narrative painting in the Confederacy in "Race, Gender, and Confederate Nationalism: William D. Washington's *Burial of Latané*," 148–59 in this volume. See also "Altars of Sacrifice," 113–40.

2. John Keegan, *The Face of Battle* (New York: Viking, 1977).

3. Margaret Mitchell, *Gone with the Wind*, quoted in *Behind the Lines: Gender and the Two World Wars*, ed. Margaret Randolph Higonnet, Jane Jensen, Sonya Michel, and Margaret Collins Weitz (New Haven: Yale University Press, 1987); Julia Le Grand to Mrs Shepherd Brown, November 17, 1862, in Julia Ellen (Le Grand) Waitz, *The Journal of Julia Le Grand, New Orleans, 1862–1863*, ed. Kate Mason Rowland and Mrs. Morris L. Croxall (Richmond: Everett Waddet Co., 1911).

4. [Augusta Jane Evans], *Macaria; or, Altars of Sacrifice* (Richmond: West and Johnston, 1864). Evans's biographer, William Perry Fidler, believes that the original edition of *Macaria* was published in 1863 in Charleston by Walker, Evans, and Cogswell. He refers to a single copy of the volume that he had heard of in 1940, more than a decade before the publication of his own book. Confederate bibliographers Marjorie Crandall and Richard Harwell have found no extant copy of this edition and date *Macaria* as 1864. William Perry Fidler, *Augusta Evans Wilson, 1835–1909: A Biography* (Tuscaloosa: University of Alabama Press, 1951).

5. See Chapter 6, "Altars of Sacrifice"; *I Would Like to Change My Name: A Favorite Encore Song . . . by Theodore von La Hache* (Augusta: Blackmar and Bro., 1863); "Our Mothers Did So Before Us," in *Songs of the South* (Richmond: J. W. Randolph, 1862), 70–71.

6. *Mobile Daily Advertiser*, October 11, 18, 30, and November 6, 1859; June 29, 1864, Ella Gertrude Clanton Thomas Diary, Manuscripts Division, Duke; Jane Tompkins, *Sensational Designs: The Cultural Work of American Fiction, 1790–1860* (New York: Oxford University Press, 1985). On the genre of the nineteenth-century domestic novel, or in Nina Baym's term, *woman's fiction*, see also Nina Baym, *Woman's Fiction: A Guide to Novels by and about Women in America, 1820–1870* (Ithaca: Cornell University Press, 1978); Mary Kelley, *Private Woman, Public Stage: Literary Domesticity in Nineteenth-Century America* (New York: Oxford University Press, 1984); Anne Goodwyn Jones, *Tomorrow Is Another Day: The Woman Writer in the South, 1859–1936* (Baton Rouge: Louisiana State University Press, 1981); Nina Baym, *Novels, Readers and Reviewers: Responses to Fiction in Antebellum America* (Ithaca: Cornell University Press, 1984); Cathy N. Davidson, *Revolution and the Word: The Rise of the Novel in America* (New York: Oxford University Press, 1986).

7. On her brothers' objections to her nursing, see Augusta Jane Evans to Ella

King Newsom, quoted in J. Fraise Richard, *The Florence Nightingale of the Southern Army; Experiences of Mrs. Ella K. Newsom, Confederate Nurse in the Great War of 1861–65* (New York: Broadway, 1914), 93.

8. Augusta Jane Evans to General P. G. T. Beauregard, August 4, 1862, quoted in Fidler, *Augusta Evans Wilson*, 95. See *Macaria*, 141, 163 for almost identical comments. For circulation figures see advertisement on back of M. E. Braddon, *John Marchmont's Legacy* (Richmond: West and Johnston, 1865). Evans's political views, her opposition to "Demagogism" and universal suffrage are often transposed from her correspondence to the mouth of Russell Aubrey in *Macaria*. See Evans to J. L. M. Curry, December 20, 1862; July 15 and October 16, 1863, J. L. M. Curry Papers, Duke. See also Drew Gilpin Faust, *The Creation of Confederate Nationalism: Ideology and Identity in the Civil War South* (Baton Rouge: Louisiana State University Press, 1988).

9. Carolyn G. Heilbrun, *Writing a Woman's Life* (New York: Norton, 1988), 48; Jones, *Tomorrow is Another Day*, 352. See also Sandra Gilbert and Susan Gubar, *The Madwoman in the Attic* (New Haven: Yale University Press, 1978).

10. On women and the language of bourgeois liberalism in the Old South see Elizabeth Fox-Genovese, *Within the Plantation Household* (Chapel Hill: University of North Carolina Press, 1988). Fox-Genovese argues that although such language had entered the South, the social experience of a slave society limited its relevance and encouraged the persistence of organic social views much like those Evans advocates in her diatribes against "selfishness." In her own life, Augusta Jane Evans had a relationship with a minister much like that of Irene with Harvey Young. See Fidler, *Augusta Evans Wilson* on Walter Harriss, 49–55.

11. For discussions of dreaded uselessness, see, for example, Diary entry, August 20, 1863, Sarah Lois Wadley Papers, SHC; Diary entry, April 19, 1862, Amanda Chappelear Papers, VHS; Clara to My dear friend Jesse, May 4, 1863, Warren Ogden, Collector, Miscellaneous Civil War Letters, Tulane University; *The Diary of Miss Emma Holmes, 1861–1866*, ed. John Marsalek (Baton Rouge: Louisiana State University Press, 1979), 251, 323; Sarah Morgan Dawson, *A Confederate Girl's Diary*, ed. James I. Robertson (Bloomington: Indiana University Press, 1960), 119; February 13, 1865, Caroline Kean Hill Diary, VHS. See Lee Virginia Chambers-Schiller, *Liberty a Better Husband: Single Women in America: The Generations of 1780–1840* (New Haven: Yale University Press, 1984), and Linda K. Kerber, *Women of the Republic: Intellect and Ideology in Revolutionary America* (Chapel Hill: University of North Carolina Press, 1980).

12. DKW, "Macaria, or the Altars of Sacrifice," *The Age* 1 (January 1865): 388, 390, 391, 392.

13. FIDELIA, "Macaria," *Mobile Evening News*, August 1, 1864.

14. Augusta Jane Evans to P. G. T. Beauregard, November 20, 1867, Brown

University Library; on her intentions, see Evans to J. L. M. Curry, October 7, 1865, Curry Papers, Duke and Evans to Alexander H. Stephens, November 29, 1865, Alexander H. Stephens Papers, Robert Woodruff Library, Emory University, Atlanta.

"Trying to Do a Man's Business": Gender, Violence, and Slave Management in Civil War Texas

1. I would like to thank the Johns Hopkins Historical Seminar, Todd Barnett, Nancy Bercaw, John Boles, Barbara Fields, Linda Gordon, Sally Graham, Nancy Hewitt, Shan Holt, Beverly Jarrett, Demie Kurz, Reid Mitchell, Charles Rosenberg, and Steven Stowe for comments and suggestions. For statistics on Confederate military service, see Chapter 6, "Altars of Sacrifice: Confederate Women and the Narratives of War." The literature on U.S. slavery is voluminous. For a recent overview and introduction see Peter J. Parish, *Slavery: History and Historians* (New York: Harper and Row, 1989). The concept of paternalism has been most fully analyzed by Eugene D. Genovese, *Roll, Jordan, Roll: The World the Slaves Made* (New York: Pantheon, 1974). For a contrasting perspective, see Norrece T. Jones, *Born a Child of Freedom, Yet a Slave: Mechanisms of Control and Strategies of Resistance in Antebellum South Carolina* (Middletown, Conn.: Wesleyan University Press, 1990). For a study of how paternalism operated on one plantation, see Drew Gilpin Faust, *James Henry Hammond and the Old South: A Design for Mastery* (Baton Rouge: Louisiana State University Press, 1982), 69–104. For a statement indicating the desirability of using whipping as last rather than first resort, see "Governor Hammond's Instructions to His Overseer," in Willie Lee Rose, ed. *A Documentary History of Slavery in North America* (New York: Oxford University Press, 1976), 353, and the Hammond Plantation Manual in James Henry Hammond Papers, SCL.

2. On women and southern households, see Elizabeth Fox-Genovese, *Within the Plantation Household* (Chapel Hill: University of North Carolina Press, 1988); on Confederate women as slave managers, see George Rable, *Civil Wars: Women and the Crisis of Southern Nationalism* (Urbana: University of Illinois Press, 1989), 114–21, and Anne Firor Scott, *The Southern Lady: From Pedestal to Politics* (Chicago: University of Chicago Press, 1970).

3. Randolph B. Campbell, *An Empire for Slavery: The Peculiar Institution in Texas, 1821–1865* (Baton Rouge: Louisiana State University Press, 1989), 231. See also *East Texas Historical Journal* 28 (January 1990): James Marten, "Slaves and Rebels: The Peculiar Institution in Texas, 1861–1865," 29–36; Ralph A. Wooster and Robert Wooster, "A People at War: East Texas during the Civil

War," 3–16. B. P. Gallaway, *The Dark Corner of the Confederacy: Accounts of Civil War Texas As Told by Contemporaries* (Dubuque: William C. Brown, 1968); Ernest Wallace, *Texas in Turmoil* (Austin: Steck-Vaughn, 1965); Randolph B. Campbell, *A Southern Community in Crisis: Harrison County, Texas, 1850–1880* (Austin: Texas State Historical Association, 1983); Vera Lea Dugas, "A Social and Economic History of Texas in the Civil War" (Ph.D. diss., University of Texas, 1963).

4. Amanda Walker to the Confederate Secretary of War, October 31, 1862, Letters Received by the Confederate Secretary of War, RG 109, M437, R79, W1106, NA; Lizzie Neblett to Will Neblett, April 26, 1863, and January 3, 1864, Lizzie Scott Neblett Papers, Eugene C. Barker Texas History Center, Center for American History, University of Texas, Austin.

5. See notation of March 18, 1864, Compiled Service Records of Confederate Soldiers Who Served in Organizations from Texas, NA. Clippings of Lizzie's publications appear under pseudonyms such as "Agnes Lyle" and "Meg Merrilies" in her Scrapbook, 1851, Lizzie Scott Neblett Papers. Quotation is from Lizzie Scott Neblett's Diary, April 14, 1852.

6. Eighth Census of the United States, 1860, Free Schedule, Slave Schedule and Agricultural Schedule, Navarro and Grimes Counties, Texas, NA. Campbell, *Empire,* 193, 68; Richard G. Lowe and Randolph B. Campbell, *Planters and Plain Folk: Agriculture in Antebellum Texas* (Dallas: Southern Methodist University Press, 1987), 82; Lizzie Neblett to Will Neblett, March 20, 1864. See also Randolph B. Campbell and Richard G. Lowe, *Wealth and Power in Antebellum Texas* (College Station: Texas A & M University Press, 1977). See *Navarro Express,* March 24, July 28, and December 21, 1860. On slavery and society in east Texas see Abigail Curlee, "A Study of Texas Slave Plantations, 1822–1865" (Ph.D. diss., University of Texas, 1932). Lizzie and Will's son William wrote a letter in 1935 indicating that he was sending Curlee a personal reminiscence of slavery for use in her work. W. T. Neblett to Mattie Hutcher, March 19, 1935, Lizzie Scott Neblett Papers. On Grimes County, see Irene Taylor Allen, *Saga of Anderson* (New York: Greenwich Book Publishers, 1957); Grimes County Historical Commission, *History of Grimes County* (Dallas: Taylor Publishing Company, 1982); Eric Lee Blair, *Early History of Grimes County,* (n.p., 1930). On women in Texas, see Annie Doom Pickrell, *Pioneer Women in Texas* (Austin: E. L. Steck, 1929); Evelyn M. Carrington, *Women in Early Texas* (Austin: Jenkins Publishing Company, 1975); Ruthe Winegarten, *Texas Women: A Pictorial History* (Austin: Eakin Press, 1986).

7. Lizzie Neblett to Will Neblett, April 26, 1863.

8. Eighth Census of the United States, Slave Schedules, Navarro and Grimes Counties, Texas, 1860. Lizzie Neblett to Will Neblett, January 9 and 3, 1864. On Thornton's marriage, see Will Neblett to Lizzie Neblett, August

2, 1856. On Sam's abroad wife, see Lizzie to Will Neblett, August 5, 1863; Lizzie to Garrett Scott, [1850s]. On Joe's family see Lizzie to Sallie Scott, March 3 and September 19, 1858; Lizzie to Will February 12 and April 26, 1863. For examples of transfers of slaves within the family, see the Nebletts' exchange of Miele, an unsatisfactory female slave, for Nance, Will Neblett to Lizzie Neblett, July 25 and August 2, 1856. Re-creating the Nebletts' agricultural operations slave force is complicated by their move in 1861 from Navarro back to Grimes County.

9. Lizzie Neblett to Will Neblett, August 18, 1863.

10. Ibid., November 17, 1863; Lowe and Campbell, *Planters and Plain Folk,* 162.

11. Lizzie Neblett to Will Neblett, November 23 and 17, 1863.

12. Ibid., November 23, 1863.

13. Ibid., November 29, 1863.

14. Ibid.

15. Ibid., December 6, 1863.

16. Ibid.

17. On this and other occasions Lizzie seems to acknowledge a special bond with Sarah, a slave woman, that enables Lizzie to use her as an intermediary and a source of information about other slaves. There is apart from these references very little in Lizzie's letters and diary that directly addresses the issue of the relationship between white and black women. It is clear, however, that on Lizzie's farm at least, it is the male slaves who are seen both as the more significant discipline problems and as potential objects of fear.

18. Lizzie Neblett to Will Neblett, April 26, 1863. On Sarah's eavesdropping on other slaves see also Lizzie Neblett to Will Neblett, November 4 and 25, 1863. Lizzie's comments on whipping appear in an undated fragment of a letter from Lizzie Neblett to Will Neblett.

19. Ibid., November 17, 1863.

20. Ibid., December 13, 1863.

21. Ibid., February 6–7, 1864, and December 13, 1863.

22. On slave hiring in Texas see Campbell, *Empire*, 82–92. On another Texas woman's preference for hiring out over personal management during the Civil War, see Campbell, *A Southern Community in Crisis*, 221–41. Lizzie Neblett to Will Neblett, undated fragment [1864].

23. Lizzie Neblett to Will Neblett, April 19, 1864, and May 3, 1864. On Joe's intention to use the mule to visit his family, see Lizzie Neblett to Will Neblett, February 12, 1864.

24. Lizzie Neblett to Will Neblett, April 23, 1864.

25. Ibid., April 15 and 23, 1864.

26. Ibid., February 12, July 3, and June 5, 1864. Lizzie wrote similarly of her

management elsewhere, noting, "I *pretend* to be chief of affairs" (emphasis added). Lizzie Neblett to Will Neblett, October 25, 1863.

27. Lizzie Neblett to Will Neblett August 28, 1863, and April 15 and 5, 1864.

28. [Augusta Jane Evans], *Macaria; or, Altars of Sacrifice* (Richmond: West and Johnston, 1864), 163. On honor and violence, see Bertram Wyatt-Brown, *Southern Honor* (New York: Oxford University Press, 1982), and Edward L. Ayers, *Vengeance and Justice: Crime and Punishment in the 19th Century American South* (New York: Oxford University Press, 1984).

29. Catherine Clinton cites an unpublished study by Elizabeth Craven that finds, based on slave narratives and WPA interviews, that only 10 percent of slaves claimed to have been whipped by mistresses, 30 percent to have been ordered whipped by mistresses. Eighty percent reported that mistresses had little or no authority (*The Plantation Mistress: Woman's World in the Old South* [New York: Pantheon, 1982], 187). On women's assumption of their incapacities as slave managers see also Clarence L. Mohr, *On the Threshold of Freedom: Masters and Slaves in Civil War Georgia* (Athens: University of Georgia Press, 1986), 221; Anne Firor Scott, *The Southern Lady: From Pedestal to Politics* (Chicago: University of Chicago Press, 1970), 88; Elizabeth Fox-Genovese, *Within the Plantation Household*, 206, 313. For a perspective on women and violence in the postwar South, see Laura F. Edwards, "Sexual Violence, Gender, Reconstruction and the Extension of Patriarchy in Granville County, North Carolina," *North Carolina Historical Review* 88 (July 1991): 237–60.

30. Lizzie Neblett to Will Neblett, August 13, 1863; December 13, 1863; October 28, 1863; May 17, 1864; March 12, 1864. Contemporary scholars of family violence emphasize the importance of distinguishing between punishment and abuse. Linda Gordon, in particular, stresses the significance of cultural and historical perspectives in establishing that distinction. I view the disapproval of Lizzie's aunt and the anticipated disapproval of Will as indications that whipping a ten-month-old baby was not generally regarded as acceptable child-rearing in white families of nineteenth-century Texas. See Linda Gordon, *Heroes of Their Own Lives: The Politics and History of Family Violence* (New York: Viking Penguin, 1988), 5, 180. Historian Philip Greven makes the case for regarding all physical punishment as abuse in *Spare the Child: The Religious Roots of Punishment and the Psychological Impact of Physical Abuse* (New York: Alfred A. Knopf, 1991). For a view of the repercussions of the violence of slavery within the black family, see Brenda Stevenson, "Distress and Discord in Virginia Slave Families, 1830–1860," in Carol Bleser, ed., *In Joy and Sorrow: Women, Family and Marriage in the Victorian South, 1830–1900* (New York: Oxford University Press, 1991).

31. No one has as yet systematically explored the role of lower-class white women as agents of violence. Because I am here dealing with slave managing women, I am, of course, addressing the issue of privileged women. Gender prescriptions for southern women, as I have argued elsewhere, tended to try to deny class differences, but for contrasts in terms of behavior by class, adequate research simply has not been done to serve as the foundation for generalization. See p. 114, herein. On family violence generally, see Linda Gordon, *Heroes of Their Own Lives;* Demie Kurz, "Social Science Perspectives on Wife Abuse: Current Debates and Future Directions," *Gender and Society* 3 (December 1989): 489–505; Wini Breines and Linda Gordon, "The New Scholarship on Family Violence," *Signs* 8 (1983): 490–531. In keeping with my perspective here, Breines and Gordon emphasize the social context of family violence and its patterning in accordance with wider dimensions of social power. They also note that "child abuse is the only form of family violence in which women are assailants as often as men." See also Linda Gordon, "Family Violence, Feminism and Social Control," *Feminist Studies* 12 (Fall 1986): 453–78; Elizabeth Pleck, *Domestic Tyranny: The Making of Social Policy against Family Violence from Colonial Times to the Present* (New York: Oxford University Press, 1987) uses some data from the South. For other examples of slave mistresses demonstrating the tension between ideology and behavior regarding white women whipping slaves, see Emily Lyles Harris who whips but finds it a "painful necessity," and Alice Palmer, who wants to whip but does not because she finds "the idea of a lady doing such a thing . . . repugnant." Diary entry, February 22, 1865, Emily Lyles Harris Papers, Winthrop College; Alice Palmer to Hattie, July 20, 1865, Palmer Family Papers, SCL.

32. Ninth Census of the United States, Population Schedules and Agricultural Schedules, NA. Lizzie Neblett to Will Neblett, March 20, 1864. Lizzie Neblett, Reminiscence, May 25, 1912; Lizzie Neblett, Scrapbook [1880s]. After the war, baby Bettie came to be called Lizzie, like her mother.

Index

Abolitionism, 21–22, 72, 73, 79, 145, 146
Acors, Almira, 136
Agricultural oration: and agricultural reform, 49–52; and agriculture as symbol of moral condition, 35–37; "apologetic preface" in, 38; avoidance of political controversy in, 43–44; compared with Protestant sermon, 46; and establishment of cognitive consistency in time of change, 41–42; historical sketch of progress of agriculture in, 39; identification of people with land in, 42–43; importance of, 30–32, 52–53; lament for existing inadequacies in, 39–40; literary device of "identification" in, 37–38; in North, 38, 204n31; paean to agriculture in, 39; religion in, 40–41; science in, 39–40; shared southern identity in, 43; slavery in, 44–46; in South Carolina, 31–32, 35–53; wealth justified in, 40–41
Agricultural societies, 46–49
Agriculture: agricultural depression in 1830s and 1840s, 32, 37; and agricultural oration, 30–32, 35–53; and agricultural societies, 46–49; cotton production, 32–33, 51, 180, 192; decline in social and economic importance of, 29–30, 31, 35, 41; reform movement in, 49–52; and soil depletion, 33, 35; in South Carolina, 29–53; as symbol of moral condition, 35–37; and western lands, 33, 35
Alonzo (slave), 68
Anti-Mission Baptists, 197–98n25
Antietam, battle of, 94
Aristotle, 37
Avary, Myrna Lockett, 142

Banner, James M., Jr., 38
Banner, Lois W., 197n12
Baptist church, 17–18, 24–25, 91, 92, 94–95, 99, 100
Barnwell, Rev. R. W., 124
Barrott, J. P., 50
Beauregard, P. G. T., 163, 172
Blacks. See Slavery
Bodo, John R., 197n18, 197–98n25
Brightwell, Frances, 135
Brisbane, John S., 48
Burial of Latané, 148–59
Burke, Kenneth, 29
Butler, Pierce, 171
Byrd, J. E., 50

Calhoun, Andrew P., 40, 44, 51
Calhoun, John C., 69
Cash, W. J., 74
Chappelear, Amanda, 118
Chattanooga, battle of, 95
Chesnut, James, 139, 145, 146, 147
Chesnut, Mary: ambition of, 8; biography of, 141, 146–47; after Civil War, 146, 147; dissatisfactions of, 142, 144; on gender roles, 144–45; importance of, 146; Martin and Avary's edition of journals of, 142; and nursing, 10, 130; portrait of, 143; relationships with men, 142, 144; resistance to ideology of sacrifice, 139; on slavery, 8, 142, 145–47; wifely role of, 144, 146, 147; Williams's edition of journals of, 142; Woodward's edition of journals of, 141–42
Chunn, Lila, 134
Churches. See names of specific churches
Civil War: battle of Antietam, 94; battle of Gettysburg, 94, 136; battle of Ma-

247

1850s, 72–73, 74–87; of Stringfellow, 15–28, 79–80, 198n38

Randall (slave), 179–80
Ravenel, Henry William, 42, 43
Reform movement, 16, 18, 19–21, 27, 197n18, 197n23
Religion: in agricultural oration, 40–41, 46; evangelicalism and proslavery argument, 15–28, 79–81, 88–89; in Evans's *Macaria*, 170–71; of northern army during Civil War, 91; revivalism in Confederate Army, 88–109; of slaves, 57–59, 102, 208n4; symbolism in Washington's *Burial of Latané*, 151–53. *See also* names of specific churches
Revis, Martha, 136–37
Revivalism. *See* Evangelicalism
Rhett, Edmund, 37, 53
Richards, I. A., 29
Rodgers, Daniel T., 97
Roper, Robert William, 45
Ruffin, Edmund, 33, 34, 75, 84, 85, 209n16
Runaway slaves, 65–69, 209–10nn19–20

Sam (slave), 179, 180, 182–86
Sams, Sarah Jane, 134
Sarah (slave), 179
Sassoon, Siegfried, 104
Scott, Sir Walter, 114, 149, 161
Seabrook, Whitemarsh Benjamin, 41, 45
Sea Islands, 71
Seddon, James, 135
Sellers, Charles, 74
Shell shock, 103–7, 227n35
Shubrick, John, 69
Simms, William Gilmore, 210n20
Slavery: in agricultural oration, 44–46; and alcohol, 63–64; Chesnut on, 142, 145–47; during Civil War, 9, 70–71, 154–55; Confederate women's responsibility for slave management, 10, 127–28, 175–92, 244n29, 245n31; disease and injuries of slaves, 64-65, 185–86; and distribution of provi-

sions, 62–63; domesticity of, 175; evangelicalism and proslavery argument, 15–28, 79–81, 88–89, 154–55; Genovese on, 55, 77, 78, 86, 210n28, 214n20, 217n46; and insubordination of slaves, 65, 127; literacy of slaves, 210n26; master-slave relationship, 54–55, 57–71; outside forces to increase slave dissatisfaction, 69; and paternalism, 7–10, 127, 174–75; physical violence against slaves, 59, 61, 174–75, 180, 182–83, 188–91, 244n29; and plantation management, 61–62; proslavery argument on, 15–28, 72–87, 174–75, 198n38; and religion, 57–59, 102, 208n4; runaway slaves, 65–69, 209–10nn19–20; in Texas, 176–92; and thefts by slaves, 63, 208–9n16; in Washington's *Burial of Latané*, 149, 155, 158–59; work patterns of slaves, 59–60
Sledd, Rev. R. N., 98
Smith-Rosenberg, Carroll, 198n30
Soldiers. *See* Confederate Army
South. *See* New South; Old South
South Carolina: agricultural reform in, 49–52; agricultural societies in, 48; agriculture in, 29–53; cotton market in, 32–33; emigration to the West, 33; plantation society in, 54–71; Sea Islands of, 71; secession of, 52; and sectional conflict, 31–32, 43–44; slavery in, 44–46; soil depletion in, 33, 35
Southern Baptist Convention, 24–25
Stephens, Alexander, 172–73, 175, 211n2
Stephenson, Harriet, 135
Sterkx, H. E., 115
Stone, Kate, 138
Stowe, Harriet Beecher, 145, 155
Stowe, Steven M., 141
Stringfellow, Amelia, 17
Stringfellow, Rev. Thornton: Bell Air home of, 18–19; during Civil War, 25–26; education of, 17; and evangelicalism, 15–28; family of, 16–17; humanitarian and reform concerns of, 16, 18, 19–21, 27, 197n18, 198n39; last